Palmers
gardenworld

Real Gardening
Real Easy

Clematis paniculata

Palmers
gardenworld

Real Gardening
Real Easy

SUE
LINN

RANDOM
HOUSE
NEW ZEALAND LTD

Cover photograph: New Zealand Picture Library

Random House New Zealand Ltd
(An imprint of the Random House Group)

18 Poland Road
Glenfield
Auckland 10
NEW ZEALAND

Sydney   New York   Toronto
London   Auckland   Johannesburg
and agencies throughout the world

First published 1996
Reprinted 1997

© Palmers Gardenworld 1996
The moral rights of the Author have been asserted.

Printed in Hong Kong
ISBN 1 86941 293 1

Contents

Acknowledgements

PHOTOGRAPHER PHILLIPA TURLEY

Pictures are as important as words in any gardening book. The inspirational photographs that help to tell the story in *Real Gardening Real Easy* are largely the work of Phillipa Turley. I am forever grateful to Phillipa, not just for her photographs, but also for her moral support and practical assistance in the completion of this book.

My thanks to those people whose wonderful gardens appear in the photographs: Pamela Wolfe, Maryan Bishop, Carmel Hare, Don O'Connor, Bernice and Ken Williams, June Marshall, Heather and Alan Makgill, Margaret Mitchell, Judy Laity, and Bev McConnell. Visiting such gardens in the quest for pictures was a treat in itself.

Real Gardening Real Easy might never have reached an end had it not been for the support of two special friends, Denise Cleverly and Libby Gormley. A general gardening book requires research for those topics where personal experience is incomplete. Denise is a knowledgeable, experienced gardener who spent valuable hours on my behalf. Libby helped in endless ways, with childcare, loads of encouragement and actual, hands-on assistance.

Finally, I need to thank my husband, Brent. He had little choice, but coped admirably well with me and our chaotic lifestyle during the writing of this book.

SUE LINN

Introduction

ABOUT THIS BOOK

Gardening can be as easy or as difficult as you like to make it. This book is about how to approach it the easy way.

The intention is not to mislead by oversimplifying complex gardening topics, but to present the important ones in a way that might hopefully open some doors. Gardening is both a science and an art. You don't have to know all the science to gain pleasure from the art.

Except for the 'highly desirables' with no near substitutes, the plants featured in *Real Gardening Real Easy* are those that are easy to grow in a wide range of soils and climates.

It is hoped that this book is a starting point — something to arm you with enough knowledge to get you started and eliminate the soul-destroying mistakes. There will always be more to discover about gardening. That is essentially its charm.

WITH REGARD TO PLANT NAMES

For the beginner, one of the most alienating things about gardening is its language — those dreaded Latin plant names, seemingly designed as a secret code to make life difficult for the uninitiated. Good reason for any respectful book daring to call itself an easy guide to gardening to go easy on the botanical names.

Unfortunately, there is a hitch: a common name often belongs to more than one plant. For example, 'black-eyed Susan' is the common name for an orange-flowered vine, *Thunbergia alata*. It is also one of the names used for the golden-flowered perennial, *Rudbeckia hirta*, which is also known as 'gloriosa daisy'. There are many other examples of plants having a number of different common names. The only way to be precise about which plant we are talking about is to use a botanical name.

To confound things further, you can't even always trust a botanical name. These are susceptible to constant revision by dedicated botanists who seem to have nothing better to do than confuse us by changing a name to something even more unpronounceable, when we've only just got the hang of the old one. An example is *Hyacinthoides* (bluebells), which used to be *Endymion*, which used to be *Scilla*. Some botanists retain the bluebells in *Scilla*. Luckily, in this case the common name is pretty universal! Actually, it's not all that bad. Botanical names are largely constant and when they do change, most references will give the old name as well.

So, as a newly committed gardener, it pays to get comfortable with botanical names. The first few you learn will be the hardest to retain, but the more you learn the easier it somehow gets. An understanding of how botanical names work will help.

Botanical names are made up of two parts: a 'surname' and a 'christian' name. The 'surname' comes first and is called the genus (plural genera). The 'christian' name comes last and identifies a species.

For example, take the botanical name for French lavender: *Lavandula dentata*. *Lavandula* is the genus and *dentata* is the species. Take another kind of lavender:

English lavender *(Lavandula angustifolia)*. It belongs to the same genus but is a different species. Spanish or Italian lavender is *Lavandula stoechas*. Note that botanical names are always either printed in italics or underlined. The genus should always have a capital letter, but the species name is in lower case.

The common name will often be the same as the genus (e.g., *Pittosporum*, *Citrus*, *Agapanthus*, *Viola*) and sometimes the same as the species name (e.g., *Lychnis viscaria*, *Podocarpus totara*). The notation 'spp.' after a genus name is often used to refer to all species within a genus, for example, *Rosa* spp. meaning 'roses'.

The meanings of both species and genus names give clues to the characteristics or origin of the plant. Learning these meanings can become an interesting pastime and certainly helps with remembering names.

Some plants have a third name, the 'cultivar' name, for example, *Lavandula angustifolia* 'Hidcote'. A cultivar is a cultivated form selected or bred by man. Sometimes so much breeding has gone on that a cultivar can no longer be attributed to a single species (it has too many ancestors to mention) and so is simply known by its cultivar name. Roses are a case in point, for example, *Rosa* 'Aotearoa'.

The genus name should not be confused with the plant's family name. A plant family contains a collection of genera, its members sharing common features such as similar flower forms. For example, when you look at the flowers of hibiscus and the perennial lavatera, it's easy to see why they are members of the same family. Once you start getting to know more plants, you will often be able to identify a plant by guessing which family it is in and working from there. Members of the same family will often share soil or climatic preferences, but not always. Family names always end in 'ae'. Some examples of plant families are:

> **Rosaceae** — includes roses (*Rosa*), apple trees (*Malus*), peach and plum trees (*Prunus*).
>
> **Leguminosae** — includes peas (*Pisium*), beans (*Phaseolus*), kowhai (*Sophora*) and gorse (*Ulex*).
>
> **Myrtaceae** — includes pohutukawa (*Metrosideros*), manuka (*Leptospermum*) and gum trees (*Eucalyptus*).
>
> **Rutaceae** — includes all citrus trees (*Citrus*), the shrub Mexican orange blossom (*Choisya*), and the herb rue (*Ruta*).
>
> **Umbelliferae (syn. Apiaceae)** — includes parsley, coriander, carrots and the poisonous weed hemlock.
>
> **Liliaceae** — includes lilies (*Lilium*), English bluebells (*Hyacinthoides*), agapanthus (*Agapanthus*) and chives (*Allium*).

When it comes to pronouncing botanical names, the best way is to say it the way it looks. In many cases one expert will differ from another as to the correct pronunciation.

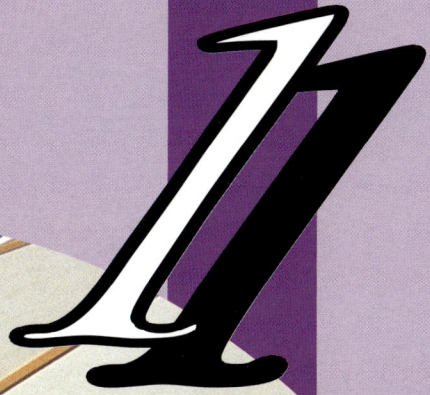

An intimate courtyard setting with a cottage garden style. The pink rose is 'Flower Carpet'. Ivy on the fence creates a solid green backdrop.

Getting started

Planning

Devising a plan and putting it on paper helps you to focus on what you want from your garden and to evaluate the constraints and opportunities of your site. The resulting design becomes the vision of the future garden, giving you something to work towards and making decisions on the way to the dream garden (such as choosing the right plants) so much easier.

Getting someone else to help you plan your garden is an excellent option and gives better value for money than is usually assumed, especially when you consider how much money is saved on avoiding expensive mistakes. You can buy advice on any scale from a quick site visit with sketch plan to the full-blown landscape plan with planting details right down to the last annual. A one- or two-hour session in your garden with someone who knows what they are talking about is often all that's needed and is a great way to get over the initial 'where do we start' barrier. Then, if need be, you can call the adviser in for more help at a later stage. Good designers can be found through garden centres or garden groups. A recommendation from a source you trust is best as those advertising themselves as 'landscape gardeners' vary greatly in expertise.

Whether you are designing your garden yourself or employing someone else, you need to sort out what you want from your garden.

There are the practical considerations:
- ❏ How much space is required for children's play, for entertaining, for car parking?
- ❏ Do you need a vegetable garden or a compost heap?
- ❏ What about space for storage, clotheslines, play equipment now or in the future?
- ❏ Do you need extra privacy or shady areas?
- ❏ How much time will you have to spend in your garden? (If you enjoy gardening, divide that by two. If you don't, divide by four or budget for a gardener!)

And the aesthetic:
- ❏ Do you have a certain style in mind? What style best suits your house?
- ❏ Which style of garden best suits your street or environment (coastal, bush, etc)
- ❏ Are there unattractive views or features that need screening?
- ❏ Which are the attractive views or features you wish to preserve or enhance?
- ❏ How is the garden viewed from inside the house?

Then the things that are hard to change need to be considered — things like:
- ❏ Property boundaries.
- ❏ Position of the house and other buildings.
- ❏ Soil type.
- ❏ Climate.
- ❏ Drainage.
- ❏ Shady and sunny areas.
- ❏ Powerlines, cables, drains, water pipes, gas lines, etc.
- ❏ Slope.

The job is then to come up with the best solution to turn what you have into something that you want. Often the more limiting your site is, the easier it is to come up with a design as there may be only one solution that fits. A huge site with perfect soil and a temperate climate can overwhelm with possibilities.

The Soil

S oils are composed of clay and sand particles and organic matter (humus); the relative amount of each determines the quality of the soil. Loam is a desirable blend of these materials, yielding fertile soils with good drainage and aeration.

Nothing will make gardening more frustrating than trying to grow plants that are wrong for your soil. Although some soils are better than others, the universally perfect soil doesn't exist. It depends on what you want to grow. Rich clay loams produce beautiful roses, but they are not ideal for plants such as echiums, proteas and English lavenders, which prefer a light sandy soil. The easiest way to garden is to select plants suitable for your soil type. Those essential favourites that fail to thrive in your soil could find a home in a pot. Meanwhile, there are things you can do to make your soil more hospitable to a wider range of plants and generally make life better for all the plants in your garden. Few soils are beyond the potential for improvement.

So, what makes a soil good? On each end of the see-saw are two essential qualities. A soil needs to be able to hold on to water and nutrients, making them available to the plants as they need them. At the same time it needs to have air spaces to enable plant roots to breathe. A sandy soil has plenty of air spaces but water and nutrients will wash straight through it. A clay soil has the opposite problem.

Compost is touted as the magic, fix-all ingredient because it contains humus. Humus is fabulous stuff — an amorphous, dark-coloured, practically odourless material — but close to gold as far as gardeners are concerned. Its greatness lies in its affect on the soil structure, making it able to hold on to water and nutrients while keeping the air spaces open. A good compost is worth paying for, but if you have the means to make it yourself — even better. Compost does wonders, but to make the best of a soil by growing the right plants you need to understand something about its make-up. The topsoil is the layer that contains the humus, hence its dark colour. The deeper and darker your topsoil, the luckier you are. Beneath the topsoil is the subsoil, which determines the basic texture of your soil.

How to make compost: Go to page 196.

CLAY, SAND, SILT OR LOAM?

A clay soil sticks to your boots when wet. It bakes hard and opens up in gaping cracks in summer. A clay-based soil with good humus content is a *clay loam*. The boot-sticking, summer-baking qualities are not so extreme in clay loams, but you can tell the clay content by rolling a lump of soil in your fingers. If it feels sticky and can be rolled into a cylinder, it contains clay. If the cylinder can be bent into a ring, it is closer to clay than clay loam. Clay and clay loam soils are very common in New Zealand. Pure clay is the worst kind of garden soil, but a clay loam holds water well and is a good fertile soil for many plants, especially trees, shrubs and roses.

Plants for clay soils: Go to page 72.

PLAN OF ATTACK TO DESIGN YOUR OWN GARDEN

1. THE BASE PLAN

Start with what you have:

❑ Measure your site to the nearest metre, drawing in the outline of your house.

❑ Add any trees and other existing features you want to keep.

❑ Add an arrow to show north in relation to your site and identify shady and sunny locations. Remember that shadows are longer in winter than they are in summer. It takes a whole year to really get to know the microclimates in your garden. Show poorly drained areas or frost pockets.

❑ Mark any other relevant details that will affect the design: tap positions, underground services, powerlines, vehicle access, etc.

2. THE CONCEPT PLAN

Next divide your site into areas and make a rough layout of what goes where.

❑ Define areas for the front entranceway, outdoor entertaining, play, vegetable garden, rose garden, flower garden, clothesline . . . swimming pool and tennis court? Determine the relative size of each area depending on your needs and the time you will have for maintenance. Don't worry about exact shapes and materials until you have worked out the locations and relative size of each area.

❑ Show where screening, shade or shelter is needed and what height it needs to be.

3. THE DESIGN

Now you can firm up the framework of the garden. Work from the most to the least permanent.

❑ *Screening for privacy and shelter:* Decide on planting, walls, fences or a combination.

❑ *Garden walls:* Decide on hedges, mass shrub plantings, walls or fences to separate different areas of the garden.

❑ *Shade:* This can be provided instantly by covering overhead structures (gazebos, pergolas, etc) with fast-growing climbers or with trees in the longer term.

❏ *Feature trees:* Decide where you want your biggest trees and choose the trees to suit your needs. Think about how they will be seen from various points around the garden and from the house, how they will frame views from within or frame the view of your house or garden from outside, as well as the shade they will cast in winter and summer. How quickly do they need to grow and how big do you want them to get? Small gardens may only have room for one small tree, so it needs to be carefully located for best advantage.

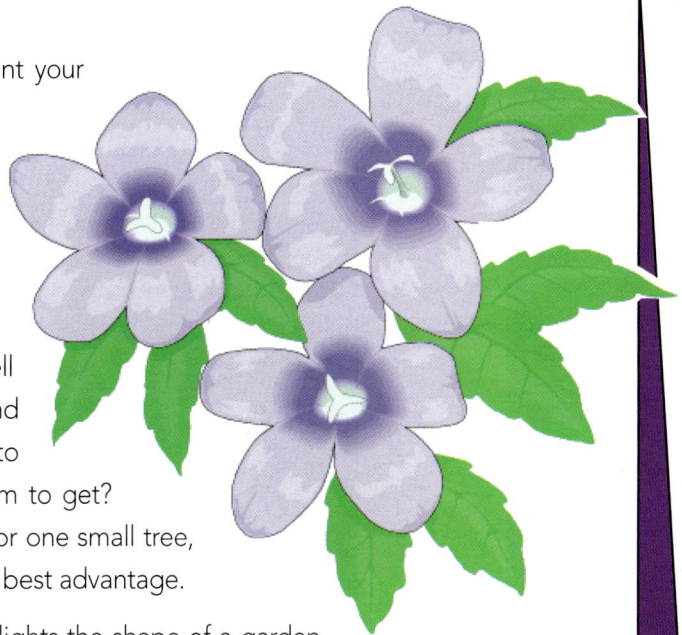

❏ *Garden floors:* The ground plan highlights the shape of a garden room. Finalise the design of driveways, decks, paved areas and lawns.

❏ *Garden beds:* The shapes of planted areas, mixed shrub borders and flower beds should basically be decided for you. They are the spaces remaining after everything else has been decided.

Section two of this book deals with the basic structure of a garden. Well designed, with a solid framework, a garden will always be easy on the eye, even at down times of the year, or when it is overdue for attention.

4. PLANT SELECTION

Your design should determine areas of tall and low planting, where there are hedges, trees, rose and flower gardens, etc. Now the fun starts. Before choosing the plants for each area on your plan, mark out the various microclimates: for example, sunny, shady, semi-shade, cold and wet in winter, hot and dry in summer, dry, boggy, windy, or sheltered positions. Taking into account your soil type and climate, you can now start drawing up your list of plants to consider. You may decide to include other parameters such as flower colour.

Select trees and shrubs first (see section two), then perennials and roses, then annuals (see section three).

A *sandy soil* feels gritty. One with a fair amount of humus in it (a sandy loam) will roll into a ball, but it will crumble easily when dropped. It will not stick to your boots, and will not roll into a cylinder. Pure sand is erosion prone, difficult to keep moist and often has a high salt content, rendering it unsuitable for most plants. Sandy loams, on the other hand, have a better water-holding capacity. They are ideal, well-drained garden soils that are easy to cultivate and are fit for a wide range of plants, especially if the humus content is regularly replenished.

There are many soils between these two extremes, including silty soils, which contain very fine clay particles, sandy clay loams, volcanic soils (various mixtures of sand and silty clay), and peat soils, which tend to be overly acidic and are often boggy.

RICH OR POOR?

Rich means a fertile soil containing lots of nutrients. Clay soils are the most naturally fertile. Sandy soils are constantly having the nutrients stripped by water draining through them. Humus is essential for soil fertility. Its crucial role is to keep the soil in good physical condition so that nutrients can be taken up by plant roots. Organic matter is also the sole supplier of the soil's natural reserves of nitrogen, containing significant amounts of other nutrients as well.

Among the most impoverished soils are the ones that have been cultivated for hundreds of years. We constantly need to be putting back what we take away, by adding compost and fertilisers.

ACID OR ALKALINE?

Soil acidity, the concentration of hydrogen ions, is measured on the pH scale of one to fourteen. A pH of one is highly acidic, pH 14 is highly alkaline, and pH 7 is neutral. Clay soils tend to be on the acid side. Sandy soils are frequently alkaline. The pH affects some plants' ability to absorb the right nutrients. Most plants are not too fussy. Excess acidity is the most common condition with New Zealand soils, especially where there is high natural rainfall. It is corrected by the addition of lime. Some plants like acid soils and should not be given lime: camellias and rhododendrons are well-known examples.

Simple, inexpensive soil tests are available if you want to find out your soil pH. Ask at your garden centre.

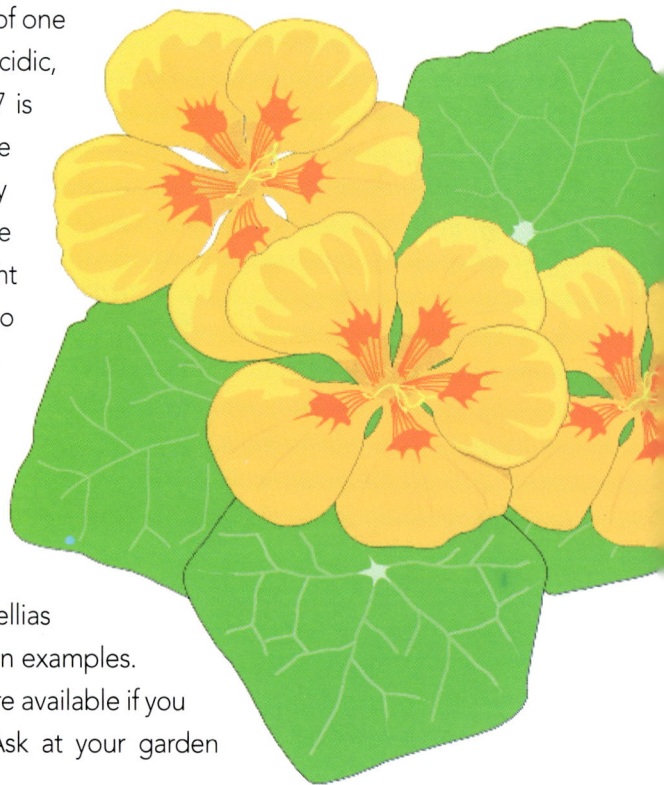

Plants for sandy soils:
Go to page 73.

More about soil improvement:
Go to page 190.

Fertilisers:
Go to page 200.

Climate

Having spent centuries adapting for survival in their natural habitat, it's not surprising that many plants don't respond well when grown in a climate that is different from that of their origin. But we often try, usually with disappointing results or a lot of fuss. The best-looking gardens specialise in plants that are suited to the prevailing climate, whether it be windy, wet, dry, hot or cold.

New Zealand's temperate climate, especially in milder regions, makes it possible to grow plants from a huge range of climatic zones. This luxury of choice may be at the expense of good design — it is difficult to resist the temptation to overdo the variety and end up with a mishmash of plants and garden styles.

Most cool-climate plants will grow in a mild climate, but it is things like foliage colour, flowering performance and overall disease resistance that suffer. In cold climates, frosts will dispatch warm-climate species unless they are grown in containers indoors or in a well-protected situation. Thus warm-climate perennials are often grown as annuals in cold climates.

Humidity has an effect on plant growth that is often overlooked. In warm climates with high rainfall, such as Auckland, the high levels of moisture in the air are well suited to growing many subtropical plants such as palms, but it makes rose-growing practically impossible without spraying for disease control.

Gardeners on the coast or in the country often have the advantage of stunning views, but also have to contend with wind. Anything more than a gentle breeze causes discomfort for both people and plants, so it's worth diverting it away from your garden in the earliest stages of development. While shelter trees grow or where, for the sake of views, the wind must be tolerated, plants tolerant to exposed conditions should be planted. Coastal gardeners also need to consider salt spray.

Subtropical gardens:
Go to page 65.

Trees and shrubs for shelter:
Go to page 24.

Coastal plants:
Go to page 78.

MICROCLIMATE

A plant that thrives in one part of your garden may do poorly in another. Sometimes the difference between the two places is not at first obvious. Each spot in the garden has its own unique set of climatic circumstances. This is the microclimate and it can be quite different from the microclimate even a metre away.

One of the most important examples of microclimate is the amount of sunlight. Most plants grown for their flowers prefer full sun, but there are some magnificent plants that prefer shade or part shade.

The shade cast on an area by a wall, building or tree varies greatly between summer and winter. A small courtyard with a high wall along its northern boundary will be almost entirely shaded through winter, but receive almost full sun in summer. A big advantage of deciduous trees is that they cast shade in summer but let light through in winter.

There will be warm and cold spots in the garden. Temperature variances are closely related to sun and shade, but are also affected by topography and the position of buildings. A north-facing wall will absorb the sun's warmth and radiate it

*Plants for shade:
Go to page 76.*

*Plants for coastal gardens:
Go to page 78.*

back out to the plants nearby. Brick and stone walls will be warmer than wooden ones, but both will provide shelter from cooling winds. On the other hand, a wall may trap the cold air and create a frost pocket in winter if it is at the bottom of a slope.

Even if the natural rainfall is high, there will be dry places in the garden. Areas under the eves of houses are a classic example. If such places are to be planted they will need dry-tolerant plants or careful irrigation. Dry shade, such as under large trees, is one of the most difficult situations to find plants for.

Then there is the question of shelter. Most plants put up with some wind, but some are very sensitive and need to be given the most sheltered corner of your garden. Where there is minimal air movement you are likely to have summer humidity and a risk of disease — not a good place for the roses! As the garden matures, and trees and hedges grow, the amount of shelter in the garden will increase, allowing different plants to be grown.

Soil type may also vary from place to place in one garden.

It can take years to thoroughly get to know the different microclimates in a garden. Just when you've sorted it all out and have perfect plants in perfect places, the neighbours could cut a tree down or add another storey to their house and you have to start all over again!

Garden Style

Garden style is a personal and ever-evolving quality. There is no finite list of garden styles. Some gardens are so unique that their style is hard to define. Others are a blend of many influences, including fashion. Often the restrictions of site or climate dictate the style of the garden.

It is wise to start out with some sort of style in mind, for strength of character and to avoid incongruent conglomerations of planting. The personal touch can then be added to make the garden distinctively yours. Listed here are some popular styles with a checklist of plants and features that are commonly found in each.

A COTTAGE GARDEN

GOOD FOR GARDENS THAT:

✓ are small city gardens ✓ surround older-style houses

GOOD FOR GARDENERS WHO:

✓ love flowers and like to pick them ✓ like lots of colour

✓ prefer informality ✓ are romantic at heart

✓ enjoy gardening and have time to garden

LIKELY FEATURES:

✓ Brick or stone pathways ✓ Picket fences

✓ Simple terracotta pots ✓ Archways

✓ Rustic timber furniture ✓ Cats

✓ Wide, densely planted flower beds ✓ Mixed plantings

LIKELY PLANTS:

✓ Fruit trees
✓ Vegetables
✓ Lavender
✓ Fragrant flowers and foliage
✓ Simple, old-fashioned flowers that self-sow, such as foxgloves, Californian poppies, forget-me-nots, love-in-a-mist, granny's bonnets, cosmos and pansies

✓ Perennials
✓ Bulbs
✓ Roses
✓ Herbs

An informal, closely planted mass of roses and perennials, typical of the cottage style; white 'Seafoam' rose, pink rose 'The Fairy', white *Lychnis coronaria* and purple *Scabiosa* 'Blue Butterfly'.

A MEDITERRANEAN-STYLE GARDEN

GOOD FOR GARDENS THAT ARE:

✓ in a warm climate
✓ on small rectangular sites
✓ around concrete/stucco houses

✓ near the coast
✓ sunny
✓ townhouse courtyards

GOOD FOR GARDENERS WHO:

✓ appreciate formal design
✓ like elaborate pots and ornaments

✓ entertain a lot more than they garden

LIKELY FEATURES:

✓ Extensive paving
✓ Concrete walls
✓ Statues, urns and pots
✓ Stylish garden furniture

✓ Ceramic tiles
✓ Water features, e.g., fountains, formal pools
✓ Topiary

LIKELY PLANTS:

✓ English box (*Buxus sempervirens*)
✓ Citrus trees
✓ Lavenders
✓ Olive tree (*Olea europaea*)
✓ Palms
✓ *Yucca* spp.
✓ *Carex* spp.
✓ *Pratia* spp.
✓ Lavender cotton (*Santolina chamaecyparissus*)

✓ Formal-shaped conifers
✓ Rosemary
✓ Sweet bay (*Laurus nobilis*)
✓ Indian bead tree (*Melia azederach*)
✓ *Agave* spp.
✓ Mondo grass (*Ophiopogon japonicus*)
✓ *Pennisetum setaceum* (syn. *P. ruppellii*)
✓ Laurel (*Prunus lusitanica*)

A COUNTRY GARDEN

GOOD FOR GARDENS:

✓ that are large
✓ with big rambling houses

✓ with long-distance views
✓ in rural settings

GOOD FOR GARDENERS WHO:

✓ love flowers
✓ don't mind mowing lawns
✓ like space

✓ love gardening or have a gardener
✓ have children and pets
✓ aspire to the 'English' look

- ✓ Large sweeping lawns
- ✓ Wide shrub and flower borders
- ✓ Vistas
- ✓ Summerhouses
- ✓ Large trees
- ✓ Labradors
- ✓ Lots of curves
- ✓ Expansive views
- ✓ Wide steps and grass pathways
- ✓ Pergolas
- ✓ Lakes

LIKELY PLANTS:

- ✓ Large deciduous trees
- ✓ Camellias
- ✓ Rhododendrons
- ✓ Azaleas
- ✓ Perennials
- ✓ *Pieris* spp.
- ✓ *Syringa* spp. (lilac)
- ✓ *Agapanthus* spp.
- ✓ Native evergreen trees (e.g., totara, puriri, kahikatea)
- ✓ Magnolias
- ✓ Roses
- ✓ Bulbs
- ✓ *Viburnum* spp.
- ✓ *Spiraea* spp.
- ✓ Bearded irises

Subtropical drama created by palms, hibiscus and strongly 'architectural' container plants; *Dracaena draco*, a cycad, and *Xeronema callistemon*.

A SUBTROPICAL GARDEN

GOOD FOR GARDENS THAT:

- ✓ are in warm subtropical climates
- ✓ are sheltered from strong winds and have high rainfall (e.g., Auckland northwards, Bay of Plenty)
- ✓ have existing mature palm trees
- ✓ surround modern homes

GOOD FOR GARDENERS WHO:

- ✓ have a passion for palms
- ✓ want a dramatic look
- ✓ enjoy luxuriant foliage and vibrant blooms
- ✓ don't like mowing lawns

LIKELY FEATURES:

- ✓ Swimming pools
- ✓ Natural, informal pathways and steps
- ✓ Paving and mass planting in preference to lawns

LIKELY PLANTS:

- ✓ Palms
- ✓ Cycads
- ✓ Vireya rhododendrons
- ✓ Jacaranda
- ✓ Bromeliads
- ✓ Frangipani
- ✓ Hibiscus
- ✓ *Bergenia cordifolia*
- ✓ *Metrosideros* 'Tahiti'
- ✓ Banana palm
- ✓ Puka (*Meryta sinclairii*)
- ✓ Climbers with fragrant or flamboyant flowers (e.g., *Bougainvillea, Mandevilla, Passiflora, Petrea, Pyrostegia, Stephanotis, Tecomanthe, Trachelospermum*)
- ✓ *Clivia miniata*
- ✓ *Cordyline*

A New Zealand native garden

Good for gardens:

✓ situated in a native bush environment

✓ around modern timber houses

✓ on difficult sites, such as sloping, coastal, exposed

✓ at the beach

Good for gardeners who:

✓ prefer more informal styles

✓ want to attract native wildlife to the garden

✓ love foliage form and texture

✓ require a low-maintenance garden

✓ have an interest in native plants and conservation

✓ have children

Likely features:

✓ Mass-planted areas

✓ Rustic seats

✓ Timber structures

✓ Natural pathways and steps

✓ New Zealand-made sculptures

✓ Natural streams

Likely plants:

✓ Any New Zealand native plants

More about New Zealand native plants: Go to page 62.

A Japanese-style garden

Good for gardens that are:

✓ small

✓ in cool/temperate climates

✓ viewed from above

✓ sheltered

✓ town house courtyards

Good for gardeners who:

✓ are inspired by the uniquely contrived informality of Japanese gardens

✓ are interested in Japanese culture

✓ are attentive to detail

✓ have time to spend in the garden

✓ are interested in bonsai

✓ want a tranquil, intimate corner to escape to

Likely features:

✓ Water

✓ Rocks and pebbles

✓ Little bridges

✓ Gazebos

✓ Bamboo fences and water features

✓ Few flowers, many evergreens

✓ Goldfish

✓ Stepping stones traversing still pools

✓ Stone lanterns and other Japanese ornaments

✓ Rock-hugging mosses

✓ Bonsai and other carefully manicured plants

Likely plants:

✓ Cherry blossom (*Prunus* spp.)

✓ Japanese maples (*Acer palmatum* cultivars)

✓ *Liriope muscari*

✓ Bamboo cultivars

✓ Azaleas

✓ Ferns

✓ *Aucuba japonica* cultivars

✓ Green conifers (e.g., *Pinus, Cedrus, Cupressus*)

✓ Grasses, e.g., mondo grass (*Ophiopogon*), *Carex* spp., fountain grass (*Pennisetum*)

✓ Mosses
✓ *Pratia* spp.

A COASTAL GARDEN

GOOD FOR GARDENS THAT ARE:

✓ on or near the coast
✓ on dry sandy soils

✓ exposed to wind and salt spray

GOOD FOR GARDENERS WHO:

✓ want a successful, easy garden in a coastal location

✓ want to create a garden at the beach house

LIKELY FEATURES:

✓ Sea views
✓ Mass planting
✓ Shell or pebble paths

✓ Garden furniture
✓ Rocks

More about cacti & succulents: Go to page 138.

More plants for coastal conditions: Go to page 78.

LIKELY PLANTS:

✓ Cacti
✓ *Agapanthus* spp.
✓ *Ceanothus* spp.
✓ *Coprosma* spp.
✓ *Corokia* spp.
✓ *Hebe* spp. and cultivars
✓ *Leucospermum* spp.
✓ Puka (*Meryta sinclairii*)
✓ NZ flax (*Phormium* cultivars)
✓ *Yucca* spp.
✓ Red hot poker (*Kniphofia*)
✓ *Lavatera* spp.

✓ Succulents
✓ *Agave* spp.
✓ *Cistus* spp.
✓ *Cordyline* spp.
✓ *Echium* spp.
✓ Lavender
✓ Pohutukawa (*Metrosideros* cultivars)
✓ *Olearia* spp.
✓ *Protea* spp.
✓ Daisies (e.g., *Argyranthemum, Brachycome, Felicia, Erigeron, Gazania*)

Basic framework

In Praise of Trees and Shrubs

Camellias:
Go to page 44.

Rhododendrons and
azaleas: Go to page 47.

Lavenders:
Go to page 41.

Hedges:
Go to page 25.

Screening and shelter:
Go to page 24.

New Zealand native
plants: Go to page 62.

Trees:
Go to page 14.

Climbers:
Go to page 49.

A garden jam-packed full of roses, flowering perennials and annuals is a wonderful sight in spring but it won't be so appealing in the middle of winter unless it has a solid framework of trees and shrubs. On the other hand, a garden planted entirely in trees and shrubs can be extremely successful, looking good for twelve months of the year. What's more, it will be virtually maintenance free after the first few years of establishment.

Permanent mass plantings of trees, shrubs and groundcovers are an excellent substitute for lawns, especially when the would-be lawn is a 'dead' area with no particular use, or a difficult-to-mow corner or slope. When there is limited time available for gardening, the areas devoted to lawns, perennials, roses, annuals and vegetables are best kept to a minimum. An area mass planted in easy-care trees and shrubs, although it may take a few years to cover the ground and block out the weeds, will in the long run take a lot less looking after.

Trees and shrubs are essential to the basic garden structure, providing a background setting for other less-permanent plants, but not without the ability to put on a seasonal show all of their own. Some of the best displays of flowers, fruit or berries, or autumn foliage come from trees and shrubs.

In a formal garden, much of the evergreen framework will be in the form of hedges dividing different areas or low borders enhancing the planting behind them. Tall unclipped hedges are ideal for screening and shelter planting. The excellent New Zealand pittosporums are a popular choice for this purpose.

Pittosporums are not the only natives worthy of attention. There is a whole host of New Zealand native trees and shrubs, many of which are all too often overlooked. They include some of the most easy-care trees and shrubs for screening, shelter, permanent groundcover and every other landscape purpose. A garden devoted to native trees and shrubs is the ultimate low-maintenance solution.

New gardens often lack shade. Trees provide the nicest kind of shade — for both plants and people. While trees grow, shade (or screening) can be produced by the planting of quick-growing climbers.

Trees

Well-placed trees are an asset. They anchor a house into its surroundings, enhancing its street appeal and framing views into or out from the site.

Even when the rest of the garden is new, trees can make a garden look established. Tree planting should be the first step in new subdivisions, but the selection and positioning of trees needs more careful deliberation than any other planting. It's heartbreaking to see a tree chopped down because it was planted in the wrong place.

The smaller the garden the more careful you have to be. When choosing a tree for a very small garden or garden space, make sure you know what the label means by 'small' tree. The height given may be a ten-year height. Ten years might convert to five in your soil. Look around your locality to see which trees do well, how big they get and how fast they grow. Some large shrubs are really trees in a small garden. Consider how you want your tree to look from various points around the garden, from inside the house and from across the street.

Think about where your tree will cast its shade. Shape, size and growth rate are the most important criteria when choosing a tree.

You also must decide at the outset whether your tree should be deciduous or evergreen.

Trees for small gardens: Go to page 17.

❑ Deciduous trees let the sun through in winter and shed all their leaves in autumn (a disadvantage if they land in the guttering, but very useful for the compost heap).

❑ Evergreen trees are not without the ability to drop leaves, in fact they are likely to do it all year round, which can be more annoying than a one-season mass. Evergreen trees are the best choice when year-round privacy or shelter is the objective, but they create drier, more dense shade than deciduous trees.

Once you have narrowed down your list of trees based on size, shape and growth rate, it's time to consider the foliage and flowers. Foliage is the most important as this is what you will be looking at most. There are purple- and yellow-leaved trees, but also every shade of green: pale green, bright green, dark green, grey green and blue green. Leaf textures vary enormously too. In addition, the branch pattern of deciduous trees becomes important in winter.

Flowering is for a limited duration, but during this time, the tree will be the most noticed thing in the garden and should be positioned with that in mind. The plantings around a flowering tree should be chosen to complement rather than compete with the tree when it is in flower.

Buying trees

Once you have made your choice, it's time to track down the best possible specimen for your garden. Price should not be the main priority if this is to be a permanent, dominant garden fixture. Invest in the best quality tree you can find.

Deciduous trees are sometimes sold bare-rooted in the winter, directly dug from an open-ground nursery and held in the garden centre in sawdust for winter sales. It is important to check that the roots of such trees are in good order and have not dried out.

If you lack time or patience, there are nurseries specialising in large specimens for instant gardens. Not all trees transplant well in an advanced state but many do, especially if they have been grown for the purpose. Good advice is available from reputable big-tree suppliers. With such an investment, it may also pay to go the extra mile and have your tree transplanted into your garden professionally.

More about buying plants: Go to page 192.

Planting trees

Care in planting your carefully selected tree will ensure that it makes good growth and grows into the best possible shape.

1. First dig a hole at least twice the width and at least 20 cm deeper than the trees roots. Break up the hard surface at the bottom of the hole with your spade.

2. Mix compost and slow-release fertiliser into the soil you have dug out.

3. Backfill the hole with this mixture to the depth of the roots.

Malus floribunda.

4. Remove the tree from its container, loosening any matted roots and pruning off any damaged ones. Centre the root ball in the hole.

5. Position stakes firmly into the ground.

6. Water the tree in its hole, making sure the root ball is thoroughly wet.

7. Backfill with the soil mixture around the edges, firming it gently with your foot.

8. Water again.

Staking is important for most young trees to anchor them against wind while the roots get established. The best way is to have two stakes, one each side of the tree. A single stake can result in damage via the tree rubbing against the stake. Tie firmly with flexible ties. Old nylon stockings work well. On exposed sites, windbreak or frost-protection cloth may be necessary for the first few years, depending on the tree.

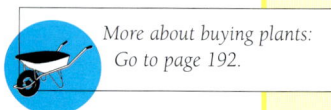

EVERGREEN

Citrus
LEMON, ORANGE, MANDARIN, GRAPEFRUIT
Functional yes, but not to be missed in a list of the best small evergreen trees for ornamental purposes, at least in warm climates. Citrus have wonderful glossy foliage, fantastic floral fragrance and a neat rounded shape. The fruit gives colour in winter. They are easy care as long as they have well-drained soil and are fed occasionally.

More about citrus:
Go to page 169.

Camellia
The larger-growing camellias make excellent feature trees in small gardens, flowering at times of the year when little else is, from autumn through to spring, depending on the cultivar. The reticulata camellias are tall growing and can be used to create tropical effects with their large leaves and flowers.

More about camellias:
Go to page 44.

Franklinia axillaris (syn. Gordonia axillaris)
GORDONIA
3 m x 2 m
This tall, winter-flowering shrub resembles its close relatives, the camellias. The flowers are large, creamy white, single with prominent yellow stamens, flowering right through winter. There is a dense covering of attractive dark green leaves. It enjoys the same growing conditions as camellias.

Hoheria populnea cultivars
LACEBARK
This graceful native tree resembles a silver birch tree, though it is evergreen and doesn't grow as large. Lacebark is quick growing, useful for fast screening or as a single specimen. It has an appealing open habit and small white flowers. The species has plain light green leaves and will grow up to 5 m. The variegated leaf forms are smaller growing.

Laurus nobilis
BAY TREE
4 m x 3 m
Bay trees are capable of becoming quite large, but respond so well to trimming that they are a perfect small-garden tree — whether you grow them in the garden or in a container, or whether you trim them as a standard or let the natural pyramid shape prevail. They tolerate coastal conditions and will grow in clay soils, sun or part shade.

Michelia figo
PORT WINE MAGNOLIA
2.5 m x 2 m
Glossy bright green foliage in spring and summer is interspersed with little yellow and purple flowers that would largely go unnoticed if it wasn't for their fragrance. It is a sweet banana-like scent, hard to miss, too much for some, but cherished by others. *M. figo* is easy to grow in any reasonable soil, in sun or part shade. Pruning is optional to control size and shape, but this is a densely covered, well-shaped shrub without it.

Myrsine australis
MATIPOU
3 m x 2 m
Usually grown amongst other native shrubs or as a screen, this small New Zealand native tree is a worthwhile specimen tree for a small garden. It grows quickly to form a well-shaped, densely covered tree, not unlike the better-known pittosporums, and is easily kept to a moderate size with trimming. Useful in floral art, the stems are a pretty reddish brown standing out against the dainty pale green leaves with their wavy margins. Matipou will cope with coastal conditions and clay soils.

Pittosporum tenuifolium cultivars
KOHUHU
The species is large and quick growing, ideal as a screen or shelter planting. The numerous cultivars are smaller growing with more outstanding foliage, better suited as stand-alone feature trees for small gardens.

More about pittosporums:
Go to page 39.

DECIDUOUS

Acer palmatum cultivars
JAPANESE MAPLE
4 m x 3 m
Among the most beautiful foliage trees of all, Japanese maples come in an extensive array of forms, varying in colour, leaf shape and growth habit. They are very versatile, used as container plants, as lawn or patio trees, planted in groups (very effective with azaleas and rhododendrons) or as bonsai. The autumn colour is most spectacular where winters are cold, but Japanese maples will grow in any New Zealand climate. What they must have is shelter, especially from hot, dry wind. The best soil is a cool, deep, well-drained one with plenty of humus and no shortage of moisture. Still small enough to suit the average town garden, the largest Japanese maple is the species *A. palmatum* itself. The round-headed tree with its delicate airy appearance will eventually reach about 5 m tall. It has something special to offer every season: red new growth in spring, cool soft green foliage in summer, flaming autumn tones and attractive winter branch patterns. Of smaller proportions are the many different cultivars. Among those qualifying as small trees (rather than shrubs) are: 'Katsura' (gold in spring, green in summer, orange in autumn), 'Osakasuki' (bright green in spring, scarlet orange in autumn), 'Roseomarginatum' (variegated green, white and pink), 'Senkaki' (lime green, margined red in spring, green in summer, canary yellow in autumn), 'Atropurpureum' (crimson in spring, dark purple in summer, red in autumn, purple stems through winter), 'Dissectum Seiryu' (bright green intricately dissected foliage, gold with orange tints in autumn).

Cedrela sinensis 'Flamingo'
CHINESE TOON
4 m x 3 m
Pink foliage is the distinctive mark of the Chinese toon. It appears in all its glory in very early spring, dominating everything else around it. The gracefully divided leaves on straight upright branches are still an attractive feature in summer after they

17

Note: The dimensions given for each tree can only be approximate, for average garden conditions, and within the first five to ten years.

turn green. Best against a dark green backdrop and easily grown in a sheltered position. Prune in winter to keep the tree compact and encourage better foliage displays.

Cornus 'Eddie's White Wonder'
DOGWOOD
4 m x 3 m

Dogwoods are pretty trees for cool-climate gardens, producing beautiful spring flowers and vibrant autumn colours. The hybrid 'Eddie's White Wonder' has white flowers, an attractive semi-weeping habit, and performs better than other *Cornus* varieties in warmer climates. Generally cold winters and hot dry autumns are ideal. They like a well-drained composty soil and full sun. Provide mulching and frequent watering when young and protect from harsh winds.

Cotinus coggygria
SMOKE BUSH
3 m x 3 m

A large shrub in a large garden or a small tree in a small garden, smoke bush is grown mainly for its amazing autumn colour, but it is also very attractive in spring and summer. It is the early summer flower display that is responsible for the common name. The large heads of fuzzy pinkish flowers cover the entire bush. The cultivar 'Royal Purple' is smaller growing with purple foliage in spring and summer. Autumn colour is more intense in a cold climate. Prune in winter for the best foliage displays.

Lagerstroemia indica
CREPE MYRTLE
3 m x 2 m

Large multi-stemmed shrubs that are easily converted to an attractive round-headed, single-trunk tree with early training. Quite slow growing, crepe myrtle prefers a hot dry summer, being susceptible to mildew in the more humid climates. Both flowers and bark are features, the large clusters of crêpe-paper-like flowers smothering the plant throughout summer. The bark is smooth grey-brown and flakes off to reveal pinkish inner skin. Depending on the cultivar, the flowers are in various shades of pink, lilac, bright cerise, red or white. Crepe myrtle requires full sun and well-drained, lime-free soil. Water in dry periods.

Remove spent flower heads through summer and prune in winter to maintain shape and promote new growth.

Magnolia xsoulangiana hybrids
TULIP MAGNOLIA

Bare branches are crammed with upward-facing, tulip-shaped blooms in early spring. These are among the most spectral of flowering trees. With a natural multibranched habit, they make a great anchor tree in the corner of a garden. They often make a sizeable tree to 5 m or more, but there are smaller examples among the cultivars. 'Lennei' has large fragrant flowers with rosy purple outer petals and white inner petals. The flowers of 'Lennei Alba' are creamy white. Plant in well-drained, lime-free, composty soil and add a layer of mulch. Prune after flowering to control shape or size.

Malus floribunda
JAPANESE FLOWERING CRAB APPLE
3 m x 2.5 m

This is one of the earliest flowering and most spectacular of the spring blossom trees. It contributes to the garden scene all year round with its long arching branches and delightful spreading habit. The flower buds are red, opening to pink single blossoms, fading to white. The sheer mass of flowers, with some at each different stage of opening, is a breathtaking sight in early spring. Underplant with spring bulbs to complete the picture. Plant in a well-drained soil in full sun, with shelter from strong winds.

Malus 'Jack Humm'
CRAB APPLE
3 m x 2.5 m

A good tree for winter colour, producing a spectacular late summer display of bright red miniature apples, which remain on the tree till late winter (only very hungry birds will eat them). The fruit can be harvested for making jelly. Well-proportioned as a small garden tree, or available on a dwarfing root stock to grow into a 2 m shrub.

Prunus subhirtella
WEEPING CHERRY
2.5 m x 2 m

These excellent little trees are

shaped like a miniature weeping willow and smother themselves in spring with dainty cherry blossom. *P. subhirtella* 'Falling Snow' has white semi-double flowers. *P. subhirtella* 'Pendula' (weeping rosebud cherry) is covered in layer upon layer of single pink flowers. Both make a stunning lawn specimen or underplant with groundcover perennials, bulbs or annuals. Give them well-drained soil and full sun.

Stachyurus praecox
EARLY SPIKETAIL
2.5 m x 2 m

A beautiful Japanese shrub that makes an ideal small tree for a small garden, *Stachyurus* is at its most stunning in early spring when the bare branches hang with drooping racemes of pale yellow, bell-shaped flowers. The buds appear in autumn and the flowers hold well into spring, as the coppery-coloured new leaves appear. The mature foliage is green through summer turning oranges and yellows in autumn. The shrub grows quickly and is easily shaped with pruning into a more tree-like form. Any reasonable soil in sun or part shade will suit. Flowers are good for cutting.

Viburnum opulus 'Roseum' (syn. V. opulus 'Sterile')
SNOWBALL TREE
3 m x 2 m

A large, old-fashioned shrub that makes an unforgettable show in spring when it covers itself in creamy white balls of flowers. The attractive maple-like leaves turn vibrant autumn tones in cooler climates. Grow in any reasonable soil in sun or part shade.

Flowering crab apple,
Malus floribunda.

EVERGREEN

Alectryon excelsus
TITOKI
7 m x 4 m
Dark glossy-green foliage forms a dense covering on this shapely native tree. It is very hard wearing, as popular for street planting as it is for gardens. Give titoki space to develop its natural rounded canopy. Young trees need protection from frost and strong winds while they establish.

Hymenosporum flavum
AUSTRALIAN FRANGIPANI
6 m x 3 m
A tall, slender, open tree with glossy foliage and beautiful fragrant flowers. The flowers are creamy yellow, produced in spring and summer for long periods. Though unrelated, the flowers are reminiscent of the island frangipani. Because of its open form, the tree, though tall, easily fits into smaller gardens and lets light through its widely spaced branches. It is a fast-growing tree for a warm subtropical climate. Provide a free-draining soil in a sunny sheltered position.

Magnolia grandiflora cultivars
LAUREL MAGNOLIA
7 m x 5 m
Laurel magnolias are capable of growing into enormous trees but these beautiful flowering evergreens from the USA are well suited to an average garden situation. They are easily pruned to control size if necessary. Among the various cultivars are some relatively compact forms. Thick leathery leaves with brown felt on the undersides are the perfect foil to magnificent huge cream flowers with a fragrance. M. grandiflora can be grown in a large container against a wall espalier style or as a lawn tree. They tolerate heavy soils and coastal conditions but need a warm climate and a sunny location.

Meryta sinclairii
PUKA
4 m x 3 m
The New Zealand native puka is treasured for its huge prominently veined leaves, which lend a dramatic tropical mood to any garden. Given space in a well-drained garden soil, they will grow into sizeable round-headed trees. They also make superb container plants — the bigger the container the better they will grow. Puka needs protection from frost when young. Mature plants may be burned but will generally recover from light, infrequent frosts.

Metrosideros excelsa cultivars
POHUTUKAWA
5 m x 4 m
An obvious choice for a coastal garden, a pohutukawa will also grow well in ordinary garden conditions, forming an attractive round-headed tree. Densely foliaged and wind tolerant, pohutukawas also make impressive shelterbelts for exposed sites. They respond well to heavy pruning where necessary, but if space allows are at their most picturesque when allowed to grow into their natural mature form. They will tolerate dry, poor soils but being a coastal tree need protection from frost while young. Pohutukawas grow easily from seed. In the wild, each tree will be slightly different from the next. Various named cultivars have been cloned from selected seedling trees, with attributes such as exceptional flowering performance, colour, and growth habit. M. excelsa 'Scarlet Pimpernel' is a small compact-growing form suitable for a large container. It flowers prolifically for long periods in summer. 'Fire Mountain' is larger growing with large orange-red flowers.

Michelia doltsopa 'Silver Cloud'
4.5 m x 2.5 m
In late winter or early spring M. doltsopa is alight with masses of creamy-white, magnolia-like, fragrant blooms. All year round it is a shapely upright tree with large dark green leaves. 'Silver Cloud' is recommended as it commences flowering at a younger age and is more compact than the species. Lime-free, well-drained soil and full sun are best. Michelia enjoys the same conditions as its close relatives the magnolias.

Olea europaea
OLIVE TREE
6 m x 5 m
Ever more popular in this country as we acquire a taste for the fruit and discover the great landscape versatility of these lovely Mediter-ranean trees. Olive trees thrive in the same climatic conditions as grapes. They require a warm summer to fruit well, but are worthy ornamental trees in most New Zealand gardens. Their main requirement is excellent drainage. They are very attractive in large containers.

Pittosporum eugenioides
LEMONWOOD, TARATA
5 m x 3 m
A fast-growing native tree often used in screening and shelter planting but also good as a small specimen tree. Young trees are bushy and upright, growing into bare-trunked, round-headed trees. The light green foliage is lemon scented when crushed, and the otherwise inconspicuous yellow flowers are sweetly scented. Tarata is tolerant of poor soils and exposed conditions.

Prunus lusitanica
PORTUGUESE LAUREL
5 m x 4 m
Popular for trimming to shape or as a hedge, the Portuguese laurel also makes a fine background or feature tree in its natural shape. The foliage is very dark green and glossy with attractive red stalks. Scented white flowers appear in long, grape-like clusters in summer and are followed by purplish fruits in autumn. Hardy and easy to grow in any average soil or climate.

Sophora tetraptera
KOWHAI
4 m x 3 m
A kowhai tree in full spring bloom is hard to resist. The golden yellow flowers appear in great profusion in spring. Some trees flower in early spring, others later, depending on location and each tree's genetic make-up. Kowhai trees are relatively slow growing and form a slender trunk with a semi-weeping canopy of lacy foliage. They have a graceful airy appearance, ideal as a lawn specimen, shade tree or planted amongst shrubs. Kowhai will grow happily throughout New Zealand, tolerating poor soils and exposed conditions.

Note: The dimensions given for each tree can only be approximate, for average garden conditions, and within the first five to ten years.

DECIDUOUS

Albizia julibrissin
SILK TREE
5 m x 4 m

The best vantage point from which to view a silk tree in flower is from above, for example, from an upper-storey window. The fuzzy brush flowers are soft apricot pink appearing all over the tree in mid-summer. The ferny foliage is also attractive, falling in autumn to reveal attractively arranged branches. This popular tree has a spreading umbrella shape, appealing arching over entranceways or as a shade tree for sitting under. Remove the lower branches as young trees grow to enhance the umbrella shape. *Albizzia* is a quick-growing tree that needs space. It revels in a hot dry summer.

Ginkgo biloba
MAIDENHAIR TREE
7 m x 4 m

Ginkgos are the most ancient trees still in existence. They are also among the most beautiful — of graceful form with unusual-shaped leaves (like a maidenhair fern) that are light green when they first appear in spring, and gold when they drop in autumn. Ginkgos can grow quite large but their relatively slow growth rate makes them well suited to the average-sized garden. Ginkgo trees are either male or female. It is a male (grafted) that you want, unless you would like your garden to smell something like dinosaur droppings! The fleshy fruit that drops from a female tree makes a smelly mess. Ginkgos are easy to grow in any climate in any reasonable soil.

Gleditsia triacanthos cultivars
HONEY LOCUST
6 m x 5 m

Gleditsias are quick-growing, very pretty trees with soft lacy foliage and an attractive spreading shape. They make good shade trees and are ideal as a front lawn highlight. The shade cast through the feathery foliage is of a lovely dappled quality, allowing lawns to keep growing and providing a nice microclimate for both people and shade-loving plants. The species *G. triacanthos* is a thorny tree best suited to farms, but its cultivars are thornless. 'Sunburst' is deservedly popular. It has golden-yellow young

spring foliage deepening to cool greens as it matures. The new growth continues through summer, giving a very delicate two-tone effect of gold on green. 'Emerald Cascade' provides an all-green look for spring and summer. It is significantly smaller growing than 'Sunburst'.

Jacaranda mimosifolia
JACARANDA
7 m x 5 m

Amazing lilac-blue summer flowers are what makes this such a coveted tree. Also the foliage is pleasantly light and airy. Jacarandas need a warm frost-free climate and well-drained soil. Stake young trees and prune lower lateral branches to create a strong single trunk as they grow. Evergreen in the tropics.

Magnolia denudata
YULAN MAGNOLIA
5 m x 3 m

Through winter, furry buds perch like little birds on the bare branches. In spring they unfold into the most magnificent creamy-white, tulip-shaped blooms, which are fragrant. In the summer they are a relatively unremarkable but not unattractive tree, with large green leaves and a rounded shape. Plant in well-drained, lime-free, composty soil and add a layer of mulch. If you wish to prune to control shape or size, do it immediately after flowering.

Melia azederach
INDIAN BEAD TREE
7 m x 5 m

Bigger-than-average examples exist, but this is generally a good-sized tree for the average suburban garden, and one of the loveliest. The foliage is glossy green and finely divided. The tree has a tidy rounded umbrella shape with a clean straight trunk. Clusters of fragrant purple flowers in spring lead to attractive yellow berries that remain on the branches after the leaves fall in autumn. The berries bring birds into the garden. This is an ideal shade or front-garden feature tree, thriving in warmer climates and tolerating coastal conditions. Deservedly well used as a street tree, showing just how hard wearing it is.

Prunus 'Accolade'
FLOWERING CHERRY
6 m x 5 m

This is a lovely hybrid cherry with an early spring display of rich pink blossom. The flowers are semi-double, 4 cm across and hang in clusters from the wide-spreading branches. A nice shade tree for summer picnics and a good one for autumn foliage.

Prunus campanulata
TAIWAN CHERRY
5 m x 3 m

One of the earliest blossom trees, flowering in late winter before the leaves appear. Deep cerise bell-shaped flowers hang in clusters and are full of nectar to attract birds. An upright vase-shaped tree, attractive planted in groups where there is room. Underplant with early flowering daffodils. Better in mild climates as the blossoms can be damaged by frost.

Prunus cerasifera 'Nigra'
PURPLE LEAF CHERRY
4 m x 3 m

If you like the rich foliage colour of the copper beech but need something faster growing and less grandiose in maturity, then this may be your tree. The dark purple foliage persists through spring, summer and autumn, and contrasted with green-foliaged trees is dramatic. Small pink flowers in spring are a bonus.

Prunus 'Shimidsu-sakura'
FLOWERING CHERRY
4 m x 5 m

An umbrella-shaped blossom tree, ideal as a shade tree, 'Shimidsu Sakura' has clusters of pink buds opening to white hanging on the branches from October to November (later than 'Accolade') at the same time as the fresh green young foliage. The foliage is brilliantly coloured in autumn.

Prunus 'Shirotae'
MT FUJI CHERRY
5 m x 5 m

This nicely shaped tree is a visual treat in mid-spring when wide-spreading branches are clothed in drooping clusters of large snowy-white flowers. It has good autumn colour too.

Prunus xyedoensis 'Awanui'
YOSHINO CHERRY
5 m x 8 m
A mature Yoshino cherry has a distinctive horizontal shape, significantly wider than it is tall. A perfect specimen for a Japanese-style garden, as a shade tree or wherever a spectacular spring-flowering tree is in demand. The flowers are pale shell pink, produced in great volume in mid-spring.

Robinia pseudacacia 'Frisia'
ROBINIA
4 m x 3 m
Perhaps the loveliest yellow-foliage tree, R. 'Frisia' quickly forms a rounded, spreading tree with soft and airy, golden yellow foliage from spring through autumn. It will grow in any average garden soil, tolerating dry conditions once established. Robinia 'Mop Top' is a compact form, grafted on to a tall standard, effective for pots or small gardens. It requires annual pruning to maintain its neat rounded 'mop top'.

Magnolia campbellii.

EVERGREEN

Agathis australis
KAURI

8 m x 3 m

The king of the forests, a mature kauri tree would hardy fit into an average garden, but one you plant today won't reach such proportions in your lifetime. The straight upright form of a young kauri tree with its distinctive bark and bronze foliage is an attractive garden feature. They will grow in most parts of New Zealand, in any reasonable soil provided they get frost and wind protection in the first few years. Water during dry periods.

Dacrydium cupressinum
RIMU

6 m x 3 m

Another New Zealand native with a distinctive growth habit and slow enough growing to allow its presence in an average-sized garden. It will grow anywhere except in coastal conditions. The ideal soil is deep, rich and well drained with plenty of moisture, though it will tolerate periods of dryness once established.

Eucalyptus ficifolia
RED FLOWERING GUM

7 m x 5 m

E. ficifolia is a single-trunked tree with a dense round head, becoming clothed in fuzzy orange-red flowers throughout summer into autumn. The stringy fibrous bark is an added attraction and the leaves are pretty throughout the year. Best in warm climates, requiring protection from frost while young.

Grevillea robusta
SILKY OAK

8 m x 5 m

Silky oak is a large, fast-growing tree. It can be trimmed but is best grown in a bigger garden. The leaves are distinctively fern-like and enough of a feature in themselves, but in spring the tree becomes covered in masses of golden-orange flowers. Grow in any average soil. Silky oak is an Australian native, best in warm climates.

Knightia excelsa
REWAREWA

7 m x 2 m

A tall narrow tree that will always be noticed, rewarewa is also very attractive to native birds when in flower. Flowers are reddish brown with an unusual brush-like form. The leaves, too, are unusual: long and narrow with toothed margins, making an interesting textural contrast when viewed from a distance. Being slender of habit, rewarewa will fit into an average-sized garden and suits coastal conditions.

Podocarpus totara
TOTARA

6 m x 4 m

Dense, dark olive-green foliage is an attractive permanent asset in a garden. Totara can be clipped to almost any size or shape provided it is trimmed from a young age. It is ideal as a hedge. Where there is space it makes a handsome specimen tree, but as such is at its best where it can be given space. Totara is easy to grow in any climate or soil but does not enjoy coastal conditions.

Schinus molle
PEPPER TREE

6 m x 5 m

Not unlike a willow tree at first glance, but much more beautiful, pepper tree grows quickly in warm climates and with age develops into a gracefully weeping tree with soft feathery foliage and lovely gnarled branches. It makes an attractive shade tree, letting through enough light so that lawn and groundcover plants can be grown beneath it. Once established a pepper tree will stand up to drought, wet conditions and light frost.

DECIDUOUS

Betula pendula
SILVER BIRCH

8 m x 5 m

The silver trunk and branches make this tree stand out at any time of the year, but it is particularly appealing in winter when the tree is leafless and the bark shines brightly, even on dull days. Planted in informal groups underplanted with spring bulbs they are perhaps at their very best, but it's a look for a larger-than-average garden. Young trees have brown bark, the silver developing as the trees mature, but it is better to plant young trees than to transplant very large ones. Water through dry spells in the first few years after planting. Silver birch grows in any reasonable soil in any climate.

Fagus sylvatica 'Purpurea'
COPPER BEECH

10 m x 6 m

Possibly the finest foliage tree you could ever plant. The colour and texture of the copper beech leaves, artistically arranged on their branches, is unmatched by any other tree. Slow growth means that it can be kept in a large container or accommodated in a small garden for a number of years. Copper beech ultimately grows into a magnificent pyramid-shaped tree with a wonderful branch pattern. The foliage is prized for picking. Copper beech grows in any average soil in any climate, but is not one for the coast. Protect from strong winds, especially while young.

Fraxinus angustifolia 'Raywood' (syn. F. oxycarpa 'Raywoodii')
CLARET ASH

8 m x 5 m

This fast-growing pyramid-shaped tree is one of the favourites for autumn colour, turning a deep claret red and holding well into winter. It will tolerate boggy soils and climatic extremes once established. It is popular as a street tree, especially in climates cold enough to make the most of the autumn foliage. In spring and summer it is attractive with its dense canopy of finely textured bright green foliage.

Liquidambar styraciflua
AMERICAN SWEET GUM

8 m x 5 m

Liquidambars will produce good autumn colour even in a mild climate,

Note: The dimensions given for each tree can only be approximate, for average garden conditions, and within the first five to ten years.

producing a magnificent blend of red, orange, purple and yellow all on the same tree. Getting a seedling tree can involve a bit of pot luck. The degree of autumn colour is genetically variable, some trees not colouring up at all well. To get around this, buy a grafted or cutting-grown tree of a named variety. The different cultivars have been selected for various characters. *L. styraciflua* 'Palo Alto' has an upright form with red, orange and gold autumn colour. 'Kia' has a broad pyramid form with orange-red and purple tones.

Magnolia campbellii
PINK TULIP TREE
7 m x 5 m
The earliest-flowering magnolia, *M. campbellii*, is covered in giant-sized, soft pink blooms in late winter. They are more like waterlilies than tulips, sitting on horizontal, bare branches. The only drawback is that trees can take up to 10 years to flower. Plant in well-drained, lime-free, composty soil and add a layer of mulch.

Quercus coccinea
SCARLET OAK
7 m x 5 m
There are lots of different oak trees. All are lovely in the right place. *Q. coccinea* is one of the best for autumn colour and branch pattern, with a spreading pyramidal form. The open branch structure allows lawn to grow underneath it. Autumn colour is bright red, but best in colder climates. It is easy to grow, establishing very quickly in good soils and resisting drought once established.

FEATURE TREES FOR SEASONAL HIGHLIGHTS

WINTER FLOWERING

Franklinia axillaris	white
Magnolia campbellii	white
Prunus campanulata	dark pink
Michelia doltsopa 'Silver Cloud'	cream
Cornus 'Eddie's White Wonder'	white

SPRING FLOWERING

Prunus 'Accolade'	pink
Prunus 'Shimidsu-sakura'	pink
Prunus 'Shirotae'	white
Prunus subhirtella 'Falling snow'	white
Prunus subhirtella 'Pendula'	pink
Prunus xyedoensis 'Awanui'	pink
Sophora tetraptera	yellow
Magnolia denudata	white
Magnolia xsoulangiana	pink, white
Magnolia stellata	white, pink
Malus floribunda	pink
Stachyurus praecox	cream
Viburnum opulus 'Roseum'	white

SUMMER FLOWERING

Jacaranda mimosifolia	blue
Callistemon citrinus 'Splendens'	red
Metrosideros excelsa cultivars	red
Magnolia grandiflora	white, cream
Albizia julibrissin	pink
Lagerstroemia indica	pink
Eucalyptus ficifolia	red

AUTUMN FOLIAGE

Acer palmatum
Cornus 'Eddie's White Wonder'
Cotinus coggygria
Fraxinus angustifolia 'Raywood'
Ginkgo biloba
Gleditsia triacanthos 'Sunburst'
Liquidambar styraciflua
Prunus serrulata 'Shirotae'
Quercus coccinea
Robinia pseudacacia
Viburnum trilobum

BERRIES OR FRUIT

Citrus cultivars
Malus 'Jack Humm'
Melia azederach
Viburnum trilobum
Olea europaea
Prunus lusitanica

Star magnolia,
Magnolia stellata.

Screens, Backgrounds and Shelter Planting

In the creation of a new garden there are some things that need seeing to very early in the piece. Privacy and the screening of unwanted views are key to the enjoyment of a garden. Shelter also tops the list of priorities, for the sake of the occupants of the garden — both plants and people. As well as serving practical purposes, such planting provides a visual backdrop for the rest of the garden.

Screen and shelter planting can be made up of a mixture of different trees and shrubs or a single species. The planting may be quite wide and fill an irregular-shaped space or in a line as a hedge. If you decide on a combination of plants, try not to have too many different textures and colours. Simplicity is best if the screen planting is to double as a visually effective background planting. Generally it works best to have three, five or more of each species in a mixed shrub planting. With one of each you can end up with a patchy, restless look.

New Zealand natives work well together as mixed background plantings. Many are quick growing and they also tend to be tolerant of difficult soils and climatic extremes. Important attributes for screen and shelter plants are rapid growth, a good covering of evergreen foliage, and, in the case of shelter planting, the ability to stand up to wind.

More about hedges: Go to page 25.

More about New Zealand natives: Go to page 62.

FAST AND EASY SCREEN AND SHELTER TREES

BOTANICAL NAME	COMMON NAME	HEIGHT	SCREEN	SHELTER	COASTAL	FROST TENDER
Banksia integrifolia	Coast banksia	8 m	✔	✔	✔	✔
Buddleia davidii	Butterfly bush	3 m	✔		✔	✔
Casuarina glauca	Swamp sheoke	6 m	✔	✔		
Corokia cotoneaster	Wire netting bush	2.5 m	✔	✔	✔	
Cupressocyparis leylandii	Leyland cypress	5 m	✔	✔	✔	
Feijoa sellowiana	Feijoa	3 m	✔	✔		✔
Hoheria populnea	Lacebark	5 m	✔			
Lagunaria patersonii	Norfold Island hibiscus	8 m	✔	✔	✔	✔
Metrosideros excelsa	Pohutukawa	5 m	✔	✔	✔	✔
Olearia albida	Tanguru	4 m	✔	✔	✔	
Pittosporum crassifolium	Karo	3 m	✔	✔	✔	
Pittosporum eugenioides	Lemonwood	5 m	✔	✔		
Pittosporum tenuifolium	Kohuhu	5 m	✔			
Prunus lusitanica	Portuguese laurel	5 m	✔			
Salix chilensis	Pencil willow	8 m	✔			✔
Syzygium australe	Australian rose apple	7 m	✔	✔	✔	✔
Thuja plicata	Western red cedar	8 m	✔	✔		

Hedges

Every garden needs its walls. The provision of privacy, screening, shelter and security is often the first consideration when creating a new garden. Garden 'walls' may be built from brick, stone or timber. Alternatively, they may comprise living plants in the form of hedges.

Because it generally takes longer to grow a wall than it does to build one, fences win out over hedges as the most popular choice for property boundaries. Hedges also require more space and more looking after, but is the softer, friendlier option. A street full of hedges is a lot kinder on the eye than the more commonly seen rows of fences, each one different to the next. A small city garden needs as much greenery as possible for visual relief from the buildings and artificial surfaces that surround it.

Although a fence or masonry wall can be a strikingly attractive feature of a garden, it can also detract if the materials and design are not chosen carefully to suit the house and style of garden. A hedge will meld into the garden easily with little risk of looking out of place. It is simply part of the structure of the garden, forming a solid background for other plantings. A good hedge will unify the garden, holding it all together even if the rest of the planting tends to get bitsy.

Low hedges, although not for screening or privacy, still define spaces and provide solidity. In a small formal garden, the entire framework may consist of hedges without any other tree and shrub planting. Box hedging (*Buxus sempervirens*) is widely used in this manner to 'hold together' rose and perennial gardens. Small evergreen hedges are particularly useful as borders around beds of roses or other deciduous shrubs and perennials that have no presence in winter.

By screening parts of the garden so that all is not revealed in one sweeping glance, hedges make a garden all the more enticing and can make small gardens appear larger. Not that I am suggesting you turn your garden into a maze. A feeling of spaciousness is important too, but it's nice to create a sense of discovery and, by doing so, draw attention to all the best features of your garden.

Hedges are common in formal gardens but they are not out of place in any style of garden. They can be tall or short, clipped or unclipped, straight or curved. Mostly they consist of small-leaved evergreen shrubs, but deciduous shrubs can also be used where it doesn't matter about bare branches in winter or when the leafless period is relatively short.

The silver foliage of *Teucrium fruticans* contrasts with bright green *Buxus sempervirens* in a two-tier border hedge.

MAKING A HEDGE

1 Decide how tall you want your hedge to be and choose a suitable plant for your soil and climate. It helps to find out what hedge plants are already thriving in your locality. Bear in mind that some hedges grow faster than others, and the faster they grow the more regularly they will demand trimming to maintain shape and height.

2 Measure the length of your hedge and how many plants you will need. Planting spacings are given on page 28. The closer you plant the more quickly your hedge will become established. It is better to be over-generous than to risk a gappy hedge.

3 Shop around to buy your plants. You may need to order ahead to get the required amount. You should be able to get a good price for a bulk lot of plants. Small healthy plants will establish more quickly and more evenly than larger ones that have been in their containers too long. If planting in winter you may be able to buy bare-root plants dug directly from the ground, which should be less expensive for their size than container-grown plants.

4 Mark out the line of your hedge and prepare the ground. If the soil has been unworked for a while, you'll need to dig it over to about a spade's depth, breaking up the heavy clods. Add any soil improvers or fertilisers and work them into the soil. Exactly what you add will depend on how well your soil meets the plant's requirements but in general a shovel of compost and a sprinkling of slow-release fertiliser for each plant will aid rapid establishment.

5 The ideal planting time is autumn but any time will do as long as you remember to water new plantings during dry weather. For this reason summer planting is best avoided. Using a string line as a guide, lay out your plants and plant as for any tree or shrub.

6 Keep the newly planted hedge deeply watered and weed free, especially in the first growing season. To retain moisture and assist with weed control add a thick layer of mulch.

Soils:
Go to page 190.

Watering:
Go to page 202.

Mulching:
Go to page 204.

KEEPING A HEDGE LOOKING GOOD

Regular trimming is what keeps a hedge looking lush and in good shape. If left too long the hedge will grow untidy and out of shape, often to a point where permanent damage is done. How often you need to trim depends on the growth rate of the species in your particular soil and climatic conditions, but most will require trimming at least once a year. Flowering hedges, such as camellias and lavender, should be pruned immediately after flowering.

If you have a lot of hedge to trim, investing in a set of electric hedge sheers is highly recommended.

If the base of a hedge receives too little light, it will often lose its bottom storey of leaves and get that leggy look. Try and avoid this by tapering your hedge so that it is narrowest at the top. It's all too easy to end up with the reverse situation if you're not careful.

Some hedges are very efficient at drawing deep and wide into the soil for food once they are established and grow fast enough without any encouragement. However, most will benefit from a dose of fertiliser every few years to keep them healthy and green. Every time you trim a hedge you dispose of a good helping of its energy in the form of clippings, so trimming and feeding at the same time is a good idea.

A rosemary hedge.

A neatly clipped, curved hedge of silver grey *Teucrium fruticans*.

Lonicera nitida 'Aurea', an appealing alternative to *Buxus* in this coastal garden.

RECOMMENDED HEDGES

FOLIAGE HEDGES

Small

BOTANICAL NAME	COMMON NAME	HEIGHT RNAGE	FOLIAGE COLOUR	SPACING
Berberis thunbergii 'Atropurpurea'	Purple barberry	1 m	`wine red	30–50 cm
Buxus semperivrens cultivars	English box	30 cm – 1 m	dark green	30–50 cm
Coprosma 'Beatson's Gold'		1 m – 1.5 m	green & gold	50–75 m
Lonicera nitida	Box honeysuckle	50 cm – 1.2 m	green	30–50 cm
Lonicera nitida 'Aurea'	Golden box honeysuckle	50 cm – 1.2 m	gold	30–50 cm
Santolina chamaecyparissus	Lavender cotton	50 cm	silver grey	20–3- cm
Teucrium fruticans	Silver germander	80 cm – 1.5 m	silver grey	30–50 cm

Medium to tall

BOTANICAL NAME	COMMON NAME	HEIGHT RNAGE	FOLIAGE COLOUR	SPACING
Corokia cotoneaster	Wire netting bush	1.5–2.5 m	grey-green	50–60 cm
Escallonia cultivars	Escallonia	1.5–2 m	dark green	50–60 cm
Feijoa sellowiana	Feijoa	2–3 m	grey-green	1 m
Hydrangea	Hydrangea	1–2 m	dark green	50–60 cm
Ilex aquifolium	Holly	2–3 m	dark green	1 m
Juniperus chinensis	Chinese juniper	2–3 m	dark green	1 m
Lauris nobilis	Bay tree	1–3 m	dark green	80–100 cm
Prunus lusitanica	Portuguese laurel	2–3 m	dark green	1 m
Syzygium australe (syn. Eugenia australis)	Australian rose apple	2–3 m	dark green	1 m
Tecomaria capensis	Tecoma, Cape honeysuckle	1–3 m	dark green	50–60 cm
Thuja plicata	Western red cedar	2–3 m	dark green	1 m
Viburnum tinus	Laurustinus	1.5–2 m	dark green	80–100 cm

FLOWERING HEDGES

BOTANICAL NAME	COMMON NAME	HEIGHT RNAGE	FOLIAGE COLOUR	SPACING
Camellia 'Debbie'	Camellia	2.5 m	bright pink	80–100 cm
Camellia 'Donation'	Camellia	2.5 m	pink	80–100 cm
Camellia sasanqua 'Hiryu'	Camellia	2.5 m	red	80–100 cm
Camellia sasanqua 'Jennifer Susan'	Camellia	2.0 m	lavender pink	80–100 cm
Camellia sasanqua 'Mine-no-yuki'	Camellia	2.0 m	white	80–100 cm
Camellia sasanqua 'Plantation Pink'	Camellia	2.5 m	light pink	80–100 cm
Camellia sasanqua 'Setsugekka'	Camellia	2.5 m	white	80–100 cm
Choisya ternata	Mexican orange blossom	1–1.5 m	white	50–75 cm
Hebe cultivars	Koromiko	50 cm – 1 m	pink, white, lavender	30–50 cm
Lavandula 'Helmsdale'	Lavender	70 cm	lavender	30–50 cm
Lavandula angustifolia cultivars	English Lavender	30–60 cm	lavender	30–50 cm
Lavandula dentata	French Lavender	1–1.2 m	lavender	30–50 cm
Lavandula 'Marshwood'	Lavender	1 m	lavender	30–50 cm
Lavandula stoechas varieties	Lavender	80 cm	lavender	30–50 cm
Rosmarinus officinalis	Rosemary	80 cm – 1.5 m	blue	30–50 cm

More about camellias:
Go to page 44.

More about English box:
Go to page 31.

More about lavender:
Go to page 41.

More about other shrubs in this list:
Go to pages 30–40.

Shrubs A to Z

Shrubs look good and are easy to care for. They may take the form of hedges, mass plantings or as backgrounds to the more labour-intensive perennials and annuals. If your garden looks bare and uninteresting in winter, you probably need to plant more evergreen shrubs.

Choose shrubs that are suitable for your climate, soil and the planting position (microclimate). Base your selection first on dimensions, then consider form and texture (leaf size and shape). Try to think about time of flowering as much as flower colour. It is possible to colour coordinate flowering and, for example, to have a pink garden in early spring and a yellow theme in summer.

Deciduous shrubs provide some of the most spectacular seasonal flower displays or autumn foliage, but you should stick to a solid grounding of mainly evergreen shrubs.

The list of shrubs that follows includes the deservedly popular top performers. Some are best reserved for sandy, very well-drained soils, but the great majority will grow well in any average soil.

Note that the dimensions given for each plant can only be approximate for average garden conditions.

Cistus incanus,
rock rose.

Acer palmatum Dissectum Hybrids
WEEPING MAPLE
1 x 1.5 m
Intricately divided, lacy leaves are closely arranged on graceful cascading branches, eventually weeping to the ground — slow to get to this state but worth the wait. A wide range of colours for each season is represented amongst the cultivars. The autumn colours are particularly attractive. These shrubs are perfect for water gardens, Japanese gardens, containers and for mass planting. They must have shelter from wind and prefer a deep, cool, well-drained soil with plenty of compost. Sun or part shade. Deciduous.

Adenandra uniflora
CHINA FLOWER
60 cm x 1 m
A compact spring-flowering shrub that smothers itself in delicate, porcelain-like white flowers in spring and summer. An attractive pathside feature, good for banks and pots. China flower likes full sun and a sandy soil or can be grown in a pot. Evergreen.

Anigozanthos hybrids
KANGAROO PAW
60 cm to1 m x 50 cm
Kangaroo paws are a superb feature for a dry garden or pot. Flowering over long periods in spring and summer, they are prized for striking and long-lasting vase displays. The long-stemmed flowers are appropriately named for their shape and come in a range of interesting colour combinations, including orange, yellow, red and emerald green. Recent developments have led to disease-resistant strains, which are far superior to earlier forms. Full sun, a frost-free location, and a sandy, well-drained soil are needed to grow them successfully. Evergreen.

Aucuba japonica
JAPANESE LAUREL
Among the most attractive foliage plants for shady corners and excellent for pots, aucubas have the bonus of bright red winter berries. A. japonica has large, deep green shiny leaves with coarsely toothed margins. There are numerous cultivars with variously patterned variegated leaves. Some are male, some female. At least one

Aucuba japonica.

of each is needed for berries. A. japonica 'Crotonoides' is a female, boldly splashed and spotted with golden yellow. A. japonica 'Mr Goldstrike' is male with similar but smaller markings. Frost tender.

Azalea evergreen hybrids
1 m x1 m
About as showy and colourful as a small shrub gets, azaleas are at their most brilliant mass planted under and around deciduous trees. They are also fine tub specimens. Plant a selection with different flowering times for long season displays in autumn and spring. Colours range from white through pinks, apricots and purples to every shade of red. Semi-shade is best in a warm climate, but most will tolerate full sun in cooler climates. Too much shade will inhibit flowering. Mulch to keep roots cool. Evergreen.

More about azaleas: Go to page 47.

Berberis thunbergii 'Atropurpurea'
PURPLE BARBERRY
1.3 m x 1 m
Great for foliage colour contrasts and a superb low hedge, this hardy shrub is without leaves for only a very short time in mid-winter. Tolerant of difficult clay soils, but best in full sun. Deciduous.

Brachyglottis (syn. Senecio) 'Otari Cloud'
1.2 m x 1.2 m
A neat rounded native shrub sporting some of the best silver foliage. It is good as a filler, massed with other shrubs, and does well on the coast. Full sun and a well-drained soil are ideal. Dry conditions are tolerated. Yellow daisy flowers appear in summer. Trim each year to maintain compactness. Evergreen.

Brunfelsia calycina 'Eximia'
YESTERDAY, TODAY, TOMORROW
1 m x 1 m
Fragrant flowers progress from deep to pale lavender, then to white, the different colours displayed on the bush all at once. The dark green foliage is covered in flowers in spring and summer. This is a much-loved shrub for a warm, frost-free climate. Evergreen.

Callistemon 'Little John'
DWARF BOTTLEBRUSH
75 m x 75 cm
A hardy, charitable little shrub forgiving of heavy soils, windy, dry and coastal conditions. Good in a mixed shrub planting, mass planted or in pots. Flowers profusely in full sun with a covering of red fuzzy flowers, mainly in spring. The foliage is an attractive grey green and the habit even and compact. Evergreen.

Ceanothus 'Blue Cushion'
CALIFORNIAN LILAC
75 cm x 1.5 m
A quick-growing prostrate shrub, useful as a groundcover on a hot dry bank, 'Blue Cushion' smothers itself in bright blue flowers in spring. It needs good drainage and full sun, tolerating dry and coastal conditions. Good for a pot. Evergreen.

Ceratostigma willmottianum
CHINESE PLUMBAGO
60 cm x 1m
Rich royal blue flowers over a long summer/autumn season are the main attraction but orange and red autumn tones, even in a mild climate, add value to this charming little shrub with its low spreading form. Best in a warm sunny spot. It will suffer frost burn but recovers well. Prune in spring. Deciduous in colder climates.

Note: The dimensions given for each plant can only be approximate, for average garden conditions.

Boronias

Boronias are quick-growing shrubs valued for their stunning spring flower displays. They are good for picking and some are delightfully perfumed. They need a well-drained soil that is not allowed to dry out. Boronias are relatively short-lived shrubs, but worth planting even for just one season. Extend their life by pruning bushes back to half their height after flowering.

Boronia heterophylla
RED BORONIA
1.3 m x 75 cm
A massive display of fragrant rosy-red flowers like miniature tulips right through spring.

Boronia megastigma 'Heaven Scent'
BROWN BORONIA
50 cm x 30 cm
The best fragrance from masses of deep purple-brown flowers.

Boronia megastigma 'Lutea'
YELLOW BORONIA
1m x 75 cm
Light green foliage and greenish-yellow flowers.

Boronia muelleri 'Sunset Serenade'
1m x 1m
Star-shaped flowers, cream turning to pink to bright cerise, blooming profusely from late winter to the end of spring. Prune lightly after flowering

English Box

The dense dark green foliage of English box is unbeatable for trimming and shaping and looks good in the garden all year round, being extremely useful as permanent framework in small garden spaces. English box is happy in any average garden soil or in a container, trained as a standard by removing lower branches and trimming the top into a ball shape, or grown as a neat rounded shrub, trimmed to any size. English box is relatively slow growing, but long lived and trouble free — very, very easy. It tolerates drought, frost, wind and heavy soils, growing in sun or shade in any climate.

Buxus sempervirens
ENGLISH BOX
The most widely planted box, famous as a border hedge and for topiary. Evergreen.

Buxus sempervirens 'Marginata'
VARIEGATED ENGLISH BOX
The same as plain English box except for its variegated gold and green leaves. Use it in conjunction with green box as interesting contrast. Adds brightness to dull areas. Evergreen.

Buxus sempervirens 'Suffruticosa'
MINIATURE ENGLISH BOX
Smaller leaves, smaller and slower growing than the species, miniature box is great for a low border or pots. Evergreen.

Chamaecyparis obtusa 'Nana'
50 cm x 75 cm
This small neatly shaped conifer has been a favourite with the Japanese for centuries. It has dense clusters of dark green foliage arranged in upward-facing fans. Famous for rock gardens and good in pots. Grow it in full sun or part shade. Evergreen.

Choisya ternata
MEXICAN ORANGE BLOSSOM
1.5 x 1.5 m
This is a very popular landscaping shrub for good reason. It has a year-round dense covering of glossy three-fingered leaves and a long show of white flower clusters centering around late winter and spring. The flowers look and smell like orange blossom.

Quick growing, it is a good shrub for a background filler, mass planting, or bold-textured hedges. It needs to be trimmed to maintain a compact habit, best done after the main flower flush. *Choisya* is easy to grow in any reasonable soil in sun or part shade. Evergreen.

Cistus cultivars
ROCK ROSE
75 x 75 cm
Cistus grow well in dry soils, tolerating coastal conditions, heat and wind. They do not like heavy clay soils that are cold and damp in winter, but can be grown in a container. *C.* 'Lusitanicus' has grey-green mounding foliage and is covered in spring and summer with single rose-like flowers, white with crimson blotches. 'Bennett's White' is a cottage gardener's favourite with large white flowers. Evergreen.

Coleonema pulchrum 'Sunset Gold'
75 cm x 1 m
A very popular low-spreading shrub with soft-textured golden-yellow foliage. In early spring it becomes covered in tiny pink starry flowers. Plant in well-drained soil in full sun and trim after flowering to maintain a dense covering of foliage. Good in containers or mass planted as a groundcover. Evergreen.

The golden foliage of *Coleonema pulchrum* 'Sunset Gold'.

Coleonema pulchrum 'Winter Charm'
PINK DIOSMA
1.2 m x 1.5 m
Graceful branches with small close-packed leaves form a dense bushy shrub, which in spring is covered in starry pink flowers perfect for picking. Requires full sun, a well-drained soil and a light trim after flowering. It is intolerant of heavy frosts.

Convolvulus cneorum
60 cm x 1 m
Here is an easy, quick-growing shrub with a wonderful combination of silver foliage and white flowers. The foliage has a delightful silky texture and the flowers continue through spring, summer and autumn. The shape is low and semi-weeping. As long as it has excellent drainage this is one of the best white-flowered shrubs for mass planting along walls, as a border to taller shrubs (e.g., roses), cascading over banks, or in pots. It tolerates coastal conditions. Evergreen.

Coprosma 'Middlemore'
1 m x 1 m
A neat and reliable shrub, ideal where a plain green foliage shrub is needed. Rich green glossy leaves and compact growth. Useful for a low hedge, mass coastal planting and basic background planting, it survives harsh coastal conditions, dry spells and and heavy clay. Good in sun or shade. Evergreen.

Coprosma 'Pride'
80 cm x 80 cm
This is one of a range of colourful-leafed coprosmas. The leaves are highly polished, bright green splashed with yellow and hints of orange, turning brighter in autumn. The neat compact shrub copes easily with poor soils and harsh environments, in sun or shade. Evergreen.

Coprosma 'Yvonne'
1.5 x 1 m
A brave survivor for tough environments, this native hybrid is also very pretty. The foliage is glossy as if given a coat of polyurethane and

coloured dark bronzy green. It makes an excellent contrast amongst other shrubs. Trim to keep it in good shape. Good on the coast, and in clay or dry soils. Evergreen.

Eriostemon myoporoides 'Stardust'
WAX FLOWER
1 m x 1.5 m
Waxy citrus-scented foliage is covered in winter and spring with small starry white flowers. It copes with dry soils and most climates but prefers good drainage and semi-shade. Prune after flowering to maintain shape and vigour.

Genista 'Yellow Imp'
1 m x 1 m
An accommodating little shrub, good for garden or container, displaying masses of small yellow flowers from spring. Trim after the first flowering flush to encourage more flowers in autumn. Tolerates dry soil but needs good drainage and full sun. Evergreen.

Grewia occidentalis
1.5 m x 1.5 m
Bright lavender-pink star-shaped flowers occur for a long spring and summer season on a compact dark green shrub. Grewia is frost tender and prefers a well-drained soil in full sun or part shade. Good for a hedge in a warm climate. Evergreen.

Lavandula spp. & cultivars
LAVENDER
Fragrant foliage and fragrant flowers on compact shrubs used for hedges, backgrounds, in pots, and planted amongst roses, perennials and other

Daphne

The daphne fragrance is impossible to resist. The fact that they flower in winter or early spring adds to their attraction. They will perform well in most climates as long as they have well-drained soil. Yellow leaves usually mean poor drainage. Part shade is best, especially in a warm climate, but full shade will limit flowering. Daphnes also like cool, lime-free conditions. Feed with camellia and azalea plant food. If yellow leaves persist in well-drained conditions your daphne may well have an iron-deficiency problem, which can be remedied with a dose of iron chelates.

The most reliable daphnes in any climate are the *Daphne odora* cultivars.

Daphne odora 'Leucanthe'
UPRIGHT DAPHNE
1 m x1 m
A neat rounded bush with large clusters of deep pink and white flowers on short stems all along the branches.

Daphne odora 'Rubra'
PINK DAPHNE
60 cm x 1 m
A more spreading, informal habit. Flowers are good for picking, being produced in tight pink and white clusters on extended stalks

Erica

Ericas (heaths) are generally cool-climate shrubs, but there are a number that will flower in mild climates. They are easy to grow with a wide range of growth habits, foliage and flower colours. Flowering seasons also vary to the extent that careful selection can provide flowers for every month of the year.

Growth habits range from prostrate groundcovers to large bushes. Mass planted they provide a low-maintenance patchwork of colour. Flowers, which are good for picking, range in colour from pink, through reds, purples, white, cream and oranges.

There are few problems with pests and disease, and they are known for their wind tolerance.

Ericas prefer an open, sunny position. A peaty, sandy soil enriched with compost is ideal. They enjoy the same lime-free soil conditions as rhododendrons and camellias, which make ideal companions. Avoid heavy fertiliser applications.

Annual trimming keeps plants compact and free flowering. Prune winter- and spring-flowering varieties after flowering and summer-flowering varieties in spring.

Closely related to ericas, the heathers (*Calluna* spp.) are another cold-climate shrub, some of which provide excellent foliage colours ranging from bright yellows to orangey bronze and silvery greys.

Erica carnea 'Snow Queen'
15 cm x 25 cm
Flowers are lemon in bud, opening to large white flowers on a plant with a neat compact habit. Evergreen.

Erica carnea 'Springwood Pink'
20 cm x 40 cm
Winter- and spring-flowering, 'Springwood Pink' makes a neat spreading mound covered in pink blooms. Fast growing and very tough, this is a good companion for spring bulbs. It is tolerant of chalky and dry soils. Evergreen.

Erica carnea 'Springwood White'
20 cm x 40 cm
'Springwood White' is the snowy-white-flowered version of 'Springwood Pink'. Evergreen.

Erica xdarleyensis 'Darley Dale'
45 cm x 60 cm
An extremely hardy winter-flowering variety with lilac-rose flowers. Best suited to cold climates. Evergreen.

Erica subdivaricata 'Autumn Snow'
75 cm x 75 cm
Masses of fragrant, tiny, white, bell-shaped flowers appear in late summer. A South African form suited to mild climates.

Erica walkeri
40 cm x 70 cm
One of the most beautiful ericas, growing well in a warmer climate, though tolerant of mild frosts. China pink, fragrant, star-shaped flowers appear in spring on a compact mounding bush.

Erica 'Winter Charm'
1m x 1m
A South African heath suitable for a warmer climate, 'Winter Charm' produces masses of deep pink bells throughout winter. Evergreen.

---

shrubs. About the most popular and useful of small garden shrubs, lavenders warrant a chapter all of their own.

Loropetalum chinense
FRINGE FLOWER
1 m x1 m
A low cascading shrub from China, ideal for walls, in rock gardens or pots. Interesting greenish-white tassel flowers appear in great numbers in spring, giving the plant a distinctly oriental appearance. Fringe flower prefers well-drained, lime-free soil and full sun or part shade. Evergreen.

Metrosideros 'Tahiti'
1 m x 1 m
One of the best evergreen shrubs for a container, and exceptional in the garden too. 'Tahiti' is closely related to the New Zealand native pohutukawa and has similar red fuzzy flowers. These appear mainly in winter on a compact shrub with a semi-weeping habit and charming grey-green rounded leaves. The new shoots are bright red. An excellent coastal shrub, but damaged by frost. Evergreen.

Myrtus communis
COMMON MYRTLE
1 x 1 m
An easily grown, densely foliaged shrub, good as a solid year-round filler, for small hedges or containers. The small white flowers are sweetly fragrant, appearing in summer. They are followed by blue-black berries. A variegated form, *M. communis* 'Variegata' is useful for foliage contrast

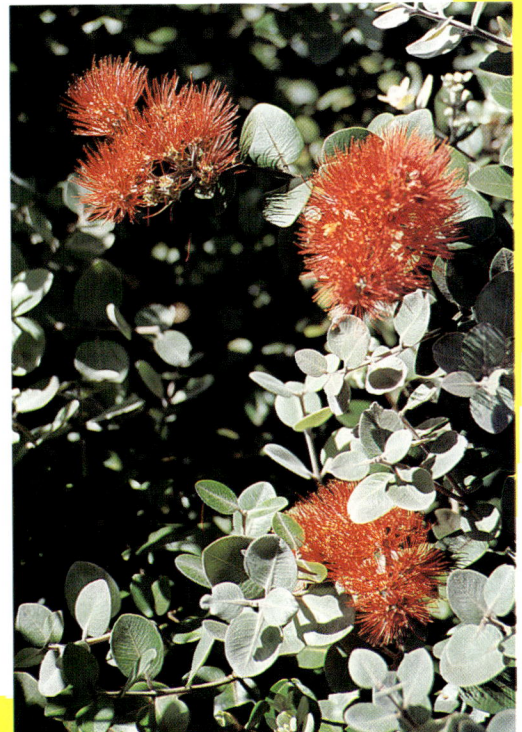

Metrosideros 'Tahiti'.

Lavender: Go to page 41.

Hebes

Hebes are the largest group of New Zealand native flowering plants, found naturally from one end of the country to the other.

Those listed here are the most suitable for average garden conditions. Sheltered inland gardens require disease-resistant varieties (e.g., *H. diosmifolia*, *H. 'Wiri Mist'*), whereas exposed coastal areas require wind-resistant varieties (e.g., *H. 'Inspiration'*, *H. speciosa*).

Give hebes a sunny spot with plenty of air movement to prevent diseases caused by humidity. They need a well-drained soil but will not tolerate excessive dryness.

To maintain compact shapely shrubs, trim immediately after flowering by cutting just below the flowers into healthy green growth. Young plants require protection from frosts for the first season.

Hebe diosmifolia
up to 75 cm x 1 m
Pale lavender flowers fade to white as they age. There is one main flush in early summer, with more flowers in autumn. This is a good northern-climate variety with small bright green foliage.

Hebe xfranciscana 'Blue Gem'
1.5 m x 1.5 m
An excellent hebe with violet-blue, summer flowers and large, glossy, deep green foliage and a bushy rounded form. Tolerant of wind and coastal conditions. Evergreen.

Hebe 'Inspiration'
1 m x 1m
Widely planted for its generous flower production and excellent health in warmer climates. The flowers are purple fading to mauve, appearing in several flushes in spring, early summer and autumn. It has a compact mounding habit with dark green shiny foliage. Handles coastal conditions.

Hebe 'Lavender Lace'
75 m x 1 m
'Lavender Lace' makes a good hedge with several flower flushes per year. The flowers are lilac fading to white.

Hebe 'Oratia Beauty'
75 cm x 75 cm
A compact bush with mid-summer flowers, which are pale pink fading to white, and deep green foliage. It is frost tender.

Hebe speciosa
1.2 m x 1.2 m
Large beetroot-purple flowers look luxuriant against the fleshy, dark green, glossy leaves. It flowers for extended periods but mainly in summer. Good for mass planting or as a hedge. This stunning shrub tolerates coastal conditions and drought but is frost tender.

Hebe topiara
90 cm x 75 cm
Named for its form, which looks as though it has been shaped by trimming, *H. topiara* has white flowers in summer and very tidy blue-green foliage.

Hebe 'Wiri Mist'
50 cm x 80 cm
Ideal for mass planting and as a border plant in cottage gardens, this hebe has white flowers in spring. It is very disease resistant.

Hebe 'Wiri Splash'
40 cm x 60 cm
A disease-resistant variety with lavender-lilac flowers in summer, a nice compact habit, and narrow golden-green foliage.

---

and to lighten up dull corners. Withstands clay soils, dry conditions and most climates. Evergreen.

Nandina domestica 'Richmond'
HEAVENLY BAMBOO
1.5 m x 1 m
This shrub produces masses of scarlet-red berries in winter, attractive to the eye but not so to birds. The form of the plant is nice and compact, and the foliage is valued for its colour. It grows well across most of New Zealand, and is particularly good for rock or feature gardens as it requires little or no maintenance.

Osmanthus heterophyllus
HOLLY OLIVE, CHINESE HOLLY
1.5 m x 1 m
An evergreen shrub with small white flowers prized for their sweet spicy fragrance, making an attractive cut flower. Useful shrubs for hedges and screens, *Osmanthus* does well in clay and prefers part shade. It grows well around all parts of New Zealand.

Phormium hybrids
NEW ZEALAND FLAX
1 m x 1 m
One of the most evocative images of New Zealand, *Phormium* (or flax as it is commonly known) is one of the most versatile and useful plants in the garden. Its foliage creates interest through both shape and colour, and its uses include attracting birds to the garden and controlling erosion in poor soils. Flax copes incredibly well with sun, shade, wind, clay, wet and coastal conditions and, as a feature point in the garden, is effective both singly and in groups. It grows virtually anywhere. Evergreen.

Pieris japonica
LILY OF THE VALLEY SHRUB
1.5 m x 1 m
This shrub is really good for its flowers and foliage, and is excellent for picking. The small urn-shaped flowers have a lovely light fragrance

and are displayed on beautiful swooping panicles giving the impression of cascades of flowers. The foliage is also interesting with new shoots being bronzy-pink to red, becoming deep green when mature. An evergreen, it prefers to be planted in a cooler part of the garden with a bit of shade. It grows well in most parts of New Zealand.

Rhaphiolepis indica 'Enchantress'
INDIAN HAWTHORN
1 m x 1 m
Attractive leathery, bronze-green foliage and a long spring through autumn display of pink flowers make this one of the most desirable small evergreen shrubs for any garden. It grows quickly into a neatly rounded, compact shrub useful in mixed shrub plantings, mass planted as a border or in containers. New growth is coppery red. Prefers full sun and any average soil in most New Zealand climates, including coastal. Evergreen.

Rhaphiolepis umbellata
INDIAN HAWTHORN
1.5 m x 1.5 m
Pure white, slightly fragrant flowers with pinkish centres appear in summer, followed by blue-black berries in winter. Good for filling gaps, this bush grows well in dry, coastal areas, enjoying full sun. Evergreen.

Rhododendron
VIREYA RHODODENDRONS
Vireya rhododendrons are mostly grown for the tropical appearance of the flowers and foliage. Excellent in pots, these evergreens contrast well with other tropical and subtropical plants, flowering two to three times a year throughout the four seasons. There is a wide range of varieties available, with choices of flower colour in vivid shades of pink, red, yellow and orange.

Rosmarinus officinalis
COMMON ROSEMARY
1.3 m x 1 m
Excellent for small hedges or as a small compact shrub, this wonderfully fragrant herb loves hot dry sunny spots and doesn't need much looking after. It grows just about anywhere as long as it doesn't get wet feet too often. In the summer it produces tiny blue flowers.

More about vireya rhododendrons: Go to page 71.

Ruscus aculeatus
BUTCHER'S BROOM
1 m x 1 m
A shrub for difficult shady corners with unusual prickly foliage and amazing bright red berries in winter, good for picking. Good for mass planting and tolerant of difficult soils and dryish spots

around buildings. 'Wheelers' is the one for the most reliable berry production. A cold winter is needed for berries. Evergreen.

Santolina chamaecyparissus
LAVENDER COTTON
60 cm x 1 m
Fine-textured grey foliage is the main attraction of this popular edging plant. Left untrimmed it produces a mass of yellow button flowers. Best in well-drained sandy soils and full sun, tolerating dry conditions. Evergreen.

Sarcococca ruscifolia
CHRISTMAS BOX
1 m x 60 cm
A valuable shrub for deep shade. Leaves are dark glossy green. In cold climates red berries are produced in winter. These follow small white fragrant spring flowers. Dry soil is tolerated once plants are established. Evergreen.

Spiraea japonica 'Albiflora'
1 m x 1 m
A hardy but graceful little shrub with a mass of dainty white flower clusters in summer. Spireas tolerate heavy soils and temperature extremes, but need full sun and protection from wind. Prune in late winter. Deciduous.

Spiraea japonica 'Anthony Waterer'
RED SPIRAEA
1 m x 1 m
This compact little shrub is covered with carmine-red flowerheads from early summer to autumn. Full sun is best for flowering. Semi-deciduous.

Spiraea japonica 'Little Princess'
40 cm x 50 cm
A dainty little shrub with mass displays of pink summer flowers. Prune in late winter. Deciduous.

Thryptomene saxicola 'Rosea'
ROCK HEATH MYRTLE
1 m x 1 m
A favourite with florists, *Thryptomene* has long slender arching stems packed with dainty pink flowers from mid-winter into spring. A well-drained soil is essential. Full sun is required for maximum flowering. Evergreen.

Camellias and rhododendrons are attractive evergreen shrubs, even when not in flower.

Abutilon darwinii hybrids
CHINESE LANTERN
2 m x 1.5 m

Chinese lanterns are attractive shrubs for filling in semi-shady spaces. They flower for most of the year, especially in winter, with their red, yellow, pink, orange or white hanging lantern flowers, much loved for picking. The more light they get, the more flowers they will produce. The attractive maple-like foliage is dark green. These are easy-to-grow shrubs in most average soils, best pruned by about a half each year to encourage bushy growth and lots of flowers. Evergreen.

Banksia ericifolia
HEATH BANKSIA
2.5 m x 2 m

As long as it doesn't have wet feet, heath banksia will grow just about anywhere. It takes strong winds and coastal conditions. The large amber-orange brush flowers are produced in great quantities over a long winter/spring season and make excellent cut flowers. Good for sandy soils and full sun. Evergreen.

Brachyglottis repanda
RANGIORA
3 m x 2 m

Easy to grow in most soils, Rangiora gives fabulous foliage contrast and looks especially good amongst smaller-leaved native shrubs. The large leaves have white felt-textured undersides and are effective moving in the wind. The plain green species is large growing, ultimately a small tree, but the purple-leaved form *B. repanda* 'Purpurea' is of smaller proportions, growing to about 3 metres. Evergreen.

Buddleia davidii cultivars
BUTTERFLY BUSH
3 m x 2.5 m

This is a very quick-growing shrub or small tree useful for fast screening. The fragrant flowers are in tapering spikes of pink, lavender, blue or white. They thrive in very harsh conditions but need regular hard pruning to prevent them from becoming untidy. Evergreen.

Callistemon citrinus 'Splendens'
BOTTLEBRUSH
2 m x 2 m

Brilliant red brush flowers last a long time in spring and summer, often appearing again in autumn. This is a tough and easy shrub, good for screening and tolerant of a wide range of soils and climates. Evergreen.

Camellia spp. & cultivars
CAMELLIA
Up to 3 m

Dark green foliage and attractive tidy growth habits all year round, camellias are excellent framework shrubs even when not in flower. In autumn, winter or spring they produce colourful, pickable flowers. A well-drained, lime-free compost-rich soil in partial shade provides the ideal home for camellias, which perform well in any climate. Evergreen.

More about camellias: Go to page 44.

Cassia corymbosa (syn. Senna corymbosa) 'John Ball'
BUTTERCUP TREE
2 m x 2 m

A welcome sight in early winter when it smothers itself in golden-yellow blooms, the fast-growing *Cassia* looks best as part of a mixed shrubbery with green background to enhance its brilliance. It is useful for a fast screen. Requires full sun. Evergreen.

Ceanothus papillosus 'Roweanus'
CALIFORNIAN LILAC
2 m x 1.5 m

Brilliant blue flowers cover glossy-green close-packed foliage in spring. Very easy to grow, tolerating dry and coastal conditions, enjoying a hot sunny location. Great for bank planting. Avoid heavy soils that are cold and damp in winter. Prune by half after flowering to maintain compact growth. Evergreen.

Cestrum nocturnum
QUEEN OF THE NIGHT
3 m x 2 m

Nothing spectacular to look at, this plain green shrub is appreciated most on summer evenings, when its exotic and powerful fragrance fills the air. Plant it next to a window or verandah in an otherwise out-of-the-way spot. It will tolerate dry soil in sun or semi-shade. Prune after flowering to keep it compact.

Chaenomeles hybrids
FLOWERING QUINCE
Up to 2 m

If you want spring blossom in your garden but haven't got room for a tree, a flowering quince could be the answer. The bare branches become covered in brightly coloured blossom in late winter or very early spring. Colours range from white, through soft pinks and apricots to rich oranges and reds. Great for picking, *Chaenomeles* are Japanese natives with a definite Japanese look. They make colourful winter hedges. Poor soils, wind and climatic extremes are tolerated. Best pruned during and after flowering to preserve shape and vigour. Deciduous.

Chimonanthus praecox
WINTERSWEET
2.5 m x 2 m

Another shrub with a winning fragrance and the endearing trait of producing its violet-scented flowers on bare branches in winter. As easy on the eye as they are on the nose, the twigs of little creamy-yellow flowers with purple markings look magnificent in a vase. Coveted by northern gardeners, it is really at its best in a cold climate. Flowering performance is disappointing where winters are mild. Deciduous.

Clianthus puniceus 'Kaka King'
KAKA BEAK
2 m x 2 m

One of the showiest New Zealand natives, putting on a vibrant spring show of bright scarlet-red, parrot-beak blooms. 'Kaka King' is a recently discovered form of superior performance. It can be grown as a large shrub, perfect as a feature amongst other native shrubs, in a tub, or espaliered against a wall. The flowers attract birds to the garden. Kaka beak thrives in a well-drained soil in full sun with shelter from wind. Young plants do not cope well with frost. Short lived by nature, plants should be pruned after flowering to prolong health and vitality. Evergreen.

Note: The dimensions given for each plant can only be approximate, for average garden conditions.

Corokia cotoneaster
WIRE NETTING BUSH
2.5 m x 1 m

This native shrub makes an excellent hedge and shelter plant with attractive small grey-green leaves arranged on twiggy interlaced branches. It tolerates strong winds, coastal conditions, drought, clay and sandy soils. There are tiny yellow flowers in spring and summer. Evergreen.

Cotoneaster bullatus
2.5 m x 2 m

A handsome shrub with bright red berries in autumn. In a cooler climate the foliage also takes on vibrant tones. Tolerant of dry soils and best in full sun. Semi-deciduous.

Cytisus multiflorus 'Albus'
WHITE SPANISH BROOM
2 m x 1 m

The fountain of snowy-white flowers in early spring is a breathtaking sight. The flowers are fragrant and good for picking. Best cut back after flowering. Plant in full sun. Evergreen.

Escallonia cultivars
ESCALLONIA
Up to 2 m x 1 m

Escallonia has long been a favourite hedge plant. Its small, dense, dark green leaves and quick growth mean it is ideal for clipping. Left untrimmed the small flowers are present in spring through summer, and it makes an excellent background shrub, or an informal screen or shelter. Easy to grow in any soil in any climate and good on the coast. Evergreen.

Euonymus japonicus 'Aureomarginatus'
JAPANESE LAUREL
3 m x 1 m

An old timer and very popular variegated foliage shrub. Good for contrast against green backgrounds and well used for clipping to shape in hedging and topiary. It is tolerant of tough locations and soils, sun or shade. Remove any green, non-variegated growth to prevent it reverting to its green form. Mildew problems in humid climates mean spraying along with the roses is a good idea. Relatively slow growing and tolerant of periods of dryness, it is good for pots.

Feijoa sellowiana
FEIJOA
Up to 3 m

With attractive grey-green foliage, feijoas make a good hedge or specimen tree, or quick screen and shelter. Be sure to plant grafted plants if fruiting is the objective. Crops are best when trees are planted in groups for pollination. Best in a warm climate and full sun. Protect from frost when young and water during dry periods. There are pretty red flowers in summer. Evergreen.

Grevillea glabrata
SMOOTH GREVILLEA
2 m x 1.5 m

Willowy weeping branches produce an early summer mass of wispy white flowers. This is a hardy, fast-growing shrub, good for a fast screen in a warm sunny location. Evergreen.

Grevillea hookeriana
TOOTHBRUSH GREVILLEA
2 m x 2.5 m

Showy red flowers, good for picking, last a long time over spring, summer and autumn, attracting birds to the garden. The shrub has an attractive spreading habit with finely divided leaves. Grows in most soils or climates in a warm sunny position. Evergreen.

Griselinia littoralis
KAPUKA
3 m x 2 m

A tough native shrub with large glossy-green leaves. Tolerating clay soils and coastal conditions, it makes a good filler, background shrub or hedge. Evergreen.

Hydrangea
Easy-to-grow hydrangeas flower for a long summer season with huge round heads of blue, pink or white flowers. They are perhaps at their best mass planted under deciduous trees in larger gardens. They are useful where a fast-growing filler is required and, though deciduous, make a lovely flowering hedge, lending an old-fashioned air to the summer garden. Old-fashioned H. macrophylla grows into a large shrub, but modern hybridising has led to many dwarf varieties, which make spectacular container plants and are suitable for small gardens. There are separate pink and blue forms but most will colour according to soil acidity. Acid soils give rise to blue shades, limey (alkaline) soils give rise to pink shades. White varieties are generally white in any soil. You can alter the colour of your hydrangeas by adding a sulphur-based fertiliser (e.g., aluminium sulphate) for blue colours or hydrated lime for pinks. More than one application is required. Start in October and apply fortnightly.

In winter, hydrangeas need to be pruned back hard. Note the different buds on the bare stems: fat ones and small flat ones. The fat ones will grow into stems with flowers on the ends of them. The idea is to cut back to a centimetre above a pair of fat buds. There will be more of these buds, and they will be lower down, on parts that have had more sun. Remove last year's spent flower stems and any spindly growth. The prunings can be used to make cuttings for new plants. Make cuttings 20 to 30 cm long and put them straight into prepared soil to about half their depth. Deciduous.

Ilex aquifolium 'J. C. Van Tol'
HOLLY
3 m x 2 m

Hollys have year-round attractive foliage, glossy green and good for picking. In a cold enough climate there is the bonus of shiny red winter berries. They are slow growing, so suitable for pots, and tolerant of the coldest climates. 'J. C. Van Tol' is a reliable berry producer with almost spineless dark green foliage. Evergreen.

Juniperus chinensis 'Kaizuka'
HOLLYWOOD JUNIPER
2 m x 1 m

A conifer with a unique spiralling growth habit. The natural form can be exaggerated with training to form feature trees and topiaries. Good for large pots and garden accent. Bright green, dense foliage. Very hardy in most soils, growing well in sun or shade. Evergreen.

Laurus nobilis
BAY TREE
4 m x 3 m

Bay trees are capable of becoming quite large, but respond so well to trimming that they are a perfect small-garden tree — whether you grow them in the garden or in a container, or whether you trim them as a standard or let the natural pyramid shape prevail. They tolerate coastal conditions and will grow in clay soils, sun or part shade. Evergreen.

Leonotis leonurus
LION'S TAIL
2 m x 1.5 m

A great shrub for hot dry locations, lion's tail produces spectacular flower displays in summer and autumn, with bright orange tubular flowers. The foliage is sage-like, soft grey-green. This is a drought-resistant shrub for any well-drained soil in full sun. Prune hard each year when flowering is finished. Evergreen.

Leucodendron salicifolium
LEUCODENDRON
2 m x 1.5 m

This shrub is excellent both for its foliage and for its flowers, which are very good for cutting. It is good in coastal and sandy environments, and likes acid soils and some sun. An evergreen, there is added interest in the spring when the uppermost leaves change colour, becoming a mass of yellow.

Leucospermum cordifolium
LEUCOSPERMUM
1.5 m x 1.5 m

Another shrub that tolerates coastal conditions well. Again, sandy, acid soils are preferred with full sun — don't even think about trying it in wet clay soils. Flowering in spring and summer with dome-shaped, rich orange blossoms, which make striking cut flowers, the shrub is an evergreen with gracefully curving branches and greyish-green leaves.

Luculia gratissima
PINK LUCULIA
2 m x 1.5 m

Luculia is one of the loveliest winter-flowering shrubs. The light to deep pink flowers are sweetly fragrant and are excellent for picking. Throughout autumn and winter the leaves become bronzy-red creating a superb background to the flowers. The plant needs plenty of sun and some shelter from frosts and wind. Semi-evergreen, some of the leaves will fall in autumn and winter, except in very warm areas.

Magnolia stellata
STAR MAGNOLIA
2 m x 2 m

Another winter-flowering shrub, this delightful magnolia combines all the fragrance of the more traditional magnolia flower forms with intriguing white, star-shaped flowers (hence the name 'stellata'). An acid lover, it needs some shelter as well as full sun. Despite being deciduous, the interest from the flowers over winter makes it a great feature tree suitable for most New Zealand gardens.

Mahonia lomariifolia
CHINESE HOLLY GRAPE
2 m x 1.5 m

One of the most interesting shrubs because of its leaf shape, which is quite dramatic, *Mahonia* is great planted beside stone or brick walls or other patterned structures such as stained timbers. Winter flowering, the yellow flowers and the distinctive shape of the leaves create a beautifully formed shrub. The berries are very attractive to birds. Planted in semi-shade, out of the path of strong winds, this evergreen will thrive in most parts of New Zealand.

Olearia cheesemanii
STREAMSIDE RIVER DAISY
2 m x 2 m

A great shrub for screening, this an excellent choice for coastal locations and other areas where soil conditions and watering are difficult. A native renowned for its spring flower display, with large white daisy flowers (with yellow centres) virtually covering the entire bush, it tolerates clay and sun. This evergreen will grow well in most conditions around New Zealand.

Philadelphus spp. and cultivars
MOCK ORANGE
2 m x 1.5 m

Extremely fragrant, creamy-white blossom-like flowers appear in early summer in great quantity. They are good for picking and combine well with roses or with colourful spring bulbs in the garden or in a vase. A deciduous shrub without much distinction when not in flower but easy to mix in with evergreen and summer-flowering shrubs. Tolerates all soil types and dry conditions, flowering best in full sun.

Plumbago auriculata
PLUMBAGO
1.5 m x 2 m

Plumbago is a great plant for filling and screening spaces — it is a semi-climbing or rambling plant, and thrives in places where it can get some support (fences, trellises, on banks or against walls). It has vibrant sky-blue flowers and blooms well over summer in dry, warm, sunny areas. Evergreen.

Protea cynaroides
KING PROTEA
1 m x 1.5 m

King protea has great potential as a cut flower — not only do the bright pink and white spiky flowers look good on the tree but they can be used to dramatic effect inside the house. It is a very tolerant plant, growing well in sandy soil and in coastal conditions. Evergreen, it loves warmth and full sun.

Pseudopanax laetus
FIVE FINGER
3 m x 1.5 m

A large-leaved native shrub good for tropical effect or contrasting with finer-foliaged trees and shrubs. The leaves are dark glossy green with purple stalks. A hardy shrub for sun or shade, any soil and any climate.

Pyracantha
2 m x 1.5 m

This plant has small white flowers followed by masses of clumps of bright red berries in autumn and winter. It's extremely tolerant and thrives in clay soils and in full sun. Good espaliered along sunny walls, and equally as good on banks or as a groundcover. Evergreen.

Leucospermum cordifolium.

Pittosporum

One of the most versatile evergreen shrubs available in New Zealand. Among the different forms are a wide range of leaf shapes, sizes and colours. Among the joys of pittosporums is the ease with which they can be grown, the attractive foliage, and the uses to which they can be put. Perfect for hedges and screens, they are also good as background shrubs to set off the beauty of flowering plants, and make a useful filler in most gardens.

Able to be grown in most parts of the country, pittosporums are easy to care for, generally requiring only a well-balanced, free-draining soil and full or partial sun. By pinching back the young growth you can get dense branching at ground level (great for hedges), and when fully grown they can be pruned to keep them at the size you want.

Pittosporum eugenioides 'Variegatum'
LEMONWOOD, TARATA
2 m x 1.5 m

One of the larger-growing pittosporums, *eugenioides* is very hardy and grows well in the worst soils imaginable. It has semi-glossy, pale green leaves that have a distinct lemon fragrance when crushed, hence the name 'lemonwood'. It has pale yellow flowers in spring and summer.

Pittosporum 'Garnettii'
2 m x 1.5 m

This hybrid is prized mainly for its medium green leaves, which are variegated with creamy-white and have an interesting pink to wine-red flush during cooler months. The leaves have wavy edges.

Pittosporum tenuifolium 'Deborah'
2 m x 1.5 m

'Deborah' is quite an airy shrub, better as a feature in the garden rather than as a hedge. Its small leaves, coloured green to grey-green with a wide cream margin, are also heavily flushed with pink or rosy red throughout the year, deepening over the winter.

Pittosporum tenuifolium 'Irene Patterson'
2 m x 1.5 m

This pittosporum makes a lovely contrast shrub in the garden, and is also good for contrast and background in flower arrangements. It is characterised by slender black branches with leaves that deepen in colour with age. Young leaves are almost completely white, while older leaves become a light green, often tinged by pink over winter.

Pittosporum tenuifolium 'Limelight'
3 m x 2 m

One of the larger pittosporums, 'Limelight' has interesting red stems. The leaves are dominated by a central yellow/green zone and have narrow green margins.

Pittosporum tenuifolium 'Mountain Green'
2.5 m x 2 m

A tallish pittosporum, 'Mountain Green' grows in quite a compact and bushy form, so is good for screens and background features. Its leaves are a light fresh-green colour.

Pittosporum tenuifolium 'Silver Sheen'
3 m x 1.5 m

'Silver Sheen' is a very attractive plant due mainly to the contrast of its leaves against its slender black stems. The leaves are tiny and rounded, coloured a striking silvery green. It's also attractive if you want to establish your garden quickly, as it is a fast-growing shrub with an upright habit.

Pittosporum tenuifolium 'Tandarra Gold'
3 m x 1.5 m

The leaves of this cultivar are small and rounded with big splashes of gold in the middle and irregular green margins. It has black branches and forms a neat compact bush.

Pittosporum tenuifolium 'Wendell Channon'
PITTOSPORUM
1.5 m x 1 m

'Wendell Channon' is a particularly good form, with lovely small light green leaves with wavy white margins. The leaves tend to flush a rose pink during winter.

Rhododendron

Rhododendrons are one of the most important groups of ornamental shrubs, renowned for the variety of size, wide range of colour, and form of their flowers. There are thousands of different varieties, with just a fraction of them available to gardeners. They are good fillers and can create spectacular splashes of colour over the winter months. Evergreen, they prefer to grow in part shade, with slightly acid soil.

More about rhododendrons: Go to page 47.

Solanum rantonnetii
PARAGUAY NIGHTSHADE
2 m x 1.5 m

Beautiful violet-blue flowers with yellow centres are displayed almost all year round in mild climates. This is a rapid-growing shrub of informal habit, which can be trained against a wall or grown to spill down a bank. Provide full sun and protection from frost.

Stachyurus praecox
EARLY SPIKETAIL
2.5 m x 2 m

A beautiful Japanese shrub, which makes an ideal small tree for a small garden. It is at its most stunning in early spring when the bare branches are hung with drooping racemes of pale yellow, bell-shaped flowers. The buds appear in autumn and the flowers hold well into spring, as coppery-coloured new leaves appear. The mature foliage is green in

Plumbago auriculata.

summer turning oranges and yellows in autumn. This shrub grows quickly and is easily pruned into a more tree-like form. Any reasonable soil in sun or part shade will suit. Flowers are good for cutting. Deciduous.

Steptosolen jamesonii
ORANGE BROWALLIA
1.5 m x 1.5 m
A long-flowering tropical shrub, this is another good filler in the garden. It loves sun and throughout spring, summer and autumn produces lovely orange blooms. Evergreen.

Strelitzia reginae
BIRD OF PARADISE
1.5 m x 1.5 m
'Bird of Paradise' sums it up — the flowers are stunning orange and blue, resembling in shape the bright plumage of tropical birds. An excell-ent feature in any garden, the flowers appear over spring, summer and autumn, and the large banana-shaped leaves are evergreen. Little if any maintenance is needed. It doesn't need much water but it does like lots of sun and warmth.

Syringa vulgaris cultivars
LILAC
2.5 m x 1.5 m
Charming, deliciously fragrant spring flowers make lilacs a must when you have the climate to grow them. Some cultivars will flower, if rather unenthus-

iastically, in Auckland, but lilacs really belong south of Waikato. The flowers are prized for picking. This is a shrub that enjoys limey soils and tolerates dry conditions. Full sun is best for flowering. Deciduous.

Syzygium australe (syn. Eugenia australis)
AUSTRALIAN ROSE APPLE
7 m x 5 m
A dense, fast-growing foliage shrub ideal for hedges, screening and shelter as well as shaping into standards. Leaves are glossy dark green with pretty bronze new growth. There are white flowers followed by bunches of edible purple berries, which persist into winter. This is a shrub for a warm climate in full sun and any average soil. Evergreen.

Tecomaria capensis
TECOMA, CAPE HONEYSUCKLE
Up to 3 m
A favourite and very effective hedge for warm climates. It is very quick growing to form a dense dark green hedge of any height. It must be trimmed regularly or it becomes untidy. The bright orange flowers are not the most sought-after feature, more a signal that it is time for the hedge trimmers. Tolerant of heavy soils and drought. Evergreen.

Teucrium fruticans
SILVER GERMANDER
1.5 m x 1.5 m
A good shrub for hedges or screen-ing. Its distinctive features are year-round silver foliage and light purple flowers for most of the year. Reason-ably hardy, it likes dry, sandy, poor soil, hot temperatures and full sun.

Thuja plicata
WESTERN RED CEDAR
Up to 8 m
An ideal hedge or shelter tree with deep green foliage in flat sprays. Tolerant of climatic and soil extremes, it is rapid growing for a conifer but is easy to look after, requiring a minimum of trimming. Evergreen.

Tibouchina spp.
LASIANDRA
Bright purple flowers and velvety leaves are the easily recognisable features of these warm-climate shrubs. The easiest to grow, but for frost-free climates only, is *T. granulosa*, a large rounded shrub with an open habit. It flowers in spring and autumn for several weeks. Evergreen.

Viburnum opulus 'Roseum' (syn. 'Sterile')
SNOWBALL TREE
3 m x 2 m
An old-fashioned shrub that grows and flowers well in most climates, it covers itself in creamy-white 'snowball' clusters of flowers in spring. The maple-shaped leaves, absent in winter, are attractive. They form a dense cover and in a cool climate turn rich colours in autumn. Sun or part shade. Deciduous.

Viburnum tinus
LAURUSTINUS
2 m x 1.5 m
This tough but lovely *Viburnum* has small glossy leaves, making it ideal as a hedge. It tolerates coastal conditions and dry soils. Through autumn and winter into spring there are lots of pretty white flowers, pink in bud. They are followed by blue-black berries which last into summer. Plant in sun or shade and trim to any size or shape. Evergreen.

Viburnum trilobum
CRANBERRY VIBURNUM
3 m x 2.5 m
Beautiful pickable orange-red berries even in a warm climate is the big attraction of this easy-to-grow shrub. Clusters of berries appear in summer and will remain until winter after the leaves have fallen. In spring there are cream flowers. Foliage is easily mistaken for that of the snowball tree. In a cool climate it colours well in autumn. Plant in sun or part shade in any reasonable soil. Deciduous.

Weigela 'Grace Warden'
APPLE BLOSSOM
2 m x 1.5 m
This is a compact deciduous shrub with foxglove-shaped deep rose-pink flowers in spring. It's good in poor soil and exposed areas, likes the sun, and grows well in most of New Zealand.

Lavender

Lavender has it all: fragrance, masses of flowers at any time of the year, rapid growth, attractive foliage and a multitude of landscape possibilities. Lavenders are good for pots, in cottage gardens, formal gardens, tiny inner-city gardens, country gardens and coastal gardens. They are fabulous planted *en masse*, especially as hedges. Not surprisingly, the nursery industry has had trouble keeping up with demand in recent years.

There is a confusingly huge array of lavenders to choose from these days, but it pays to work out which varieties will best suit your situation. Lavenders vary in soil and climate preference, flowering time, and growth habit. The flowers vary in colour, form and stem length.

THE 'ENGLISH' LAVENDERS

(*Lavandula angustifolia* cultivars)
The so-called English lavenders have been grown extensively in England for a very long time but the original species is native to the western Mediterranean. These are the lavenders with the best fragrance, which is present in both flowers and foliage. Flowers retain their fragrance when dried and are used for potpourris and lavender bags. Low growing and summer flowering, they make sensational border hedges.

English lavender.

English lavenders are best reserved for well-drained sandy soils. Trying to grow a hedge in heavy soil usually leads to disappointment as plants one by one surrender to the cold, wet, winter conditions. Gardeners with heavier soils will have better luck if they grow English lavenders in pots or raised beds. English lavenders grow best where winters are cool and summers are warm and sunny. They prefer a neutral to slightly alkaline soil (pH 6–8). Acid soils can be altered by adding lime or superphosphate.

Lavandula angustifolia (syn. *L. spica)* flowers earlier than its cultivars, starting in early November and continuing on with fresh blooms through summer. In flower the plant is 60 to 80 cm tall.

Lavandula angustifolia 'Alba' is a white-flowered English lavender. It grows 40 to 60 cm tall in flower.

Lavandula angustifolia 'Hidcote' is distinguished by its dark-coloured flowers. It flowers about two weeks later than *L. angustifolia* and grows to a flowering height of about 70 cm.

Lavandula angustifolia 'Lady' is one of the few lavenders that will flower in the first season when grown from seed. For seedlings, the plants are a uniform size, which makes 'Lady' a good hedge lavender. It reaches 40 to 45 cm in flower.

Lavandula angustifolia 'Munstead' was bred by the famous English gardener, Miss Gertrude Jekyll, early this century. It is 45 to 60 cm tall in flower, and apart from flower colour, which is a deeper shade of violet, it is hardly distinguishable from the parent species, flowering at about the same time.

Lavandula angustifolia 'Rosea' is a pink-flowered English lavender, growing to 60 cm when in flower. It is an early-flowering cultivar.

THE STOECHAS LAVENDERS

Distinguishing them from the English lavenders, the flower spikes of stoechas lavenders are topped with 'rabbit's ears' — technically speaking, sterile bracts — of varying degrees of prominence. Most importantly, these are the warm-climate lavenders. They tolerate the Auckland climate well and are intolerant of anything more than a mild frost. Although they tolerate a degree of humidity (much more than the English lavenders), they are not lovers of very humid or very rainy conditions. Stoechas lavenders prefer a well-drained position but they will thrive in a wide range of soil types and favour slightly acid soils, thriving in a clay loam, for example. Interestingly, they have been declared noxious weeds in parts of Australia.

Whereas English lavenders are summer bloomers, stoechas types flower for long periods at various times of the year.

Stoechas lavenders do not share the special fragrance of the English lavenders, but their fragrance is pleasant, certainly worth having.

French lavender,
L. dentata.

Lavandula dentata (French lavender): By far the most popular lavender for northern regions and deservedly so. It is a fast-growing shrub, tolerant of heavier soils and warm humid conditions. As long as it is regularly trimmed it makes an excellent hedge, densely foliaged and growing to about a metre tall. Flowers are pale lilac on long stems, good for picking. The foliage is grey-green with toothed margins. One of the greatest things about French lavender is its ability to flower all year round. A good prune after Christmas helps to keep it from growing tall and leggy, with flowers returning in autumn.

Lavandula dentata 'Monet' is a recently developed dwarf form of French lavender, better for pots than its parent form with small flowers on a much more compact plant.

Lavandula stoechas: From the Mediterranean and popularly known as Spanish or Italian lavender, this attractive plant grows about 70 cm tall. It has grey-green foliage and a mass of purple flowers starting in early summer. It makes an attractive hedge. *L. stoechas* 'Wine' is an especially good form with rosy-purple flowers.

Lavandula stoechas sub sp. *pendunculata* has longer flower stalks than *L. stoechas* and rounder flower spikes. The plant is slightly more prostrate and about 90 cm tall in flower.

Lavandula 'Helmsdale' is a compact plant with close foliage and a dense covering of burgundy-purple flower spikes on short stems. It is good as a hedge, growing to about 80 cm in flower. Bred in the South Island of New Zealand and tolerant of mild frosts.

Lavandula 'Marshwood' grows quickly and flowers early. It is a favourite for a colourful flowering hedge. The flowers are pinky-lilac on stems long enough for picking. 'Marshwood' reaches over a metre tall in flower. Again, bred in the South Island of New Zealand and tolerant of mild frosts.

Such is the appeal of lavender that there is a constant stream of new varieties being released. Many not mentioned here will be worth a try in your garden.

GROWING LAVENDER

Although some lavenders tolerate all sorts of soils, the best situation is one that is well drained. Sunshine is essential for healthy flowering plants; shade leads to leggy, stretched growth and few flowers.

Pruning is essential, especially with the stoechas types, to keep plants compact and bushy. Without pruning they soon become bare and twiggy at the base and misshapen. Prune after flowering (except in the case of French lavender, which is almost always flowering). Pruning may take place more than once a year to keep fast-growing varieties in shape. Never cut below the leaf growth. There should a good few centimetres of healthy green foliage left below your cut. For hedges, electric pruning sheers will do a good job and leave a clean topiaried look while the plants kick back into action.

Choose the variety to suit your climate and soil. English lavender is best in cold climates with well-drained, limey soil. The stoechas types grow best in warm climates and are more tolerant of heavy soils.

> **LAVENDER LOVES:**
> ✓ Good drainage.
> ✓ Warm sunshine.
> ✓ Lots of trimming.

Camellias

C amellias could be described as the roses of winter — at least in terms of their flowers. But while you might be forgiven for suggesting that roses are only worth growing for their flowers, there is no such downfall with camellias. They are as valuable for their contribution to the evergreen structure of a garden as they are for their flowers. With year-round glossy-green foliage, camellias are a wonderful backdrop for other plants, many varieties making superb hedges for screening and shelter. Smaller varieties are well suited to containers and those with more willowy growth habits are ideal for espaliering. Taller-growing varieties can be trained as small trees or made into standards.

Camellias grow best in a lime-free soil, although they will tolerate a little lime if the soil is naturally acid. In most cases it pays to avoid adding lime and to use a fertiliser specially blended for camellias and other acid-loving plants.

Most importantly, the soil should be well drained and rich in humus. Peat moss and compost are both ideal, added to the planting hole and used as a mulch. Because camellia roots grow close to the surface, protecting them from temperature extremes and other disturbances by mulching is a good idea.

Camellias will generally grow in sun or part shade. Some pale-petalled varieties are best grown in filtered sunlight to avoid scorching.

CAMELLIA TYPES

The hardiest and easiest camellias to grow are the various cultivars of *Camellia sasanqua*, known as the 'sasanqua camellias'. These have smaller leaves and softer growth habits than other camellias. They are the earliest to bloom, with massive flower displays from autumn into winter. The flowers themselves are smaller and generally more subtle than their flamboyant cousins, but sasanqua camellias are very free flowering. They are among the best plants for hedges and espalier work, and are suitable for any climate.

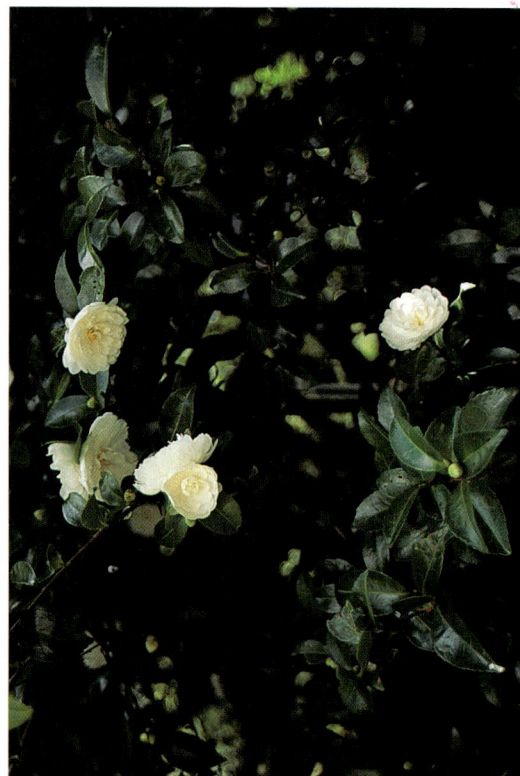

Hedges:
Go to page 25.

Making standards:
Go to page 208.

More about mulching:
Go to page 204.

RIGHT: Camellia 'Mine-no-yuki'.
BELOW: Camellia 'Plantation Pink'.

Camellia hybrids are the most recently expanded group. They comprise many exceptional miniature-flowered varieties and some ideal container plants. Some of the earlier hybrids have made a name for themselves as excellent hedge plants.

Camellia japonica is the parent species of the great majority of cultivars grown today. The japonicas are the traditional types — the first you are likely to think of at the mention of camellias. They tend to be bold flowered with dark green, coarse-textured foliage. Both flowers and leaves are generally larger than other forms. Many of them can be used to great effect in a subtropical-style garden for winter and spring colour.

The species camellias are the predecessors of modern-day hybrids. They have tiny flowers but lots of them, and are often fragrant. The leaves are small and the growth habits mainly soft and semi-weeping. They may grow into small trees but are fairly slow growing so are useful for containers.

THE BEST CAMELLIAS

SMALL OR SINGLE-FLOWERED CAMELLIAS

FLOWERING AUTUMN INTO MID-WINTER

		HEIGHT
'Crimson King'	Sasanqua. Dark wine red petals with yellow stamens. Small single flowers.	1.5 m
'Jennifer Susan'	Sasanqua. Medium sized, lavender pink semi-double flowers. Good hedge.	2 m
'Mine-no-yuki' (syn. 'Moonlight')	Sasanqua. Lots of medium-sized double white flowers. A good hedge.	2 m
'Plantation Pink'	Sasanqua. Fragrant light pink, single flowers with golden stamens. Great hedge.	2.5 m
'Setsugekka'	Sasanqua. Single white flowers with golden stamens. Favourite hedge.	2.5 m
'Yuletide'	Sasanqua. Small red single flowers and yellow stamens. A compact shrub for a tub.	2.5 m

FLOWERING MID-WINTER INTO EARLY SPRING

		HEIGHT
'Baby Bear'	Hybrid. Tiny, pale pink flowers are packed on to a compact shrub, excellent for pots.	1 m
C. lutchuensis	Species. Very fragrant,tiny white flowers in great profusion. Pretty bronze new growth.	2.5 m
C. tsaii	Species. Masses of tiny white fragrant flowers on a graceful weeping shrub.	2.5 m
'Cinnamon Cindy'	Hybrid. Scented miniature flowers, white edged pink. Easily shaped, good for pots.	1.5 m
'Little Babe'	Japonica. Small double flowers are deep red. Good for containers.	1.5 m
'Little Pearl'	Sasanqua. Pink buds open to semi-double white flowers. Slow growth, good for pots.	1.5 m
'Mansize'	Japonica. Pure white miniature.	2 m
'Nicky Crisp'	Hybrid. Pale pink, beautiful semi-double, small grower ideal for a pot.	1.5 m
'Quintesscence'	Hybrid. Fragrant pinky-white flowers. A low-spreading form good for pots and baskets.	1.5 m
'Wilhelmina'	Hybrid. Soft pink miniature camellias of formal form, perfect for picking.	2 m

FLOWERING LATE WINTER INTO SPRING

		HEIGHT
C. transnokoensis	Species. Tiny red buds open to masses of white flowers. Dense foliage. Ideal for pots.	1.5 m
'Fairy Wand'	Hybrid. Rosy-red, semi-double miniature. Fast bushy grower.	2 m
'Spring Festival'	Hybrid. Pink miniature, semi-double flowers on a strongly upright shrub. Good for containers.	1.5 m
'Tiny Princess'	Hybrid. Dainty pink, semi-double miniatures on a graceful shrub.	2 m

Large or Bold-flowered Camellias

		HEIGHT
'Beatrice Emily'	Sasanqua. Large double blooms, white, shading to pink at edges.	2.5 m
'Bonanza'	Sasanqua. Dark pink, large double flowers. Good espalier.	2 m
'Hiryu'	Sasanqua. Cerise-red semi-double blooms in huge abundance. Good hedge.	2.5 m
'Jean May'	Sasanqua. Large semi-double, soft pink. Heavy flowering.	2 m
'Showa-no-sakae'	Sasanqua. Pink, semi-double flowers on a willowy grower, great for espaliering.	2 m

Flowering mid-winter into early spring   HEIGHT

		HEIGHT
'Anticipation'	Hybrid. Large pink double flowers. A tall, narrow shrub.	2.5 m
'Debbie'	Hybrid. Hot pink, large double blooms. Good hedge.	2.5 m
'Debutante'	Japonica. Large clear pink doubles on a strong, very reliable grower.	2.5 m
'Desire'	Japonica. Large white, blushed pink double flowers.	2.5 m
'Donation'	Hybrid. Vigorous with masses of large pink, semi-double blooms. Excellent hedge.	2.5 m
'Elegans Champagne'	Japonica. Very large creamy-white, frilly flowers. Slow spreading growth.	2 m
'Elegans Splendor'	Very large, soft pink with white. Lacy petals. Spreading growth.	2 m
'Elegans Supreme'	Japonica. Large, vibrant pink flowers with a lacy, semi-double form.	2 m
'Guillio Nuccio'	Japonica. Huge, coral-red flowers of elegant, semi-double form. Golden stamens.	2.5 m
'Margaret Davis'	Japonica. Large flowers are white edged rose pink. Peony form.	2.5 m
'Roger Hall'	Japonica. Bright red double flowers and superior foliage.	2.5 m
'Silver Anniversary'	Japonica. Very large white flowers, semi-double with golden stamens. Stunning.	2.5 m

Flowering late winter into spring   HEIGHT

		HEIGHT
'E. G. Waterhouse'	Hybrid. Pink flowers are medium sized, formal. A neat tall, narrow shrub.	2.5 m
'Rendezvous'	Hybrid. Medium-sized semi-double flowers, bright red with showy golden stamens.	2.5 m
'Waterlily'	Hybrid. Clear pink flowers reminiscent of waterlilies	2 m

Camellias as Hedges

'Debbie'	2.5 m	bright pink
'Donation'	2.5 m	pink
'Hiryu'	2.5 m	red
'Jennifer Susan'	2.0 m	pink
'Mine-no-yuki'	2.0 m	white
'Plantation Pink'	2.5 m	light pink
'Setsugekka'	2.5 m	white

Camellias as Espaliers

'Bonanza'	2 m	dark pink
'Showa-no-sakae'	2 m	pink

Camellias for Pots

'Baby Bear'	1.0 m	pink
C. lutchuensis	2.5 m	white/pink
C. transnokoensis	1.5 m	white
C. tsaii	2.5 m	white
'Cinnamon Cindy'	1.5 m	white
'Elegans Supreme'	2.0 m	bright pink
'Little Babe'	1.5 m	red
'Little Pearl'	1.5 m	white/pink
'Nicky Crisp'	1.5 m	pink
'Prudence'	1.0 m	soft pink
'Quintessence'	1.5 m	white/pink
'Snippet'	1.0 m	soft pink
'Snowdrop'	1.5 m	white/pink
'Spring Festival'	1.5 m	soft pink
'Yuletide	'2.5 m	red

Rhododendrons and Azaleas

F ew shrubs can match the flowering brilliance of rhododendrons and azaleas. Starting in early spring, they transform themselves into dazzling clouds of colour. They range in size from small shrubs to trees. Azaleas are essentially small rhododendrons. They thrive under deciduous trees, their shallow roots escaping competition from the deeper-delving tree roots. A mass grouping in full bloom in the natural setting under deciduous trees is an unforgettable sight. Spring-flowering bulbs complete the picture.

Given the right growing conditions, rhododendrons and azaleas are easy to grow, but there is a vast difference between one that is thriving and one that is merely surviving. The best soil is very well drained, compost rich and lime free. When planting rhododendrons or azaleas try to make sure the top of the root ball is not below the soil surface. On heavy soils, plant in raised mounds or make raised beds. Avoid packing the soil down too tightly after planting.

Mulching is almost essential to keep the roots cool and moist. If you want to make a rhododendron unhappy, just plant it in the middle of a lawn and mow around it. They are far better off mass planted in a garden bed with other shrubs, under a generous blanket of organic mulch. However, take care not to build mulch up around the main stem.

Dappled shade is ideal for rhododendrons and azaleas, though too much shade will inhibit flowering. Too much sun, especially in warmer climates, can cause the flowers to fade. It also speeds up evaporation from the ground and the leaves, creating dry conditions more quickly. Larger-leaved varieties generally need the most shade.

Watering is as important as drainage for these fine-rooted plants. They must not be allowed to dry out. Take extra care during periods of dry or windy weather. Plants in full sun or windy locations or those freshly planted need the most frequent watering. Mulching helps to preserve moisture.

Feed rhododendrons and azaleas at the beginning of spring and again in late summer with a fertiliser designed for acid-loving plants (i.e., camellia, rhododendron and azalea food). Use a slow-release fertiliser at planting time. Yellow leaves are a sign of an anaemic rhododendron. This lack of iron is caused either by poor drainage (roots unable to absorb iron), too much lime in the soil (a high pH locks up any iron so it is unavailable to the roots) or an actual iron deficiency. The latter can be fixed by applying iron chelates. Sometimes yellow leaves are due to a magnesium deficiency. This is remedied with an application of magnesium sulphate.

Pruning is barely necessary except for size control. If you need to prune, do it immediately after flowering.

Spring bulbs:
Go to page 120.

More about planting:
Go to page 194.

More about mulch:
Go to page 204.

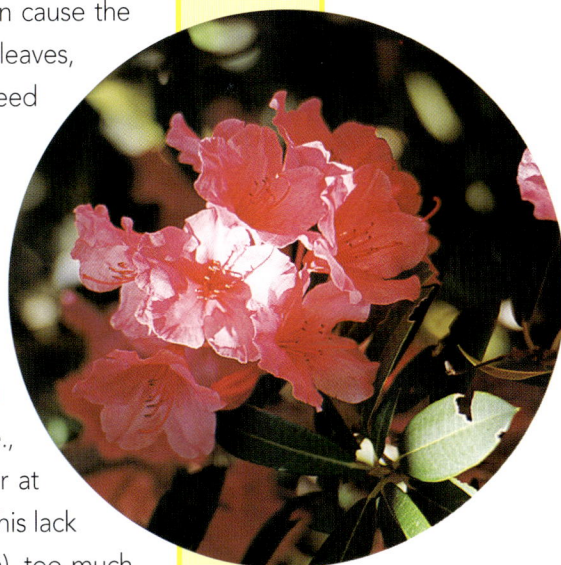

TOP 20 RHODODENDRONS

Planting a range of rhododendron varieties with different flowering times will give you flowers from earliest right through to late spring.

FLOWERING IN LATE WINTER OR EARLY SPRING		*HEIGHT*	*FLOWERING*
'Bruce Brechtbill'	Pink with cream throat.	2 m	early–mid
'Chrysomanicum'	Rich yellow flowers over a long season.	1 m	early
'Countess of Haddington'	Large flowers, white flushed pale pink. Fragrant.	2 m	early
'Dora Ameteis'	Pure white, spotted green. Fragrant.	1 m	early–mid
'Fireman Jeff'	Bright red, large flowers on a compact shrub.	1 m	early–mid
'Kaponga'	Brilliant red flowers and dense foliage.	1.5 m	early
'President Roosevelt'	Pale pink with red margins. Variegated foliage.	2 m	early
'Ptarmigan'	Masses of small white flowers on a dwarf plant.	30 cm	early–mid.

FLOWERING IN MID-SPRING		*HEIGHT*	*FLOWERING*
'Blue Peter'	Frilled, soft lavender, with purple flare.	2 m	mid
'Hydon Hunter'	Large, reddish-purple flowers, margined pink.	1 m	mid
'Lemon Ice'	Outstanding pale lemon blooms.	1.5 m	mid
'Lem's Monach'	Huge white flowers with pink margin.	2 m	mid
'Ostbos Low Yellow'	Apricot-pink buds open pale yellow.	1 m	mid
'Percy Wiseman'	Soft apricot flowers with pink tones.	1 m	mid
'The President'	Red and white variegated flowers.	2 m	mid
'Unique'	Pink buds, opening creamy yellow.	2 m	mid
'Winsome'	Hot cerise pink blooms.	1 m	mid

FLOWERING IN LATE SPRING		*HEIGHT*	*FLOWERING*
'Daphnoides'	Many tight clusters of purple flowers.	2 m	mid–late
'Mt. Everest'	Large pure white flowers.	2.5 m	mid–late
'Purple Splendour'	Frilled deepest purple blooms.	2 m	late

TOP 10 AZALEAS

The following azaleas are compact evergreen shrubs averaging around 70 cm tall and wide, perfect for containers or mass planting. They flower profusely in spring and sometimes spasmodically at other times of the year.

'Bit of Sunshine'	Soft, light red	70 cm
'Kirin'	Mass upon mass of small rose-pink flowers	60 cm
'Mission Bells'	Ruffled bright red double	75 cm
'Pacific Twilight'	Frilled soft lavender double	75 cm
'Purple Glitters'	Violet-purple centred with red stamens	60 cm
'Red Glitters'	Bright red single	75 cm
'Silver Anniversary'	Frilled soft pink	75 cm
'Southern Aurora'	Deep apricot and white	60 cm
'Vespers'	White semi-double	60 cm
'Winter Hawk'	White	75 cm

Climbers

Climbers are among the most decorative of plants. They are also extremely useful. They give a beautiful established look to a new garden in a very short space of time and are especially indispensable in the small garden. In return for a minimum of ground space, they provide fast screening and shade, and paint a permanent background of foliage and flowers that changes with the seasons.

Climbing plants are used liberally for dressing up fences, carports and pergolas, and to soften the harsh lines of buildings. As for tree stumps, old sheds and compost heaps or next-door eyesores, a vigorous climber will hide them in no time.

There are so many irresistible climbers that the existing vertical spaces can be too few. Many an archway or pergola has been built in honour of coveted climbing plants. There are some that are grown mainly for flower display or fragrance, others for their foliage. Climbers from warm tropical regions will often defy a colder climate and thrive on the warm sheltered wall of a courtyard garden.

There is a climber to suit every soil type and climate, for sunny and shady locations. Many are quick growing, others are more restrained. It is a matter of selecting the best plant for your particular set of circumstances. Evergreen climbers offer year-round cover, whereas deciduous ones (often the most flamboyant in their flowering) are a popular choice for pergolas, shading in summer but letting the sun through in winter.

Parthenocissus quinquefolia, Virginian creeper in autumn.

Some climbers are rather rampant, so thought needs to be given to how much space you have available and the effect on adjacent plantings. The good thing is that most can be kept to the desired proportions with rigorous pruning. Keep vigorous climbers such as wisterias away from guttering and downpipes. Heavy climbers need strong supports. Those with invasive habits, such as ivy and Chinese jasmine (*Jasminum polyanthum*), need particular care with placement and may well be best in pots. Many vigorous growers can be constrained by growing them in large containers. These will need to be fed and watered frequently and most will grow better if the container has some shade.

What most climbers love best is cool, well-drained soil and plenty of sunlight. When you see climbers in the wild it's easy to see why. Flowering branches are draped over the treetops with roots embedded in a shady forest floor. What's more, the forest floor has a constantly renewed natural mulch of decaying leaf litter. Approximate such conditions in the garden and your climbers should thrive.

SUPPORTING CLIMBERS

A few climbers are self-supporting by means of sucker discs or aerial roots. Such climbers are ideal for solid walls where they just need some initial guidance to start them off. They are not recommended for planting against painted wooden walls.

SELF-CLINGERS
Campsis grandiflora
Ficus pumila (Creeping fig)
Hedera (Ivy)
Hydrangea petiolaris
Parthenocissus

Some have tendrils that grow out and wrap themselves around the nearest thing handy. They are relatively self-supporting given wires or trellis to attach to, but will need training in the right direction.

CLIMBERS WITH TENDRILS
Passiflora (Passion vine)
Pyrostegia venusta (Flame vine)
Vitis vinifera (Ornamental grape)

Many climbers have a twining habit so that given something to twine on they will support themselves to some extent, but they still need training to encourage them to grow in the desirable direction. Twiners tend to be best at twining on to themselves or other nearby plants.

TWINERS
Clematis
Gelsemium sempervirens
Hardenbergia violacea
Jasminum (Jasmine)
Lonicera (Honeysuckle)

Clematis montana.

Mandevilla
Pandorea
Petrea volubilis
Solanum (Potato vine)
Stephanotis floribunda
Tecomanthe speciosa
Trachelospermum jasminoides
Wisteria

Others need to be tied, unless they reach the stage that they are scrambling through trees or draping themselves over garden buildings.

CLIMBERS THAT MUST BE TIED

Bougainvillea
Climbing and rambling roses

Pieces of nylon stocking make useful ties, strong but flexible. Slightly more aesthetic are the small plastic clips specially designed for the purpose of attaching plants to their supports. It is important not to tie too tightly and to check regularly that the plant is not being strangled by its ties as the stems thicken. Tightly tied branches are prone to breaking as the plant moves with the wind.

Support for climbers may be a trellis or wires running along the length of a fence or wall, or vertically up a post or corner of a building, secured firmly at both ends. Climbers may be trained up poles by wrapping the pole with plastic or wire netting.

With climbers on wooden fences or archways, U-shaped nails can be used to attach the ties at appropriate intervals as the plant grows.

Growing climbers in deciduous trees creates stunning effects. Plant climbers as far out from the tree as possible with a stake slanted in against the tree. Dig a big hole and provide plenty of compost and slow-release fertiliser when planting.

A similar method should be used when planting against solid walls. Plant away from the wall to give the roots plenty of room to spread and use a slanting stake to guide the young plant to the wall. English gardening books show houses sumptuously clad in climbing roses and the like. You might think this is all very well on masonry walls but not for your painted wooden house. There is a way. Attach a trellis to the wall of your house so that it can be detached and laid on the ground (climber intact) when it comes time to paint the house. Chains have been used very successfully in the same manner. Ideally, there should be at least 2 cm space behind trellis attached to solid walls to allow air circulation.

*Bougainvillea
'Raspberry Ice',
an impressive
variegated form
suitable for
containers or
hanging baskets.*

EVERGREEN

Bougainvillea cultivars
BOUGAINVILLEA
Bright summer colour — reds, oranges, pinks, purples, yellows and whites — essential for subtropical gardens. Good also in a hanging basket or large pot, but don't forget to water. A warm, well-drained soil and a warm climate are necessary. This quick-growing climber needs to be tied to its support. Rampant but easily kept in bounds with a once-yearly prune.

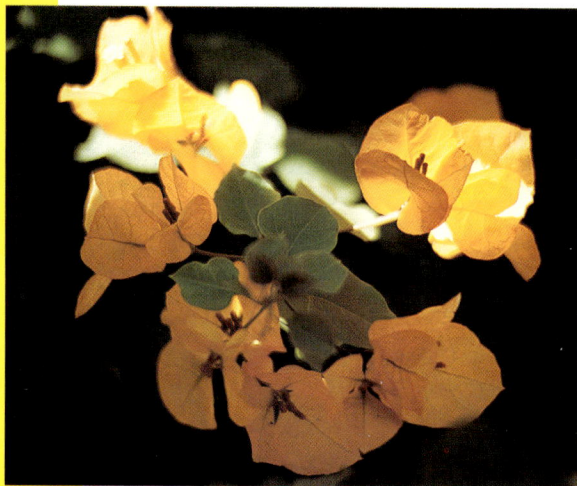

Bougainvillea cultivar.

Clematis paniculata
NEW ZEALAND CLEMATIS or PUAWHANANGA
One of the most admired of all New Zealand native plants. Smotherings of white flowers in early spring adorn treetops and pergolas alike. Fast growing with very nice dark green foliage playing the part between flowering seasons.

Ficus pumila
CREEPING FIG
A self-clinger that suits most New Zealand soil conditions but prefers cool and shady positions. Good for covering walls and foundations with tightly packed, small deep green leaves. Controlled easily with occasional pruning. Creeping fig is perfect for making quick topiaries by growing it over a shaped wire frame. 'Minima' is a smaller-growing form with smaller leaves.

More about topiary: Go to page 207.

Gelsemium sempervirens
CAROLINA JESSAMINE or FALSE JESSAMINE
Ideal where a modestly proportioned climber is needed, this is a slower growing twiner with fragrant yellow flowers from winter through to spring. Attractive glossy foliage. Grows well in sunny or semi-shady spots and suits most soil types.

Hardenbergia violacea cultivars
CORAL PEA
Masses of tiny flowers in purple, pink or white variations make their appearance for most of the winter and spring. This twiner is ideal for growing in pots or as a fast-growing screen. Prefers full sun and well-drained soil. Coral pea needs support for climbing but can also be used as groundcover if pegged down.

Hedera
IVY
Ivy can grow just about anywhere — in the sun or shade, wet or dry conditions, clay or sandy soils, or in a pot. This self-clinger grows fast and can be used for covering walls, banks and the ground, and can be helpful in controlling erosion. It is very attractive in pots or hanging baskets. Interesting foliage makes for excellent picking. There are lots of different varieties: small leaves, large leaves, different shapes, plain green or variegated. Ivy is a number one plant for making fast topiaries over wire frames. The small-leaved varieties are best for this.

More about topiary: Go to page 207.

Jasminum azoricum
AZORES JASMINE
This twiner flowers just about all year round, and is easier to control than the more rampant *J. polyanthum*, so is better for small gardens. The white fragrant flowers make wonderful picking. Grows well in most New Zealand conditions but needs frost protection when young. Plant in sun or semi-shade.

Jasminum polyanthum
CHINESE JASMINE
Beautiful sweet-smelling pink and white flowers are characteristic of this vigorous twiner, which flowers from winter to spring. Although it will grow quickly and easily, Chinese jasmine is best planted where it will not interfere with other plants, as it is inclined to take over. Avoid planting it close to buildings, but it does perform well in a pot. It is slightly frost tender but otherwise grows in full sun or part shade in almost any soil. Superb picking.

Mandevilla 'Alice du Pont'
A must for the subtropical garden, 'Alice du Pont' needs plenty of sun and warm conditions. In summer it produces stunning, large pink trumpet flowers with yellow throats. Nice for a spa pool area and grows well in a container.

Pandorea jasminoides cultivars
These indispensable long-flowering twiners with lovely deep green foliage produce their flowers from summer to winter. They prefer lots of sun for prolific flowering, growing best in rich, moist, well-drained soil. Flowers on 'Alba' are milky white. 'Lady Di' is creamy white. 'Rosea Superba' has striking pink and maroon flowers.

Pandorea pandorana
WONGA WONGA VINE
A very hardy and fast-growing twiner with beautiful creamy flowers in spring. Attractive glossy foliage that looks good all year round. Suits most soils, sun or part shade.

Petrea volubilis
PURPLE WREATH
This twiner's late spring flower show is superb, with hundreds of tiny purple flowers covering the foliage. Grows best in well-drained soil in full sun and prefers warm temperatures.

Podranea ricasoliana
PORT ST JOHN CREEPER
Bright pink flowers and lush glossy foliage characterise this rampant-growing creeper. Flowers from mid-summer to autumn. Suits most soils but needs a sunny position. Requires tying back or support to grow.

Pyrostegia venusta
FLAME VINE

For winter colour in warmer climates this twiner is a must. Its stunning bright orange flowers often carry on into spring. Climbs easily and quickly using tendrils for support. Grows well in coastal areas but needs full sun.

Solanum jasminoides 'Grandiflora'
WHITE POTATO VINE

Little white flowers can be seen all year round on this twiner. Grows very quickly and prefers sun or partial shade. A hardy climber that grows in almost all soil types. Trim occasionally to encourage foliage cover at the base of the plant.

Stephanotis floribunda
MADAGASCAR JASMINE

Deliciously fragrant white flowers cover this twiner during summer and autumn. It needs warm sheltered, frost-free conditions with plenty of sun and good drainage. Grows well in containers.

Tecomanthe speciosa

A native to New Zealand, this twiner has lovely glossy leaves with creamy yellow flowers in winter. Grows best in sun or partly shaded areas and mild climates.

Thunbergia grandiflora
SKY FLOWER

Another show-stopper for a subtropical garden, *Thunbergia grandiflora* produces the most exquisite blue trumpet flowers, present for most of the year, but mainly between spring and autumn. It needs full sun and the absence of frost.

Trachelospermum jasminoides
STAR JASMINE

This glossy-green climber is not to be missed for its superb jasmine-like fragrance. In spring and summer there are hundreds of fragrant white flowers. Star jasmine grows fast in most soils, in sun or part shade. It also grows well in pots.

Thunbergia grandiflora, sky flower.

DECIADUOUS

Campsis grandiflora
CHINESE TRUMPET VINE

A fast-growing climber with attractive foliage and vibrant orange trumpet flowers. Vibrant colour for summer pergolas, tolerant of coastal conditions and great for fast screening of sizable areas. Coastal, summer colour, fast screen. Prune after flowering to control size and renew healthy growth.

Clematis hybrids
HYBRID CLEMATIS

Twining vines with huge, exotic-looking flowers. Long-flowering favourites for combining with old-fashioned roses. 'Jackmanii' has rich purple flowers in summer. 'Nellie Moser' has pale pink flowers with crimson stripes and flowers in spring. 'Lawsoniana' has rosy-purple flowers in summer. 'Madame le Coultre' (syn. 'Marie Boisselet') is a free-flowering white, blooming in spring. Hybrid clematis need a cool root run (lots of mulch) with their tops in sun or part shade. Prune summer-flowering varieties by cutting back hard in winter. Spring-flowering varieties should be pruned lightly, immediately after flowering or not at all.

Clematis montana cultivars
ANEMONE CLEMATIS

Very hardy, very quick growing and crowded with flowers in early spring, as showy as a spring show gets. Choose from white or pink forms. Unfussy but enjoying cool roots in sun or part shade. Handles frost, wind and poor soils. Prune if necessary to control size.

Mandevilla suaveolens
CHILEAN JASMINE

Worth growing for the fragrant waxy white flowers alone, but the dark green foliage is an attractive feature in summer too. Good for a trellis in close proximity to outdoor summer-living areas.

Parthenocissus quinquefolia
VIRGINIAN CREEPER

A self-clinger that looks wonderful draped over trellis or growing up walls. Foliage changes to vibrant oranges and reds in autumn and produces little blue-black berries. Likes cooler conditions but needs to be in the sun or partial shade. Works well as groundcover on banks for erosion control.

Parthenocissus tricuspidata 'Veitchii'
BOSTON IVY

A very fast-growing self-clinging vine with attractive deep green foliage transforming in autumn to rich yellows and reds. Prefers a cooler climate in a sunny or partially shaded spot. Clusters of blue-black berries in autumn. Great for erosion control. Looks lovely growing on walls.

Solanum wendlandii
BLUE POTATO VINE

Fast cover, with stunning purple blue flowers in spring. From Costa Rica, requiring a frost-free climate and full sunshine. Prune to control size and renew growth. Fast but not easily controlled.

Solanum jasminoides 'Grandiflora', white potato vine.

Vitis vinifera 'Purpurea'
ORNAMENTAL GRAPE

Grow this one for autumn colour if you have cool winters, a dryish soil and a sunny wall or pergola. Not for the tropics, but tolerant of drought and frost.

Wisteria floribunda cultivars
JAPANESE WISTERIA

The later- and longer-flowering wisteria. The fragrant flowers appear in spring at the same time as the leaves. The foliage remains attractive right through summer, a nice backdrop to other flowering plants. A fast-growing twiner of grand proportions needing strong support. White, pink or purple varieties to choose from. Prune after flowering for size control.

Wisteria sinensis cultivars
CHINESE WISTERIA

The most famous wisteria with lovely lilac flowers on bare branches in early spring. Fragrance to spare and an encore of attractive foliage right through the summer. Fast and vigorous once it gets going and not for flimsy supports. Prune after flowering for size control. Plant grafted plants to be sure of early flowering. Seedling plants are hit and miss but generally not worth the wait.

Wisteria floribunda.

Climbing Roses

Where there is a sunny space for a climber, roses are high on the list of possibilities. While they are generally leafless in winter, they can be a sight made in heaven during spring summer or autumn.

Some are more vigorous than others, so choose carefully depending on your space. An old but sturdy shed may call for a vigorous old-fashioned rambler, but a verandah post will suit a less-rampant climbing rose.

'Alberic Barbier'	cream, fragrant, vigorous and far reaching.
'Albertine'	apricot-pink, very fragrant, vigorous and far reaching.
R. banksia 'Lutea'	yellow, wide spreading, thornless, almost evergreen.
R. banksia 'The Pearl'	white, thornless almost evergreen.
'City of London'	pink, fragrant, modestly proportioned.
'Compassion'	apricot, fragrant, moderate spread.
'Dublin Bay'	red, fragrant, moderate spread.
'Golden Showers'	yellow, fragrant, modestly proportioned.
'Graham Thomas'	yellow, very fragrant, large shrub or moderate climber.
'Iceberg'	white, moderate spread.
'Mme Alfred Carrière'	white, fragrant, vigorous and far reaching.
'New Dawn'	pink, fragrant, moderate spread.
'Veilchenblau'	purple, vigorous and far reaching.
'Wedding Day'	white, vigorous and far reaching.
'Westerland'	orange, fragrant, moderate spread.

More about these climbing roses: Go to page 97.

'New Dawn'.

Groundcovers

Groundcovers are the garden carpets, those low, mat-forming plants that cover the soil, suppress the weeds and provide a foil for the taller-growing plants above them.

The idea of groundcovers in a low-maintenance garden is to fill in all the soil spaces under and around trees and shrubs, leaving no gaps for weeds. Preferably they are evergreen and densely foliaged to make them as effective as possible as a barrier to the germination of weed seeds.

A word of caution though — do not expect your groundcovers to defeat those persistent weeds such as oxalis, couch grass and other perennial grasses. These must be eradicated as thoroughly as possible before planting your groundcover, as they are capable of growing from the smallest remnants left in the soil, and will push their way through the tightest-woven groundcovers.

Apart from weed stopping, groundcovers have a number of other virtues. Some are less rigorous at weed suppressing, but make up for it by simply looking great with attractive carpets of flowers and foliage that finish off a grouping of plants or soften the lines of paving.

Ajuga 'Jungle Beauty' forms a dense weed-stopping carpet.

A bare soil is exposed to the elements. Wind, hot sun, rain, hail and snow all do damage to the structure of the soil over time. Wind can blow it away. Water and slope combined create the worst kind of erosion. Temperature extremes are not good for the soil or the plants' roots under its surface. So a fully clothed ground surface is far better all round than a nude one.

Lawns are a form of groundcover, and the most tolerant (next to non-living alternatives) of foot traffic. But there are alternatives to lawns that stand varying degrees of walking on and don't need mowing.

Where there is more than a gentle slope that calls for low planting, alternative groundcover plants are often a better solution than lawn. Better in the sense that dangerous mowing is not required and that better erosion control will result. Plants with deeper, stronger roots help bind the soil on banks and also 'suck out' excess water, thus preventing slips.

Another place where groundcover plants come into their own is under trees. Apart from the fact that lawns grow less successfully in shade, it is not good for any tree or shrub to have its roots continuously compacted and its trunk knocked by a lawn mower. Who wants the hassle of mowing around trees anyway? Tall plantings around a tree can ruin its looks by hiding its trunk but low groundcovers display it to best effect. There is a good choice of groundcovers for shade.

FOR SHADY PLACES

Ajuga
CARPET BUGLE
Under 20 cm

A thick mat of lush foliage makes a year-round cover. In spring, upright clusters of blue flowers appear in great mass. All are easy to grow but perhaps the very best is the larger-leaved 'Jungle Beauty'. *A. reptans*, the smaller-leaved form, comes in three colours: plain green (*A. reptans*), burgundy ('Atropurpurea'), pink, edged white ('Burgundy Glow') and the green and white variegated 'Variegata' to really lighten up a shady corner. Ajuga will grow in sun or shade (more sun means more flowers), preferring a moist soil.

Bergenia cordifolia cultivars
ELEPHANT'S EARS
Under 30 cm

Lovely big leaves giving striking textural contrast make this an excellent perennial for mass planting. The flowers appear in early spring and are red, pink, lavender or white depending on the variety. Bergenias tolerate dry shade once established, growing in sun or shade but flowering best with some sun.

Ficus pumila
CREEPING FIG
UNDER 20 CM

This self-clinging climber with tightly packed, small deep green leaves, is also useful as a groundcover in shady places. It needs space as it is an enthusiastic spreader, but is controlled easily with occasional pruning.

Hedera
IVY
UNDER 20 CM

Ivy can grow just about anywhere — in the sun or shade, wet or dry conditions, clay or sandy soils, or in a pot. It grows fast and can be used for covering walls, banks or the ground, and is helpful in controlling erosion. There are lots of different varieties. The variegated forms are useful for lighting up dull areas. Ivy is a large-scale groundcover, not for small pockets in the garden.

Lamium maculatum cultivars
DEAD NETTLE
Under 30 cm

Despite the rather unflattering common name, this plant makes a useful and very attractive evergreen groundcover for shady locations. The plain species is rather rampant, but the various cultivars with their pretty variegated or mottled leaves are more easily confined. There are pink or white flowers in summer. Good also in hanging baskets or containers, but needing rich moist soil.

Liriope muscari
TURF LILY
Under 45 cm

Grassy dark green clumps sport blue, grape hyacinth-style flower spikes in autumn. Great as a border or mass planting under trees, where it will cope with dry soil as well as shade. Clumps are divided and transplanted in winter or spring.

Ophiopogon planiscapus
MONDO GRASS
Under 30 cm

Similar to *Liriope muscari*, here is another excellent grassy foliage plant for mass planting in sun or part shade. The species has dark green foliage, and there is a stunning black form, *O. planiscapus* 'Nigrescens'.

Pachysandra terminalis
JAPANESE SPURGE
Under 30 cm

Especially valuable in cooler climates, *Pachysandra* is perfect for underplanting trees and tolerates dry conditions well. It is related to English box with small glossy-green leaves making a dense weed-suppressing carpet. Slow growing but very tough.

Pratia puberula
BABY'S TEARS
Under 5 cm

Tiny leaves form a tight moss-like mat which becomes covered in a mass of tiny, starry pale blue flowers. Excellent in combination with stepping stones. There is a white-flowered form too. Very easy to grow, needing moisture.

Saxifraga umbrosa
LONDON PRIDE
Under 40 cm

A pretty spring-flowering perennial that makes a wonderful groundcover mass planted under trees or as an edging to shady pathways. The flowers are white, held on dainty stems above spreading rounded leaves.

Viola hederacea
TASMANIAN VIOLET
Under 15 cm

Lots of little purple and white, pickable flowers are crowded above dense dark green leaves. Easy to grow in a moist soil with some shade.

Viola odorata cultivars
SCENTED VIOLET
Under 20 cm

Very easy, taking care of itself in any average soil, spreading and self-seeding so it is best where it can be allowed to naturalise without interfering with other treasured plants. The winter and spring flowers are loved for their fragrance and for picking. There are a number of different varieties, both single- and double-flowered forms in shades of pink, blue and white. More sun means more flowers but perfectly happy in semi-shade. Divide every two or three years. Poor flowering is often due to overcrowding.

Pratia puberula.

Other low-maintenance plants for mass planting in shady places:

Acanthus mollis	Bear's Breeches	1 m
Agapanthus cultivars		50 cm to 1 m
Arthropodium cirratum	Rengarenga	60 cm
Clivia miniata	Clivia	50 cm
Euphorbia amygdaloides var. *robbiae*	Spurge	50 cm
Zantedeschia aethiopica 'Little Child'	Dwarf Arum Lily	60 cm

More about these plants: Go to page 103–111.

FOR SUN

Acaena microphylla
NATIVE BIDDY-BID
UNDER 5 CM
A low-spreading carpet of brownish-green leaves is covered in red spiky seedheads in summer. Spectacular around paving, rocks and stone pathways, this biddy-bid has a useful rapid spread, but is easily kept in bounds, and does not have seedheads that stick to your clothes. Some of the *Acaena* species are serious weeds.

Anthemis punctata subsp. cupaniana
DAISY
Under 30 cm
A lovely spreading plant with silver foliage and masses of white daisies about the size of a fifty-cent coin, with yellow button centres. A good one for spilling over path edges or retainer walls. Cut back after flowering to keep it compact.

Carex spp.
NEW ZEALAND SEDGE
Under 50 cm
Mass-planted grasses make excellent low-maintenance groundcovers. The New Zealand sedges lend an interesting texture to any garden, native or otherwise, with their soft foliage blowing in a breeze. They tolerate dry conditions and clay soils, wind and coastal conditions.

More about grasses: Go to page 141.

Ceanothus 'Blue Cushion'
CALIFORNIAN LILAC
75 cm x 1.5 m
A low-mounding shrub with bright blue flowers, excellent for dry banks. Needs good drainage but tolerates poor soils. Loves hot sun.

Cerastium tomentosum
SNOW-IN-SUMMER
Under 10 cm
Ground-hugging silver foliage and a smothering of little white flowers in summer. A well-drained position in full sun is best, but semi-shade will suffice. Good also in pots.

Cistus salviifolius
SAGE LEAF ROCK ROSE
60 cm x 2 m
Soft sage-like foliage with white silk-textured flowers resembling small single roses in spring and summer. Perfect for hot dry banks and coastal gardens but not for soils that are wet in winter.

Coprosma acerosa
SAND DUNE COPROSMA
45 cm x 1.5 m
An extremely tough and easy groundcover, making a dense weed-suppressing blanket very quickly. Will grow in most soils but loves a dry sandy bank as the name suggests. A hardy evergreen native for sun or part shade.

Coprosma xkirkii
30 cm x 1.5 m
Another tough native groundcover with small shiny leaves. Good on the coast or on banks, in any soil.

Gazania hybrids
AFRICAN DAISY
Under 30 cm
Bright summer yellows, oranges, reds and pinks lasting for a very long time and thriving in hot, well-drained conditions. Ideal coastal or container plant, perfect for cascading over clay banks, binding crumbling soils. Flowers are more prolific in poor soil. Protect from frost.

Grevillea 'Bronze Rambler'
30 cm x 3 m
There are lots of low-spreading grevilleas. They are ideal groundcover shrubs for sunny well-drained locations. 'Bronze Rambler' is one of the best. It has intricately divided glossy foliage on spreading branches, which form a dense weed-stopping layer. The new growth is bronzy red and the red toothbrush flowers are present from spring into autumn. Great for banks. Evergreen.

Helichrysum argyrophyllum
EVERLASTING DAISY
Under 20 cm
Silver-grey foliage and lots of little yellow paper daisies in summer and autumn. Enjoys warm sunny conditions and good drainage. A good ground-hugger or container plant.

Heterocentron elegans (syn. Schizocentron elegans)
SPANISH SHAWL
Under 5 cm
A very dense, very ground-clinging plant with fine foliage and intense cyclamen-pink flowers. Leaves and stems are coloured reddish in winter. Plant about four plants per square metre for quick cover. Spanish shawl requires free-draining soil and a frost-free climate. Water in dry periods.

Juniperus horizontalis
CREEPING JUNIPER
10 cm x 2 m
A low, wide-spreading conifer, much planted in tough locations. It tolerates clay soils, wet or dry and coastal conditions. Foliage is dark grey-green. There are a number of cultivars with various coloured foliage: blue, plum, silvery-grey.

Libertia peregrinans
NEW ZEALAND IRIS
Under 30 cm
Like a miniature flax with interesting orange-toned, spiky foliage, perfect for both colour and textural contrast. Underground rhizomes mean this plant has a useful spreading habit to form a solid groundcover, without becoming invasive. To mass plant an area, space young plants about 30 cm apart. New plants can be produced by lifting and dividing established clumps. Tiny white iris flowers appear in spring.

Lithodora diffusa (syn. Lithospermum diffusum) 'Grace Ward'
15 cm x 90 cm
Brilliant gentian-blue flowers are a show stopper on this low-spreading evergreen in spring. The foliage is rich dark green. A useful small-scale groundcover and good in pots. Must have good drainage and full sun.

Mazus radicans
SWAMP MUSK
Under 10 cm
A delightful little native thriving in good moist soil and partial shade, but flowering best in sun. Forms a good mat of small mottled leaves with dainty lobelia-like flowers, white with touches of purple and yellow.

Osteospermum cultivars
AFRICAN DAISY
Under 30 cm
A spreading daisy, fantastic as a bank cover, hardier than the gazanias, with-standing light frost. The flowers cover the plant in spring and summer, most often in shades of pink and purple, also white and yellow. Some forms are bushy, others spreading. Full sun and good drainage are essential.

Parahebe spp. and cultivars
Under 15 cm
Low cushion-forming New Zealand natives with small leaves and dainty flowers, closely related to hebes. They are free flowering and easy to grow, best in free-draining soil that doesn't dry out.

Pratia angulata
PANAKENAKE
Under 10 cm
A New Zealand pratia with pretty lobelia-like flowers of snowy-white, which cover a dense mat of tiny mid-green leaves for many months starting in early summer. Plant in a moist soil with sun or light shade. Best in a frost-free climate.

Phlox subulata hybrids
PROSTRATE PHLOX
Under 10 cm
A mass of colour in spring or summer with flowers totally covering the foliage in shades of bright pink, lavender blue, soft pink, or white. Good in pots, in rock gardens, on banks or retainer walls, with bulbs and other perennials, they need a warm sunny spot in a well-drained soil. They will tolerate dry, exposed conditions and do well in coastal gardens in any climate. Plant a variety of forms for a colourful tapestry effect.

Rosa 'Flower Carpet'
FLOWER CARPET ROSE
50 cm x 1 m
Practically evergreen in a warm climate, this rose makes an excellent groundcover or bank plant. Extensively used worldwide in city plantings, it provides a mass of flowers from spring through autumn, and is set apart from most other roses by its disease resistance and easy-care pruning.

More about Flower Carpet: Go to page 92.

Rosmarinus officinalis (syn. R. lavandulaceus)
CREEPING ROSEMARY
30 cm x 2 m
Blue summer flowers and grey-green foliage that looks like a waterfall when grown over a wall. Sprigs can be used in the kitchen. This is a hardy evergreen shrub for a well-drained position, flowering best in full sun.

Stachys byzantina
LAMB'S EAR
Under 20 cm
Unmistakable soft downy leaves in silver grey. There are pale lavender flower spikes but these are best removed for it is the foliage that is the real feature. Lamb's ear is the perfect edging plant, spreading quickly into a weed-stopping mat. It will grow in any average soil, but looks sad in cold wet winter conditions. Prefers full sun or light shade. Easily lifted and divided.

Sutera cordata
BACOPA SNOWFLAKE
Under 10 cm
A mat-forming creeper with lush green foliage and lots of little white flowers through the year. Great as an edging or for mass planting under roses, in the front of a flower border and in pots or hanging baskets. Feed and water regularly and provide a well-drained soil in sun or part shade.

Sutera cordata.

Thymus spp. and varieties
THYME
Under 20 cm

There are a number of low-growing thymes suitable as groundcover plants. The lowest of them all are the creeping thymes, which are lovely in combination with paving. 'Emerald Carpet' is an excellent example with bright green leaves all year round and white flowers in summer. There are gold- and silver-leaved forms too, with pink or white flowers. Thyme must have full sun and a well-drained soil to grow well.

More about thyme: Go to page 168.

Trachelospermum jasminoides
STAR JASMINE

This is an evergreen climber that is equally useful and attractive as a groundcover, not to be overlooked for its superb jasmine-like fragrance. In spring and summer there are hundreds of fragrant white flowers. Growing in full sun or part shade it suits most soils and grows fast, but is easily contained with pruning.

LAWN SUBSTITUTES

Dichondra spp.
MERCURY BAY WEED

Tiny, kidney-shaped leaves form a close-packed, lush green, ground-hugging carpet, plants spreading by surface runners. In full sun *Dichondra* stays low to the ground and never needs mowing. In shade it may reach up to 15 cm tall, needing frequent mowing. A *Dichondra* lawn needs ample feeding and watering. It can be sown directly on to the ground from seed, or 'plugs' of growing plants can be transplanted into prepared soil. These are available in trays from garden centres. Try small areas of *Dichondra* lawn before plunging into large-scale projects, perhaps as a feature around stepping stones.

Thymus spp.
CREEPING THYME

Thyme releases its wonderful fragrance when crushed so is lovely at the edge of a pathway, as a small lawn, or even a seat. The tricky part is that the flowers attract bees — not good for bare feet.

Chamaemelum nobile
CHAMOMILE

Chamomile makes a lush green lawn that releases a delicious perfume when walked on. The best for lawns is the variety 'Treneague' with a tidy dense growth habit and no flowers to attract the bees. Because it is a non-seed-producing variety, 'Treneague' has to be grown by division or cuttings, so a lawn takes longer, or is more expensive to establish. Common chamomile is easy to grow from seed but, although it can be mown, has a more uneven growth habit.

Mainly natives in a low-maintenance coastal garden.

Special
selections

New Zealand Native Plants

New Zealand is dotted with beautiful gardens that take care of themselves. They are pockets of native bush, full of plants that are perfectly suited to their environment.

We cannot expect to transplant an exact copy into a domestic setting, but there is much inspiration to be gained by looking at the bush. Magnificent green tapestries woven from the vast assortment of foliage textures is one of the most special qualities. It is easy to create a colourful, richly textured, all-native garden before you even start with the spectacular flowering native shrubs.

Of the most strikingly beautiful native plants are the kowhai trees, which are smothered in yellow flowers in early spring, the bright red kaka beak, the stunning native clematis vines and the puka with its handsome large leaves. There are many such dramatic examples. To provide a stage for the dramatic are the many subtly beautiful native shrubs. Native shrubs include some of the best shrubs for use as groundcovers, hedges and background planting. Some of the best windbreaks are made from natives.

Natives have a magic way of enhancing each other when planted in groups with other natives. One of the easiest ways to achieve a coherent style is to plant a native garden. A purist might only plant the green endemic species, but the wealth of cultivars developed from them are not to be sniffed at. These offer an ever-expanding choice of foliage colour and texture and include some important smaller-growing alternatives for small gardens.

Because native plants work so well together, many gardeners devote separate areas of the garden to them, but they mix well with exotic plants too. There is no reason why you shouldn't grow roses with your natives.

If you want to attract bird life into your garden, native plants are ideal. In this regard, try to provide a year-round food supply as much as possible.

Phormium cultivar.

A puka, *Meryta sinclairii*, trained as a small tree and underplanted cottage-style.

SMALL SHRUBS AND GROUNDCOVERS

BOTANICAL NAME	COMMON NAME	HEIGHT	GO TO PAGE
Acaena microphylla	Biddy-bid	5 cm	58
Arthropodium cirratum	Rengarenga	60 cm	103
Astelia chathamica 'Silver Spear'	Astelia	1.3 m	139
Brachyglottis (syn. Senecio) 'Otari Cloud'		1.2 m	30
Carex spp.	NZ Sedge	30 cm	58
Chionochloa flavicans		1 m	141
Coprosma acerosa	Sand Dune Coprosma	45 cm	58
Coprosma xkirkii		30 cm	58
Coprosma spp. and cultivars		1 m	32
Hebe spp. and cultivars	NZ KOROMIKO	1 m	34
Libertia peregrinans	NZ Iris	25 cm	59
Mazus radicans		5 cm	59
Parahebe spp. and cultivars		10 cm	34
Phormium hybrids	Flax	1 m	34
Pratia angulata	Panakenake	5 cm	59
Xeronema callistemon	Poor Knights Lily	1 m	139

SHRUBS

BOTANICAL NAME	COMMON NAME	HEIGHT	GO TO PAGE
Brachyglottis repanda	Rangiora	up to 5 m	36
B. repanda 'Purpurea'	Purple Rangiora	2.5 m	36
Clianthus puniceus 'Kaka King'	Kaka Beak	2 m	36
Corokia cotoneaster	Wire Netting Bush	2.5 m	37
Hoheria populnea 'Alba Variegata'	Lacebark	3 m	17
Meryta sinclairii	Puka	4 m	19
Myrsine australis	Matipou	3 m	17
Olearia albida	Tanguru	4 m	24
Olearia cheesemanii		2 m	38
Pittosporum crassifolium	Karo	3 m	24
Pittosporum eugenioides	Lemonwood, Tarata	5 m	39
P. eugenioides 'Variegata'	Lemonwood, Tarata	2 m	39
Pittosporum tenuifolium cultivars			39
Pseudopanax laetus	Five finger	3 m	38

(CONTINUED)

TREES

Botanical name	Common name	Height	Go to page
Agathis australis	Kauri	10 m+	22
Alectryon excelsus	Titoki	7 m	19
Cordyline 'Green Goddess'	Cabbage Tree	3 m	139
Cordyline banksii	Cabbage Tree	2.5 m	139
Dacrydium cupressinum	Rimu	6 m	22
Hoheria populnea	Lacebark	5 m	17
Knightia excelsa	Rewarewa	7 m	22
Metrosideros excelsa cultivars	Pohutukawa	4–5 m	19
Podocarpus totara	Totara	6 m	22
Sophora tetraptera	Kowhai	4.5 m	19

CLIMBERS

Botanical name	Common name	Height	Go to page
Clematis paniculata	NZ Clematis, Puawhananga		page 52
Tecomanthe speciosa			page 53

LEFT: NZ rock lily or rengarenga, *Arthropodium cirratum*, ideal for planting under trees.
BELOW: A new native garden, featuring a hebe hedge and the contrasting foliage of *Astelia*.

Subtropical Gardens

So appropriate, yet so underutilised — the stunning possibilities of a South Pacific-style garden have yet to be discovered by many warm-climate gardeners.

In warm, humid climates where roses and hollyhocks succumb to disease, peonies won't flower, and autumn colour is second best, a subtropical-style garden may be your answer. In Auckland, Northland and parts of the Bay of Plenty, where frosts are rare, there is the ideal opportunity to create a lush green paradise in your own backyard — the kind of garden that elsewhere can only exist in elaborate green-houses.

The scene is one of luxuriant abundance with lots of bold, flamboyant flowers. Bright colours — pinks, reds, yellows, oranges, bright blues and purples. In some gardens the mixing of such colours might well seem gaudy, but in a subtropical setting they happily coexist with plenty of green foliage to cool them down.

A subtropical garden can be made on any scale. Small sheltered city gardens are well suited. A humus-rich, well-drained soil is best, and you should have access to plenty of water for irrigation. On poor or heavy soils, raised beds have been known to give brilliant results with subtropical gardens.

Mandevilla sanderi 'Rosea', a long-flowering climber for a warm position.

PLANTS

THE TOP STOREY

The upper canopy of a subtropical garden is for the main part made up of palms, but other trees that provide gently filtered light are also good. Trees that suit the theme include *Robinia* 'Frisia', *Jacaranda, Hymenosporum flavum* (Australian frangipani), *Schinus molle* (pepper tree) and *Albizia julibrissin* (silk tree).

Many climbers originate from tropical regions. Their flowers and foliage play a big part in setting the scene, but as well provide dappled shade for those subtropical plants that need it. Climbers fit into the smallest gardens, taking a minimum of ground space. Your subtropical garden should include *Bougainvillea*, also one or more of *Mandevilla* 'Alice du Pont', *Pyrostegia venusta* (flame vine), *Trachelospermum jasminoides* (star jasmine), *Campsis grandiflora* (Chinese trumpet vine), *Solanum wendlandii* (blue potato vine), *Petrea volubilis, Podranea ricasoliana* (Port St John creeper), *Stephanotis floribunda* (Madagascar jasmine), *Thunbergia grandiflora* (sky flower) and *Tecomanthe speciosa*.

Palms:
Go to page 68.

Trees:
Go to page 15.

Climbers:
Go to page 49.

Vireya rhododendrons for colour, ferns and palms for lush form and texture.

THE MIDDLE LAYER

The two essential flowering shrubs for subtropical gardens are hibiscus and vireya rhododendrons — as many different varieties of each as you can fit!

Other flowering shrubs for warm climates are *Anigozanthos* (kangaroo paw), *Brunfelsia calycina* (yesterday, today, tomorrow), *Grewia occidentalis*, *Leonotis leonurus* (lion's tail), *Luculia grandiflora*, *Metrosideros* 'Tahiti', *Solanum rantonnetii* (Paraguay nightshade), *Steptosolen jamesonii* (orange browallia) and *Tibouchina* (lasiandra).

Non-tropical shrubs with a tropical look are the large-leaved, large-flowered camellias, and large-leaved rhododendrons. These are quite in keeping with the tropical style, adding to the green backdrop in summer and providing colour for winter, while the hibiscus rest.

As well as flowering shrubs you need lots of big-leaved plants, such as banana palms (*Musa* spp., *Ensete* spp.), bird of paradise (*Strelitzia* cultivars), and puka (*Meryta sinclairii*). Large-growing perennials with appropriate foliage include canna lilies, *Alocasia odora* (giant taro), *Acanthus mollis* (bears breeches) and *Zantedeschia aethiopica* (arum lily).

A treasure trove of foliage plants for subtropical gardens is the houseplant area at your local garden centre. Prime examples are peace lily (*Spathiphyllum*), fruit salad plant (*Monstera deliciosa*), *Philodendron* spp., and weeping fig (*Ficus benjamina*). There are many more. Especially when first transplanted outdoors these plants need protection from bright sun. Remember, they grow naturally in the tropics, in the dappled shade of the forest.

THE GROUND STOREY

The lacy foliage of ferns offsets and enhances the texture of the big-leaved plants. These are the ideal groundcover plants and bulk fillers for shady places in the subtropical garden, but they must have plenty of moisture so are not for dry corners.

Many commonly grown annuals and perennials are very appropriate for subtropical gardens, where they take on a whole new look. These include the brightly flowered begonias, *Portulaca*, New Guinea hybrid impatiens, *Bergenia* (elephant's ears), and those with lush strappy foliage: *Agapanthus*, *Clivia*, *Liriope* (turf lily) and *Arthropodium cirratum* (rengarenga). All make wonderful edging, filler, or container plants.

For bright spots in containers or in the ground are some well-known flowering houseplants: kalanchoes and blush begonias, easily grown outdoors in a warm climate.

Hibiscus:
Go to page 70.

Vireya rhododendrons:
Go to page 71.

Shrubs:
Go to page 29.

Camellias:
Go to page 44.

Rhododendrons:
Go to page 47.

perennials:
Go to page 102.

Indoor plants:
Go to page 221.

Ferns:
Go to page 222.

Annuals:
Go to page 127.

BROMELIADS

The low-growing masses of the tropical garden are the bromeliads. Both their flowers and foliage are colourful and eyecatching. These dramatic plants are commonly sold for indoors, but in warm climates they are extremely easy to grow outdoors. Not only do they grow on the ground or in containers, but they are just as happy growing in a tree or attached to a piece of driftwood, or even a pergola post. Most bromeliads are epiphytes. They use their roots mainly for anchorage, taking their food and water from the air and via their built-in reservoir. The vase at the centre of the plant fills with water and traps all manner of gourmet delights — from mosquito larvae to tree frogs — in their natural habitat. In the home garden they need their urns filled in dry weather and require feeding occasionally with liquid fish fertiliser, applied to the leaves. Inorganic fertilisers are best avoided, as are sprays, especially oil-based ones, which block the plant's ability to absorb water and nutrients.

Whether you grow your bromeliads at ground level or eye level, they will look best in good-sized groupings. For the beginner, the many species and varieties of *Neoregelia* are probably the easiest to grow. They like light shade, good drainage and moderate moisture.

Bromeliads and impatiens at the base of a palm tree.

EMBELLISHMENTS

Accent plants for containers or pride-of-place garden positions include cycads, palms and spiky-foliage plants like *Xeronema* (Poor Knights lily), *Agave* spp., *Yucca* spp., *Astelia* spp. (silver spear), *Cordyline* spp. and *Dracaena draco*.

More about accent plants:
Go to page 138.

Palms and cycads:
Go to page 68.

FRAGRANCE

Last, but not least, this is an all-important dimension in any garden. In a subtropical garden it comes from some of the more challenging of tropical plants, such as island frangipani (*Plumeria rubra*) and *Gardenia* spp., but also from easy-to-grow plants like *Cestrum nocturnum*, *Michelia figo*, *Hymenosporum flavum* (Australian frangipani), *Luculia grandiflora* and the very easy star jasmine (*Trachelospermum jasminoides*), which can be used as a climber or groundcover. Some of the vireya rhododendrons are also fragrant.

Textural contrast: hen and chickens ferns (*Asplenium bulbiferum*) with *Clivia miniata*.

Palms

Palms, a key ingredient in the making of a subtropical garden, are remarkably easy to grow. Widely grown as an indoor plant, in the right climate they are a whole lot easier to look after if they are grown outdoors in the ground. They are the ultimate low-maintenance tree — no pruning, no spraying, just the occasional clearing away of dead leaves. Some of them are surprisingly fast growing too.

The clean, straight trunk of a mature palm leaves plenty of space for planting underneath. In this sense they are perfect for small gardens, providing height and shade without taking up valuable ground space. Palms tend to look best planted in groups, especially if they are a mixture of ages.

Palms usually grow out rather than up in their formative years, first developing their canopy of leaves. Then the trunks start to form, growing straight upwards to form those distinctive vertical lines so fundamental to the subtropical picture. Each palm has an absolute number of leaves, which remains unchanged once developed. As each one dies a new one develops to take its place. A compact root system gives palms a number of advantages: many make ideal container plants; they are very accommodating of smaller plants grown at their feet (right up to their trunks); and they are happy to be transplanted, even when very large.

Palms vary in price depending on variety and size. The costly ones are generally slow growing or difficult to propagate.

Palms require shade when young and a moist, well-drained soil with plenty of well-rotted compost or manure. A clay-based soil will support most palms as long as it is well drained. They will not tolerate wet feet. Dig a big hole at planting time and backfill it with good soil and slow-release fertiliser. Have the palm well watered, by soaking it for an hour in advance of planting. Mulch with well-rotted compost and water deeply in the warmer months. Most palms prefer a warm humid climate, but some tolerate surprisingly cooler conditions. Warmer soil usually means faster growth.

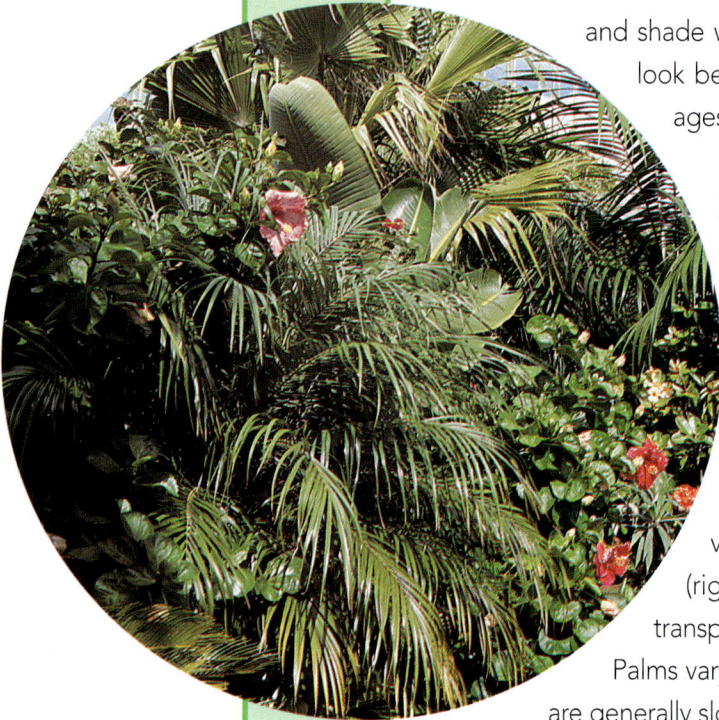

Archontophoenix cunninghamiana (syn. *Seaforthia elegans*)
BUNGALOW PALM

A very easy, very fast-growing Australian palm for warm northern regions, it has long arching feathery fronds and a slender straight trunk from which the old leaves shed cleanly. It will generally reach around 8 m in New Zealand conditions, growing in quite poor light soil but will not tolerate frost and needs shelter from wind. It is commonly grown as an indoor palm.

Cycas revoluta
SAGO PALM

The most well known of the cycads, the jewels of the subtropical garden. Cycads are very special and very valuable, but not at all difficult to grow — after all, they have survived since the days of the dinosaurs. They are among the most primitive plants in existence and very slow growing, becoming increasingly handsome as they grow. Cycads are fern-like in youth and palm-like in maturity, but botanically in a class all of their own. The leaves uncurl from a central cone into perfect rosettes. Sago palms are usually grown in containers, perhaps on account of their value, but also because they are so well suited. Plant in a well-drained soil or potting mix and provide filtered light. Avoid overwatering. They are not worth the risk as outdoor plants where frosts are likely.

Phoenix roebelinii
PYGMY OR MINIATURE DATE PALM

A delightful small palm of considerable grace, pygmy date palm is slow growing, reaching about 1 m x 1 m in 10 years and maturing at about 2 m tall. A perfect small palm for restricted spaces or small gardens, it is well used in containers indoors and out. It forms a slender, rough-textured single trunk with a dense rounded crown of curved fronds, up to 1.2 m long and wide. Pigmy date palms make very elegant poolside palms. For formal pool surrounds try them in pairs or rows. Bright indirect light is best as hot midday sun can cause the foliage to turn yellow. Plant in a frost-free location in free-draining fertile soil with ample moisture over the growing season. Be careful not to overwater in winter.

Rhopalostylis baueri var. *Cheesemanii*
KERMADEC NIKAU PALM

Closely related to the New Zealand native *nikau R. sapida* (the most southern growing of the palm family), but faster growing, Kermadec nikau is a very attractive palm. Upright glossy green leaves fan out from a prominent bulge at the top of straight slender stems, so the palm looks like a giant feather duster. It will cope with strong winds and coastal conditions. Beautiful grown in clumps of three or more. Young plants require shelter and good light, but protection from hot all-day sun. Only very mild frosts are tolerated.

Syagrus romanzoffianum
QUEEN PALM

One of the best, notable for its quick growth (to about 18 m) and ability to retain its good looks in wind, although strong winds will lead to breakages. A native to Brazil, it has bright, glossy green, long arching fronds that move gracefully in the slightest breeze. The very straight, slender trunk reaches about 10 m in New Zealand conditions. Bright light, good humidity and a warm frost-free position are needed for good growth. Lovely planted in informal groups.

Trachycarpus fortunei
WINDMILL PALM OR FAN LEAF PALM

A native of China, this is one of the toughest palms, withstanding climatic extremes, even light snowfalls, and coastal exposure. In average conditions it will grow about 4 m tall in 10 years, eventually reaching up to 10 m. Growth is moderate to fast, speeding up significantly once the trunk has formed. Best grown as a single specimen, windmill palm has a thick trunk and large fan-shaped leaves up to 1 m across. They are deep glossy green, carried on sharply toothed 45 cm stalks, giving the appearance of a windmill. Small fragrant yellow flowers produced amongst the foliage are followed by small bluish berries. This palm is reasonably wind tolerant but prefers shelter from harsh winds, which will damage the leaves.

Washingtonia robusta
CALIFORNIA FAN PALM OR COTTON PALM

This very fast-growing palm is native to Northern Mexico and is one of the most widely planted palms in California. It is extremely easy to grow. Tall and slender, it has fan-shaped leaves on long stalks over a reasonably compact crown. The leaves bend down as they mature to form a petticoat around the trunk, but they can be removed if need be. *W. robusta* is tolerant of extreme heat, some drought, and poor soil but thrives best in well-drained average garden soil, with ample moisture over the growing season. It is reasonably cold hardy but intolerant of frosts.

Sago palm in a pot.

Hibiscus

As easy-care shrubs for long summer and autumn colour, hibiscus are among the best. They are staple-diet shrubs in a subtropical-style garden. There are three main evergreen types to choose from:

Fijian hibiscus are the most cold hardy, tolerant of light frost. The flowers are smaller but more numerous, and usually double and frilly petalled.

Hawaiian hibiscus have huge flowers that are usually single, arguably the most exotic and beautiful of them all but very frost tender. They are generally smaller growing than the Fijians and ideal for pots.

Jack Clark hybrids are a New Zealand-bred cross between Fijian and Hawaiian hibiscus. The best of them exhibit the most desirable qualities of each.

To grow hibiscus choose a warm, suitably frost-free position. They detest wet feet and cold winter winds. Plant into well-drained soil or containers, and mulch, feed and water generously. Citrus fertiliser is ideal for hibiscus, which should be fertilised in early spring as new growth emerges.

Prune in early spring as new shoots appear, never in autumn, as this encourages new growth which will be damaged over winter. Prune to maintain an open structure by removing old wood. Hibiscus flower on new growth. Avoid pruning too severely or too late, as this will delay and reduce flowering.

TOP 10 HIBISCUS

'Agnes Gault'	Fijian	bright rose pink, single flowers, the largest Fijian	2.5 x 1.5 m
'Ben James'	Jack Clark	tomato red, single, medium flowers	1.5 x 1 m
'D. J. O'Brien'	Fijian	orange with red throat, large double flowers	1.5 x 1.5 m
'Gold Sovereign'	Fijian	deep yellow, double flowers, free flowering	1.5 x 1.5 m
'Golden Belle'	Hawaiian	giant, bright yellow, single flowers	1 x 1 m
'Molly Cummings'	Hawaiian	giant, deepest velvet red, single flowers	1 x 1 m
'Nathan Charles'	Hawaiian	Enormous crinkled crimson, single flowers	1 x 1 m
'Pride of Lockley'	Fijian	vigorous rosy red, double flowers, free flowering	1.5 x 1.5 m
H. rosa-sinensis	species	large red, single flowers, free flowering and the hardiest	2.5 x 2 m
'Suva Queen'	Fijian	bright cerise pink, fully double flowers, very free flowering	2.5 x 2 m

Tropical Rhododendrons

You could be forgiven for not recognising them as rhododendrons, because tropical (or 'vireya') rhododendrons are quite different from the spring-flowering rhododendrons we know so well. Different, but just as alluring.

The large clusters of waxy bell flowers are in rich apricots, reds and yellows; pastel pinks, creams and apricots; and pure white. Some are fragrant. Flowers appear at any time of year, but most commonly in late summer and autumn. The plants fit neatly into confined spaces, growing to an average of about 1 m tall by 1 m wide.

Cool-climate gardeners will have to console themselves in the knowledge that the traditional rhododendrons grow so well for them, because it is only in a warm frost-free garden that vireya rhododendrons will thrive. They will nevertheless stand up to light infrequent frosts and are so well suited to growing in containers that they can be brought into a greenhouse in cold weather.

'Java Light'.

The reason vireya rhododendrons do so well in containers is that they are epiphytes in the wild, growing in tree crevices with little root space, but plenty of air around their feet. They enjoy cramped root conditions. If grown in the garden it is imperative that they receive excellent drainage. This means raised beds if you have heavy clay soil. Add compost or peat moss to improve the soil prior to planting. Mulch to keep the roots cool and moist. Water regularly in the warm months, but avoid overdoing it. Feed with a balanced slow-release or liquid fertiliser, a light dose every month or so. Plenty of light means plenty or flowers, but some protection form the hottest afternoon sum is appreciated. The dappled shade of an overhead deciduous tree or climber can make all the difference.

Tropical rhododendrons should play a big part in the planting scheme of a subtropical garden. They look fabulous mass planted and work well in mixed plantings with other shrubs and perennials. The glossy vireya foliage is attractive, but the growth habit can be rather open, so planting alongside leafy plants such as ferns works well, further enhancing the gorgeous vireya flowers.

TOP 12 TROPICAL RHODODENDRONS

'Cameo Spice'	creamy apricot	'Flamenco Dancer'	yellow orange
'Golden Charm'	yellow, edged orange	'Hugh Redgrove'	bright red
'Java Light'	bright orange	'Pink Delight'	rich satiny pink
'Rob's Favourite'	salmon pink	'Tropic Glow'	golden yellow, shaded orange
'Kisses'	pink with lemon	'Gilded Sunrise'	bright yellow
'Princess Alexandra'	palest pink, fragrant	R. loranthiflorum	white and highly fragrant

More about soils:
Go to page 3.

Plants for Problem Soils

S uccessful gardening depends on selecting plants that do well in the given soil type and climatic conditions. Some places are more challenging than others.

The following plant lists are by no means exhaustive. Much trial and error is involved in sorting out the intricacies of each individual site.

Day lily *Hemerocallis*.

PLANTS THAT TOLERATE CLAY SOILS

Clay soils are baked hard and dry in summer, turning cold and wet in winter. The more clay your soil contains, the more pronounced these problems will be. As well as planting tolerant species, improve clay soils over time with repeated applications of organic matter, as a mulch or mixed into the soil at planting times.

ANNUALS

Botanical name	Common name	Position	Go to page
Calendula officinalis	Calendula	sun	128
Centaurea cyanus	Cornflower	sun	128
Cleome spinosa	Cleome	sun	128
Eschscholzia californica	Californian poppy	sun	128
Petunia xhybrida	Petunia	sun	130
Tagetes hybrids	Marigold	sun	130

PERENNIALS

Botanical name	Common name	Position	Go to page
Acanthus mollis	Bear's breeches	sun, shade	107
Achillea spp. & cultivars	Yarrow	sun	107
Agapanthus spp. & cultivars	African lily	sun, part shade	103
Anemone xhybrida	Japanese anemone	semi-shade	108
Arctotis acaulis (syn. A. scapigera)		sun	103
Aster novi-belgii cultivars	Michaelmas daisy	sun	108
Bergenia cordifolia cultivars	Elephant's ears	sun, shade	103
Canna spp.		sun	109
Hemerocallis cultivars	Day lily	sun	110
Leucanthemum xsuperbum	Shasta daisy	sun	105
Sedum spectabile cultivars	Stonecrop	sun, part shade	111

SMALL SHRUBS AND GROUNDCOVERS

Botanical name	Common name	Position	Go to page
Berberis thunbergii 'Atropurpurea'	Purple barberry	sun	30
Callistemon 'Little John'	Dwarf bottlebrush	sun	30
Carex spp.	NZ sedge	sun, shade	141
Coprosma spp.	Coprosma	sun, shade	32
Hebe speciosa	Koromiko	sun	34

Juniperus horizontalis	Creeping juniper	sun, shade	58
Rosa 'Flower Carpet'	Flower carpet rose	sun	92
Ruscus aculeatus	Butcher's broom	shade	35
Spiraea japonica cultivars	Spiraea	sun	35

MEDIUM SHRUBS

Botanical name	Common name	Position	Go to page
Griselinia littoralis	Puka	sun, shade	37
Lavandula dentata	French lavender	sun	42
Myrtus communis	Common myrtle	sun, shade	33
Olearia cheesemanii	NZ river daisy	sun	38
Osmanthus heterophyllus	Holly leaf osmanthus	part shade	34
Phormium hybrids	Flax	sun, shade	34
Pyracantha cultivars	Firethorn	sun	38
Rosa rugosa cultivars	Rugosa roses	sun	

TREES AND TALL SHRUBS

Botanical name	Common name	Position	Go to page
Agathis australis	Kauri	part shade	22
Callistemon citrinus 'Splendens'	Bottlebrush	sun	36
Casuarina glauca	Swamp sheoke	sun, shade	24
Cordyline 'Green Goddess'	Cabbage tree	sun, shade	139
Corokia cotoneaster	Wire netting bush	sun, shade	37
Cupressocyparis leylandii	Leyland cypress	sun	24
Euonymus japonicus 'Aureo-marginatus'	Japanese laurel	sun	37
Juniperus chinensis 'Kaizuka'	Hollywood juniper	sun, shade	37
Laurus nobilis	Bay tree	sun, part shade	17
Liquidambar styraciflua	American sweet gum	sun	22
Magnolia grandiflora	Laurel magnolia	sun	19
Myrsine australis	Matipou	sun, shade	17
Olearia albida	Tanguru	sun	24
Philadelphus coronarius	Sweet mock orange	sun	38
Prunus lusitanica	Portugese laurel	sun	19
Pseudopanax laetus	Five finger	sun, shade	38
Tecomaria capensis	Tecoma, Cape honeysuckle	sun	40

PLANTS THAT TOLERATE SANDY SOILS

Sandy soils are free draining to excess and lacking in nutrients, with little capacity to hold on to added fertilisers for long. They can be improved over time with the addition of compost, and with diligent persistence on the part of the gardener. While you work on improving the soil, your garden will need plants that tolerate such impoverished, dry conditions. Many prefer it. A dry sandy soil is the envy of the succulent or cacti enthusiast.

ANNUALS

Botanical name	Common name	Position	Go to page
Centaurea cyanus	Cornflower	sun	128
Cleome spinosa	Cleome	sun	128
Cosmos bipinnatus	Cosmos	sun	128
Digitalis purpurea	Foxglove	sun, semi-shade	129
Dorotheanthus bellidiformis	Livingstone daisy		129
Limonium sinuatum	Statice	sun	130
Lobularia maritima	Alyssum	sun, semi-shade	128

More about improving soils: Go to page 190.

Lychnis viscaria	Viscaria	sun	131
Petunia xhybrida	Petunia	sun	130
Scabiosa atropurpurea	Scabiosa	sun	130
Tagetes hybrids	Marigold	sun	130
Tropaeolum majus	Nasturtium	sun	130

SUCCULENTS

Botanical name	Common name	Position	Go to page
Agave spp.		sun	139
Aloe spp.		sun	139
Aeonium arboreum 'Schwarzkopf'		sun	140
Crassula argentea	Jade plant	sun	140
Echeveria elegans	Hen and chicks	sun	140
Kalanchoe hybrids		sun	140
Sedum spp.	Stonecrop	sun	140
Sempervivum spp.	Houseleek	sun	140

PERENNIALS

Botanical name	Common name	Position	Go to page
Achillea	Yarrow	sun	107
Agapanthus spp. & cultivars	African lily	sun, semi-shade	103
Ageratum houstonianum	Floss flower	sun	108
Alchemilla mollis	Lady's mantle	semi-shade	103
Anthemis punctata subsp. *cupaniana*		sun	103
Arctotis acaulis (syn. *A. scapigera*)		sun	103
Argyranthemum frutescens	Marguerite daisy	sun	103
Cerastium tomentosum	Snow-in-summer	sun, semi-shade	104
Dianthus	Border pink	sun	104
Echinacea purpurea	Cone flower	sun	109
Echium candicans (syn. *E. fastuosum*)	Pride of Madeira	sun	109
Euphorbia spp.	Spurge	sun	109
Gaura lindheimeri		sun	110
Gazania	African daisy	sun	104

Helichrysum argyrophyllum	Everlasting daisy	sun	105
Iberis sempervirens	Candytuft	sun	105
Kniphofia	Red hot poker	sun	110
Lavatera thuringiaca 'Barnsley'	Mallow	sun	110
Liriope muscari	Turf lily	shade	106
Nepeta xfaassenii	Catmint	sun	106
Osteospermum cultivars	African daisy	sun	106
Pelargonium xdomesticum cultivars	Regal pelargonium	sun	106
Pelargonium xhortorum cultivars	Geranium	sun	106
Phlox subulata		sun, semi-shade	106

Scabiosa cultivars	Pincushion flower	sun	130
Stachys byzantina	Lamb's ears	sun, semi-shade	107
Verbena	Verbena	sun	107

SMALL SHRUBS AND GROUNDCOVERS

Botanical name	Common name	Position	Go to page
Adenandra uniflora	China flower	sun	30
Anigozanthos	Kangaroo paw	sun	30
Brachyglottis greyii (syn. *Senecio greyii*)		sun	30
Callistemon 'Little John'	Dwarf bottlebrush	sun	30
Carex spp.	NZ sedge	sun, shade	141
Ceanothus cultivars	Californian lilac	sun	30
Cistus cultivars	Rock rose	sun	31
Cistus salviifolius	Sage leaf rock rose	sun	58
Convolvulus cneorum		sun	32
Coprosma spp. & cultivars	Coprosma	sun, shade	32
Erica cultivars	Heath	sun	33
Eriostemon myoporoides	Wax flower	semi-shade	32
Grevillea spp. & cultivars		sun, shade	58
Juniperus horizontalis	Creeping juniper	sun, shade	58
Lavandula spp. & cultivars	Lavender	sun	41
Lithodora diffusa		sun	59
Lonicera nitida	Box honeysuckle	sun, semi-shade	28
Nandina domestica	Dwarf heavenly bamboo	sun, shade	34
Rosmarinus officinalis 'Prostratus'	Creeping rosemary	sun	59
Santolina chamaecyparissus	Lavender cotton	sun	35
Thryptomene saxicola	Rock heath myrtle	sun	35

MEDIUM SHRUBS

Botanical name	Common name	Position	Go to page
Astelia chathamica		sun, semi-shade	139
Ceanothus papillosus	Californian lilac	sun	36
Coprosma spp. & cultivars	Coprosma	sun, shade	32
Leonotis leonurus	Lion's tail	sun	38
Leucodendron salicifolium	Leucodendron	sun	38
Leucospermum cordifolium	Leucospermum	sun	38
Protea spp. & cultivars	Protea	sun	38
Rosemarinus officinalis	Common rosemary	sun, hot	167
Teucrium fruticans	Silver germander	sun, hot	40
Xeronema callistemon	Poor Knights lily	sun, warm	139
Yucca filamentosa	Adam's needle	sun	139

TREES AND TALL SHRUBS

Botanical name	Common name	Position	Go to page
Banksia ericifolia	Heath banksia	sun	36
Banksia integrifolia	Coast banksia	sun	24
Cassia corymbosa 'John Ball'	Buttercup tree	sun	36
Corokia cotoneaster	Wire netting bush	sun, shade	37
Cytisus multiflorus 'Albus' (syn. *C. Albus*)	White Spanish broom	sun	37
Eucalyptus ficifolia	Red flowering gum	sun	22
Euonymus japonicus	Japanese laurel	sun, shade	37
Grevillea spp. & cultivars	Grevillea	sun	37
Lagunaria patersonii	Norfolk Island hibiscus	sun	24
Melia azederach	Melia	sun	20
Meryta sinclairii	Puka	sun, part shade	19
Metrosideros excelsa	Pohutukawa	sun	19
Philadelphus coronarius	Sweet mock orange	sun	38
Pittosporum crassifolium	Karo	sun	24

Plants for Shade

Clivia miniata 'Firelight'.

Few plants grow well in dense shade, but there are many that tolerate or prefer a degree of shade. Many flowering plants will grow in shade but flower better given some sun. Cool-climate plants often do better in a warm climate if given some shade. Those that have evolved as shade lovers will often have large or shiny leaves designed to catch the light. Be aware that shade often also means dry soil, sheltered from natural rainfall, often with tree roots absorbing any spare moisture there is. Plants that are not thriving in the shade may simply be water stressed. Long, straggly, 'stretched' growth is a sign that plants are straining towards the light and need more sun.

ANNUALS

Botanical name	Common name	Position	Go to page
Digitalis purpurea	Foxglove	sun, semi-shade	129
Impatiens walleriana	Busy Lizzie	semi-shade	128
Lobularia maritima	Alyssum	sun, semi-shade	128
Lunaria annua	Honesty	shade	129
Myosotis sylvatica	Forget-me-not	sun, shade	129
Pericallis xhybrida	Cineraria	shade	128
Primula malacioides	Fairy primrose	sun, semi-shade	128
Viola cornuta	Viola	sun, semi-shade	131
Viola xwittrockiana	Pansy	sun, semi-shade	130

PERENNIALS

Botanical name	Common name	Position	Go to page
Acanthus mollis	Bear's breeches	sun, shade	107
Agapanthus spp. & cultivars	African lily	sun, semi-shade	103
Ajuga 'Jungle Beauty'	Carpet bugle	sun, shade	57
Alchemilla mollis	Lady's mantle	semi-shade	103
Anemone xhybrida	Japanese anemone	semi-shade	108
Arthropodium cirratum	Rengarenga lily	shade	103
Astilbe hybrids	False spiraea	semi-shade	108
Bergenia cordifolia cultivars	Elephant's ears	sun, shade	103
Campanula portenschlagiana	Bellflower	sun, shade	104
Cerastium tomentosum	Snow-in-summer	sun, semi-shade	104
Clivia miniata	Clivia	shade	109
Corydalis flexuosa 'Blue Panda'		semi-shade	104
Diascia spp. & cultivars		sun, semi-shade	104, 109
Euphorbia amygdaloides var. robbiae	Spurge	sun, shade	104
Geranium 'Johnson's Blue'	Crane's bill	sun, semi-shade	104
Heliotropium arborescens	Cherry pie	sun, semi-shade	110
Helleborus cultivars	Winter rose	semi-shade	105
Heuchera spp. & cultivars	Heuchera	sun, semi-shade	105
Hosta cultivars	Plaintain lily	shade	105
Lamium maculatum cultivars	Dead nettle	semi-shade	57
Liriope muscari	Turf lily	shade	106
Myosotidium hortensia	Chatham Is. forget-me-not	shade	106
Pachysandra terminalis	Japanese spurge	sun, shade	57

Botanical name	Common name	Position	Go to page
Pelargonium tomentosum	Peppermint geranium	shade, semi-shade	106
Primula prolifera	Candelabra primula	semi-shade	111
Salvia uliginosa	Bog sage	sun, semi-shade	111
Saxifraga umbrosa	London pride	semi-shade, shade	57
Sedum spectabile cultivars	Stonecrop	sun, semi-shade	140
Sisyrinchium striatum	Satin flower	sun, semi-shade	111
Tradescantia virginiana	Spiderwort	semi-shade	107
Viola hederacea	Tasmanian violet	shade	57
Viola odorata cultivars	Scented violet	semi-shade	57
Zantedeschia aethiopica	Arum lily	shade	111

SMALL SHRUBS

Botanical name	Common name	Position	Go to page
Aucuba japonica	Japanese laurel	semi-shade	30
Azalea hybrids	Azalea	semi-shade, cool	30
Buxus sempervirens	English box	sun, shade	31
Carex spp.	NZ sedge	sun, shade	141
Daphne odora cultivars	Daphne	sun, part shade	32
Eriostemon myoporoides	Wax flower	semi-shade	32
Myrtus communis	Variegated myrtle	sun, shade	33
Nandina domestica	Dwarf heavenly bamboo	sun, shade	34
Ruscus aculeatus	Butcher's broom	shade, cool	35
Sarcococca ruscifolia	Christmas box	shade	35

MEDIUM SHRUBS

Botanical name	Common name	Position	Go to page
Abutilon darwinii hybrids	Chinese lantern	semi-shade	36
Acer palmatum Dissectum hybrids	Weeping maple	sun, shade	30
Astelia chathamica		sun, shade	139
Camellia spp. & cultivars	Camellia	semi-shade	36
Choisya ternata	Mexican orange blossom	sun, semi-shade	31
Escallonia cultivars	Escallonia	sun or semi-shade	37
Mahonia lomariifolia	Chinese holly grape	sun, shade	38
Myrtus communis	Common myrtle	sun, shade	33
Osmanthus heterophyllus	Holly leaf osmanthus	semi-shade	34
Phormium hybrids	Flax	sun, shade	34
Pieris cultivars	Lily of the valley shrub	semi-shade	34
Rhododendron cultivars		semi-shade	35

TALL SHRUBS AND TREES

Botanical name	Common name	Position	Go to page
Brachyglottis repanda	Rangiora	sun, shade	36
Camellia cultivars	Camellia	sun, semi-shade	36
Cestrum nocturnum	Queen of the night	sun, semi-shade	36
Chimonanthus praecox	Wintersweet	semi-shade	36
Cordyline spp. & cultivars	Cabbage tree	sun, shade	139
Corokia cotoneaster	Wire netting bush	sun, shade	37
Euonymus japonicus	Japanese laurel	sun, shade	37
Ilex aquifolium	Holly	sun, shade	37
Juniperus chinensis 'Kaizuka'	Hollywood juniper	sun, shade	37
Laurus nobilis	Bay tree	sun, semi-shade	37
Meryta sinclairii	Puka	sun, shade	19
Pseudopanax laetus	Five finger	sun, shade	38
Rhododendron cultivars	Rhododendron	semi-shade	48
Stachyurus praecox	Early spiketail	sun, semi-shade	18
Viburnum opulus 'Roseum'	Sterile snowball tree	sun, semi-shade	18
Viburnum trilobum	Cranberry viburnum	sun, semi-shade	40

The Coastal Garden

Seaside gardens have to put up with strong, often salt-laden winds. Many must also contend with sandy soils that are so well drained they are poor at holding on to water and nutrients. Fortunately, some plants enjoy such impoverished conditions. Others, although preferring less-challenging situations, will tolerate life in the coastal garden very well. Some of the best are listed here. There will be many more to be discovered as you get to know your site.

ANNUALS

Botanical name	Common name	Go to page
Calendula officinalis	Calendula	128
Centaurea cyanus	Cornflower	128
Eschscholzia californica	Californian poppy	128
Lychnis viscaria	Viscaria	131
Petunia xhybrida	Petunia	130
Tagetes hybrids	Marigold	130

PERENNIALS

Botanical name	Common name	Go to page
Achillea cultivars	Yarrow	107
Agapanthus cultivars	African lily	103
Anthemis spp.		103
Argyranthemum cultivars	Marguerite daisy	103
Arthropodium cirratum	Rengarenga	103
Brachyscome multifida	Swan river daisy	103
Convolvulus sabatius (syn. C. mauritanicus)	Bindweed	104
Coreopsis verticillata	Tickseed	109
Dianthus cultivars	Border pink	104
Echium candicans (syn. E. fastuosum)	Pride of Madeira	109
Erigeron speciosus cultivars	Fleabane	104
Felicia amelloides	Blue marguerite	104
Helianthemum cultivars	Sun rose	105
Helichrysum argyrophyllum	Everlasting daisy	105
Helipterum anthemoides	Paper daisy	105
Iberis sempervirens	Candytuft	105
Kniphofia cultivars	Red hot poker	110
Lavatera 'Barnsley'	Mallow	110
Lupinus Russell hybrids	Russell lupin	110
Lychnis coronaria	Rose campion	110
Nepeta xfaassenii	Catmint	106
Osteospermum cultivars	African daisy	106
Pelargonium spp. & hybrids	Geraniums & pelargoniums	106
Phlox subulata cultivars	Phlox	106
Salvia leucantha	Mexican sage	111
Santolina chamaecyparissus	Lavender cotton	35
Scabiosa cultivars	Pincushion flower	106
Verbena cultivars	Verbena	107

CACTI AND SUCCULENTS

Botanical name	Common name	Go to page
Agave spp.		139
Aloe spp.		139
Aeonium arboreum 'Schwarzkopf'		140
Crassula argentea	Jade plant	140
Echeveria elegans	Hen and chicken	140
Kalanchoe hybrids	Kalanchoe	140
Sedum spp.	Stonecrop	140
Sempervivum spp.	Houseleek	140

SMALL SHRUBS

Botanical name	Common name	Go to page
Brachyglottis greyii		140
Callistemon 'Little John'	Dwarf bottlebrush	30
Cistus cultivars	Rock rose	31
Convolvulus cneorum		32
Coprosma cultivars		32
Hebe spp. & cultivars (some)	Hebe	34
Metrosideros 'Tahiti'		33

MEDIUM SHRUBS

Botanical name	Common Name	Go to page
Coprosma cultivars	Coprosma	32
Escallonia cultivars	Escallonia	37
Lavandula dentata	French lavender	42
Leucodendron salicifolium	Leucodendron	38
Olearia cheesemanii		38
Phormium cookianum	NZ Flax	34
Protea cynaroides	King protea	38
Rhaphiolepis umbellata	Indian hawthorn	35

TREES AND TALL SHRUBS

Botanical name	Common name	Go to page
Banksia ericifolia	Heath banksia	36
Banksia integrifolia	Coast banksia	24
Brachyglottis repanda	Rangiora	36
Callistemon citrinus	Bottlebrush	36
Cordyline	Cabbage tree	139
Corokia cotoneaster	Wire netting bush	37
Feijoa sellowiana	Feijoa	37
Knightia excelsa	Rewarewa	22
Lagunaria patersonii	Norfolk Island hibiscus	24
Laurus nobilis	Bay tree	17
Magnolia grandiflora	Laurel magnolia	19
Melia azederach	Indian bead tree	20
Metrosideros excelsa	Pohutukawa	19
Olea europaea	Olive tree	19
Olearia albida	Tanguru	24
Pittosporum crassifolium	Karo	24
Pseudopanax spp.	Five finger	38
Rhopalostylis baueri var. cheesemanii	Kermadec nikau palm	69
Viburnum tinus	Laurustinus	40

The Scented Garden

Heliotropium,
cherry pie.

The delight of a garden is not only in what you see. It is also the sounds (birds, water, wind chimes) and the scents. No garden should be without fragrance. Some plants have scented flowers, some have scented foliage, some have both. Sometimes scented foliage has to be touched or trodden on to really release its scent. Flowers often need the warm sun to really bring out their perfume.

Some of the most delicious fragrances are in winter and early spring: daphne, jasmine, spring bulbs, stock . . . but in summer there is no shortage either, especially if you have roses in your garden.

Most roses require a sunny position. Those that tolerate some shade will produce more flowers and more fragrance in full sun.

ANNUALS

Botanical name	Common name	Position	Go to page
Lobularia maritima	Alyssum	sun, semi-shade	128
Matthiola incana	Stock	sun	131
Lathyrus odoratus	Sweet pea	sun	131
Phlox divaricata	Sweet William	sun	131

PERENNIALS

Botanical name	Common name	Position	Go to page
Dianthus cultivars	Border pink	sun	104
Heliotropium arborescens	Cherry pie	sun, part shade	110
Pelargonium citrosum	Scented pelargonium	sun	110
Pelargonium tomentosum	Peppermint geranium	shade, semi-shade	106
Viola odorata cultivars	Scented violet	semi-shade	57

BULBS

Botanical name	Common name	Position	Go to page
Allium moly	Golden garlic	sun, part shade	120
Freesia hybrids	Freesia	sun	121
Gladiolus tristis	Gladiolus	sun, part shade	121
Hyacinthus hybrids	Hyacinth	sun	121
Muscari cultivars	Grape hyacinth	sun, part shade	123
Narcissus hybrids (some)	Daffodils, jonquils	sun, part shade	123
Lilium	Lilies	sun	125

SMALL SHRUBS

Botanical name	Common name	Position	Go to page
Boronia heterophylla	Red boronia	sun	31
Boronia megastigma 'Heaven Scent'	Brown boronia	sun	31
Boronia megastigma 'Lutea'	Yellow boronia	sun	31
Boronia 'Sunset Serenade'		sun	31
Daphne odora cultivars	Upright daphne	sun, semi-shade	32
Lavandula spp.	Lavender	sun	41

Medium shrubs

Botanical name	Common name	Position	Go to page
Camellia spp.	Camellia	semi-shade	44
Magnolia stellata	Star magnolia	sun	38
Myrtus communis	Common myrtle	sun, shade	33
Osmanthus heterophyllus	Holly leaf osmanthus	semi-shade	34
Rhododendron cultivars (some)	Rhododendron	semi-shade	39
Rosmarinus officinalis	Common rosemary	sun, hot	35

Trees and tall shrubs

Botanical name	Common name	Position	Go to page
Buddleia davidii	Butterfly bush	sun	36
Cestrum nocturnum	Queen of the night	sun, semi-shade, warm	36
Chimonanthus praecox	Wintersweet	semi-shade	36
Citrus cultivars	Citrus	sun	17
Hymenosporum flavum	Australian frangipani	sun	19
Luculia gratissima	Pink luculia	sun	38
Magnolia grandiflora	Laurel magnolia	sun	19
Michelia doltsopa		sun	19
Michelia figo	Port wine magnolia	sun, semi-shade	17
Philadelphus coronarius	Sweet mock orange	sun	38
Syringa vulgaris	Lilac	sun	40

Climbers

Botanical name	Common name	Position	Go to page
Gelsemium sempervirens	Carolina jessamine	sun, part shade	52
Jasminum azoricum	Azores jasmine	sun, shade	52
Jasminum polyanthum	Chinese jasmine	sun, shade	52
Mandevilla suaveolens	Chilean jasmine	sun	53
Pandorea pandorana	Wonga wonga vine	sun	52
Stephanotis floribunda	Madagascar jasmine	sun	53
Trachelospermum jasminoides	Star jasmine	sun, part shade	53
Wisteria spp. & cultivars	Wisteria	sun	54

Roses

Botanical name	Type	Colour	Go to page
'Abraham Darby'	David Austin	apricot	97
'Albéric Barbier'	climber	cream	97
'Albertine'	climber	apricot-pink	97
'Ambridge Rose'	hybrid musk	apricot	97
'Aotearoa'	hybrid tea	pink	97
'Auckland Metro'	hybrid tea	white	97
R. banksia 'The Pearl'	climber	white	97
'Big Purple'	hybrid tea	purple	97
'Buff Beauty'	hybrid musk	yellow	97
'Carolyn'	hybrid tea	pink	97
'Cécile Brünner'	climber	pink	97
'Charles Austin'	David Austin	orange	97
'City of Auckland'	hybrid tea	orange	97
'City of London'	climber	pink	97
'Compassion'	climber	apricot	97
'Cornelia'	hybrid musk	apricot	98
'Deep Secret'	hybrid tea	red	98
'Dublin Bay'	climber	red	98
'Elina'	hybrid tea	yellow	98
'English Garden'	David Austin	yellow	98
'Fair Bianca'	David Austin	white	98
'Felicia'	hybrid musk	apricot	98
'Flower Carpet White'	shrub	white	98
'Friesia'	floribunda	yellow	98
'Grus an Aachen'	old-fashioned	white	99

'Just Joey'	hybrid tea	orange	99
'Lantern'	hybrid tea	orange	99
'Lavender Lassie'	shrub	lavender-pink	99
'L. D. Braithwaite'	David Austin	red	99
'Margaret Merrill'	floribunda	white	99
'Mary Rose'	David Austin	pink	99
'Mme Alfred Carrière'	climber	white	99
'Moonlight'	hybrid musk	white	100
'New Dawn'	climber	pink	100
'Old Port'	floribunda	purple	100
'Penelope'	hybrid musk	apricot	100
'Proud Titania'	David Austin	white	100
'Spek's Centennial'	floribunda	orange	101
'Super Bowl'	hybrid tea	purple	101
'Wedding Day'	climber	white	101
'Westerland'	climber	orange	101
'White Sparrieshoop'	climber	white	101
'Yellow Button'	David Austin	yellow	101

David Austin rose,
'English Garden'.

Pansies.

Colour and accent

This section is all about filling in the detail. Once the permanent framework of trees and shrubs is in place it's time to have fun sorting out the smaller, less-permanent plants and also the plants that add a touch of drama.

While flowers are the icing on the cake when it comes to trees and shrubs, smaller garden plants are grown largely for their flowers. For some of them, foliage texture and colour is the most important feature.

Small flowering plants (bulbs, perennials and annuals) are often grown together in special garden beds, which constantly change through the seasons, as well as from year to year. Depending on what you plant, these herbaceous borders, as you will hear them called, represent varying degrees of maintenance, but on the whole are more labour intensive than trees and shrubs.

In specially devoted gardens of their own or as part of the herbaceous border, roses are among the most loved flowering plants of all. They are at their most spectacular each November, but continue on to produce blooms for colour, fragrance and picking right through until late autumn.

If your garden is in need of a bit of textural contrast, try adding some strappy-foliaged plants, or grasses. For strength and focus consider some of the succulents or 'accent plants' with spiky foliage and interesting symmetrical forms.

Rudbeckia,
see page 111.

More about annuals:
Go to page 127.

More about grasses:
Go to page 141.

More about perennials:
Go to page 102.

More about accent plants:
Go to page 138.

More about bulbs:
Go to page 112.

More about succulents and cacti:
Go to page 138.

More about roses:
Go to page 85.

Roses

Roses are undeniably beautiful, the most universally loved flowers of all. Not everybody, though, has roses at the top of their list when it comes to growing plants. For roses have a reputation for being difficult, prickly to touch and just plain prickly by nature, demanding too much fuss and bother. This chapter is about removing some of that fuss and bother. Rose growing is a lot more straightforward than you may think.

The first step is to plant only the best varieties. There is a daunting number of roses to choose from, with new ones released every year. All will produce at least one irresistibly exquisite bloom (the one photographed for the label!), but not all produce consistent volumes of beautiful blooms, and not all are lush healthy plants that cope well with the onslaught of pests and diseases in a warm and humid climate. Some roses struggle to thrive, no matter how much you pamper them. These are the varieties that give roses a bad name. There must be many unsuspecting new gardeners who, based on a pretty picture and a bargain price, innocently purchase their first selection of roses. They blame themselves when the plants never reach expectations and give up on roses altogether. These same ill-fated varieties would be the underdogs in even the most experienced gardener's collection.

So select carefully. Visit the local botanic gardens to view the roses in spring and again in autumn. Look out for those that win awards and make a note of the ones recommended by other gardeners in your district. The roses listed on pages 93–6 are current leaders in their field, surpassing others in flower production, foliage, growth habit and disease resistance. Most are fragrant. Those that are not are simply too good in every other way to leave out.

'Penelope'.

Once you have your varieties sorted out, the next step to rose heaven is to have the right place in which to plant them. Half-day sun will give satisfactory results, but the best position will receive a full-day's sun. You don't want your roses in a howling gale so that all you ever get to see are scatterings of rose petals, but an overly sheltered position encourages the loitering of pests and diseases. So an open sunny spot is best.

As to soil, roses do best in a soil that holds on to its water. A soil that contains a lot of clay, as long as it is not poorly drained, will suit them well. Light sandy soils or very heavy soils can be improved with the addition of compost.

The traditional way to grow roses is in a bed of their own. The advantage here, if you have a lot of roses, is that the jobs of watering, feeding, pruning, and spraying are less time-consuming when the roses are all in one place.

More and more, however, roses are being grown in combination with other plants, especially annuals, herbs, perennials and small shrubs such as lavenders. The

About soils:
Go to page 3.

Compost:
Go to page 196.

larger shrub roses are worked in amongst evergreen shrubs. Even formal rose beds are given an evergreen border, English box being the most popular example. This companion planting takes away the starkness of the bare roses in winter. It also means more competition for the roses, so you'll need to water and feed more often. Also, the higher humidity created by lots of underplanting will compound the need to spray for pests and diseases.

To strike a balance between the easy management of a separate rose bed and the year-round appeal of the mixed planting approach, devote an area to roses and plant the edges. A hedge of English box gives a more formal look. Alternatively, you could plant leafy evergreen perennials, a single variety or a combination. (For easy perennials see pages 103–11.) Either mulch under the roses permanently (easiest for weed control) or add winter colour with flowering annuals (e.g., primula, polyanthus) or bulbs (e.g., cyclamen, daffodils, ranunculus, anemone) to be removed in the spring and replaced with a mulch for the summer.

PLANTING

Roses sold in the winter have been grown in the open ground and dug up in time to be bagged for sale, traditionally as 'bare-root' plants (with a protective cushion of potting mix or sawdust around their roots), but more often these days they are planted up in containers of potting mix. It makes little difference to the plants until they start to grow in the spring. At this point they need to be properly planted in containers or in the ground.

Bare-root plants should be planted as soon as possible after you buy them. The longer the delay, the greater the chance of the roots drying out. When planting in winter, remove the bag and other material surrounding the roots. Prune off any damaged root growth. If you think your plant may have dried out a little, soak it in a bucket of water while you prepare the planting hole.

Dig a hole 50 cm wide and deep enough to allow the bud union (see diagram) to sit just above soil level when the hole is filled in. Hold the plant in position with one hand while you fill in with soil to half way. Firm down gently. Fill to the top, firm down and water thoroughly.

The planting of containerised roses in spring is done in the same way as for any tree or shrub. It is important not to disturb the roots at this stage.

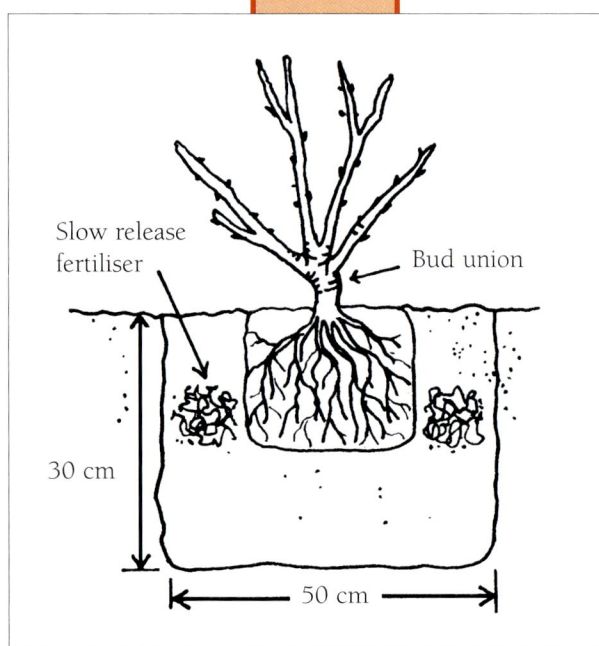

Slow release fertiliser

Bud union

30 cm

50 cm

Planting trees and shrubs: Go to page 194.

ROSE CARE — GROWING THE BEST ROSES

Selecting top-performing varieties and planting the best-quality plants you can find means half the battle is won. If you never do anything else your roses will most likely continue to grow and produce blooms, but by following a few simple procedures to care for them properly you will be rewarded with more flowers, better-quality flowers, and healthy lush growth.

To thrive a rose bush needs watering, feeding, pruning and in most cases, spraying. Mulching is highly recommended also.

WATERING ROSES

Roses need lots of water. Without sufficient water growth will be retarded and blooms will be inferior and fewer in number. A thirsty plant is also more vulnerable to attack from pests and diseases than a well-watered one.

The soil surface is the first to dry out, so plants whose roots are growing deeper in the soil will survive longer between waterings than those with shallow surface roots. The way to encourage shallow root growth is to just keep lightly wetting the surface. This is fine if you want to spend your summer on the end of a hose, but the best idea is to water as deeply as possible from the start and encourage your roses to grow deep roots. The easiest way to achieve this is to set up a trickle irrigation system for your roses, thus watering is made as simple as turning a tap. The alternative is to leave the hose trickling into the soil at the base of each rose plant for about fifteen minutes before moving it on to the next plant, an easy task while you are spending time in the garden doing other things. With deep watering you should only have to water once a week during dry periods.

'English Garden'.

The demand for water will vary with soil type and the amount of wind your roses are subjected to, but as long as your soil is well drained it is pretty difficult to over-water a rose. The more you water, the better they will be. Roses in pots will need a lot more watering — the smaller the pot and the bigger the rose bush, the more often you will need to water — up to twice a day in the summer. It is generally not a good idea to plant roses right up against buildings where they miss out on much of the rainfall. But if this is the best site you have for roses, take extra care with watering.

More about watering
Go to page 202.

The best time to water is in the coolest parts of the day, early morning or late evening, otherwise much of the water you put on will be lost to the clouds via evaporation. Also, warmth plus moisture equals humidity, just the conditions loved by diseases. The best way to water roses therefore is at ground level, not via a sprinkler.

FEEDING ROSES

All rose enthusiasts have their own magic recipe. It depends a lot on the soil type, so what works in the Waikato will not necessarily perform the same miracles in Auckland. Anyway, forget the science. The main thing is that your roses are fed.

The easiest way is to apply a special 'rose fertiliser' available from your local garden centre. Any reputable brand will do. Apply it once in early spring and again in summer for the autumn flower flush. Roses growing in poor soils will respond to an extra helping during the spring/summer season.

More about fertilisers:
Go to page 200.

In addition, it is worthwhile at planting time to add a slow-release fertiliser, such as MagAmp or Osmocote, to the planting hole. The nutrients released will be available as soon as the plants come into active growth and will tide them over in between applications of rose fertiliser.

Animal manures are very good if you have access to them. Apply as a mulch, mixed into the compost, or mix them into the soil at planting time, but avoid applying them until they are well rotted down.

PRUNING ROSES

Pruning roses is often made out to be more complex than it really needs to be. You don't require a horticulture degree to prune your roses successfully, although it's on the cards you will become intrigued to delve further once you start.

First of all, don't be timid. Unless you cut it off at ground level it is pretty difficult to kill a rose by pruning it. It is generally better to prune a rose badly than never prune it at all. Roses that are never pruned get old before their time. The bushes get tall and ungainly with blooms of ever-decreasing beauty at the ends of straggly branches. (This applies to modern bush roses, it is not so true of old-fashioned roses — see later). So, arm yourself with a good sharp pair of secateurs (important), and a pair of leather gloves and go to it.

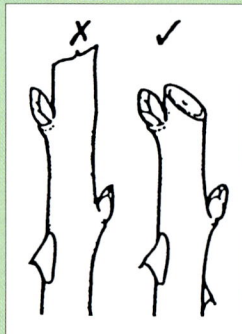

THE RIGHT CUT

Pruning cuts are always made on an angle *just above a bud*. The angle slopes away from the bud, to prevent water running into it. The cut should be around 5 mm above the bud. If you prune too far above the bud, the wood above the bud will die and turn black, risking infection of the whole stem. If you cut too close, you risk damaging the bud.

PRUNING CLIMBING ROSES

1. Remove any diseased wood. Cut back to a bud below the damaged area or cut the damaged cane right out.

2. Remove canes that cross over or are growing where you don't want them to.

3. Shorten the remaining canes by about one-third.

PRUNING OLD-FASHIONED ROSES

Old-fashioned roses need less pruning than modern roses. In general, pruning is only necessary to control size and shape and can be carried out in winter. Those old-fashioned roses that are once flowering (such as 'Albertine') should be pruned in summer, immediately after flowering.

The repeat-flowering climbers (such as 'New Dawn') should be pruned as for climbing roses above.

Removing spent flowerheads (by cutting back to a bud as you would when pruning) through summer and autumn encourages repeat flowering and means less pruning in winter.

More about prunimg:
Go to page 206.

The main rose pruning is done in July or August while rose bushes are dormant. The idea is to prune after the risk of frost damage to freshly pruned wood but before the new season's shoots emerge (i.e., the colder the climate the later you should prune).

The basic rules for winter pruning of modern bush roses are as follows:

1 **Remove any diseased wood.** Cut back to a bud below a damaged tip or cut the damaged cane (branch) right off.

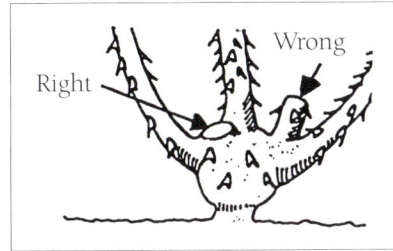

2 **Remove twiggy growth.** These are the skinniest canes, which are usually those smaller than a pencil in diameter but their actual width depends on the variety. (Some varieties have all of their canes thinner than a pencil.)

3 **Remove canes that cross closely over others or grow towards the middle of the bush.**

4 **Shorten the remaining canes back to an outward-facing bud.** The idea of the outward-facing bud is so that the next season's growth is outwards rather than towards the centre of the bush, thus avoiding a crowded mass of leaves and flowers.

How heavily roses should be pruned is a matter of much discussion. Anything from a half to two-thirds of their initial height is about right. In general, the heavier you prune, the better the size and quality of next season's blooms. An advantage of lighter pruning is a greater number of flowers, but pruning too lightly year after year will reduce the overall vigour of the bush. Some varieties are more vigorous-growing than others and should be pruned harder.

Old neglected rose bushes will not stand up to a sudden onslaught with the pruning shears. They must be rejuvenated slowly with a gentle prune the first year, gradually building up new wood. The best idea, especially with modern roses, is to replace them with new plants.

Aim for a vase shape with branches radiating (as evenly as possible) outwards from the central base.

SPRAYING ROSES

It is possible to grow roses without spraying. However, in all but the coldest climates it is difficult to grow really good roses without some assistance from the bottle. The risk of disease increases with the number of roses you grow and is greatest in warm humid climates. Recent developments hint that it won't be long before we have a good range of roses we can grow without spraying. The 'Flower Carpet' shrub roses are leading the way. These roses are highly disease resistant but still need spraying for insects.

For the time being, most rosaphiles accept the need to spray. There is no need to use lethal chemicals. Modern sprays developed for home-garden use are of a low toxicity to humans. But you should always take precautions and read the label.

The main time to spray is when the weather is warm, the plants are in active growth and the bugs are about. The worst problems are fungal diseases: mildews, black spot and rust. These can be prevented with a fortnightly spraying of fungicide starting when the flower buds appear and continuing through until the end of autumn. It is recommended that you alternate with two or three different sprays to discourage the build-up of resistance. Examples of fungicides you could use are copper, Fungus and Mildew Spray®, and Bravo®.

The easy 'one-spray-fits-all' approach for both pests and diseases is to use a combination spray, such as Gild® or Shield®, although it is better to alternate one of these with a different spray such as Fungus and Mildew Spray®. Alternatively, mix an insecticide with your fungicide spray as the need arises. Always check for compatibility when mixing sprays, as some sprays should not be mixed with others.

Mites may attack plants in summer, especially in hot dry locations. These tiny creatures cause a yellow or silvery mottling on the leaves, but are difficult to see with the naked eye. Use a mite killer and make sure you spray the undersides of the leaves.

In winter you have a golden opportunity to nab the nasties while they sleep with what is known as a 'winter clean up' spray at pruning time. Use a copper spray or lime sulphur. It is important to use lime sulphur by itself and not mix it with any other sprays.

'Graham Thomas'.

WHICH ROSES FOR YOUR GARDEN?

ROSE TYPES

There are old-fashioned roses and modern roses. Some gardeners devote themselves to one group or the other, but there is no reason why both cannot coexist in a garden. Many of the most recently bred roses are closer in looks to the roses of the turn of the century than they are to those of 20 years ago.

Old-fashioned roses are a rather base grouping. The term 'old-fashioned' is generally used to refer to those that existed prior to about the 1940s. The flowers tend to be less formal than modern roses, either single with prominent stamens or full-petalled and frilly. Most of them are large-growing shrubs or ramblers. They need space to look their best, but require less pruning than modern roses. They are generally hardy and quite disease resistant. A criticism is that many of them do not repeat flower, but the single flowering cannot be matched for the sheer volume of blooms when they are in season, usually in early summer — worth waiting all year for. One of the most popular old roses of all is the sumptuous 'Albertine', a once-a-year bloomer.

The **hybrid musks** are a group of old-fashioned roses that were developed in the twenties and thirties. These are well known for their repeat-flowering performance and fragrance. Some are moderate-sized climbers and some are shrubs, not too big for the average-sized garden. They include 'Penelope', 'Cornelia', 'Buff Beauty', 'Felicia' and 'Moonlight'.

Modern bush roses are the more recently bred varieties. They are smaller-growing bushes easily managed in a small garden, producing lots of flowers with repeat (if not continuous) flowering through spring, summer and autumn. They can be separated into two main groups: the floribundas and the hybrid teas. Floribundas have flowers closer in form to the old-fashioned roses, producing many roses per stem and ideal for mass garden colour. The hybrid teas produce one bloom per stem, so are ideal for picking. The hybrid tea rose is the classical-shaped, pointed-centre rose, larger than floribunda roses.

Sam McGredy roses: Sam McGredy is a world-famous rose breeder who happens also to be a New Zealander. Many of the best modern roses, hybrid teas, floribundas and climbers as well as patio roses have been raised by Sam. Being developed in New Zealand, they are ideally suited to growing here, but are known throughout the world. A particular strength with Sam McGredy roses is a high disease resistance.

David Austin roses (or 'English' roses) are the hit roses of the nineties. They started appearing on the scene in the early eighties, the outcome of crossing old roses with modern roses, the very clever idea of their namesake and breeder, David Austin. Deservedly growing in popularity, David Austin roses offer the romance and fragrance of the old-fashioned roses but have the colour range and repeat-flowering habit of modern roses. Most are quite large-growing in New Zealand, usually up to two metres or more, at least twice the height of the same varieties in English soil. Some, like the favourite 'Graham Thomas', are best treated as climbers and grown against a wall. Picked, they look wonderful grouped together in a vase, though they only last a few days this way.

Shrub roses and **groundcover roses** are another relatively new breed of roses. They are generally easy to care for, long flowering, and very disease resistant. Pruning is a matter of trimming them back as you would any flowering shrub. Hedge clippers are not to be ruled out! Shrub roses are densely branched with close, small foliage and lots of small to medium-sized flowers. The flowers have an informal, old-fashioned appearance.

Standard roses are simply rose bushes grafted on to the top of a long stem (the root stock). They grow into exactly the same shape and size as their non-standard equivalent but are raised up in the air a metre or so. Obviously, tall upright roses don't look so good as standards. The best effects are with floribunda roses or spreading shrub roses, and groundcover roses are transformed into very desirable weeping standard roses. Patio or miniature roses on shorter root stocks are very effective for pots.

Patio roses is the term used for those roses that are ideally suited to container growing. They also happen to be excellent garden roses where smaller-growing bushes are called for. They have small to medium flowers, often produced continuously or in flushes from late spring through autumn. Miniature roses can be included in this category. They are small-growing bushes with small flowers. Miniature roses are often offered for sale as inexpensive miniature plants. If nurtured they will soon grow into bushy specimens. As with all roses, some cultivars are stronger than others.

'Flower Carpet Apple Blossom' standard.

'FLOWER CARPET' ROSES — THE EASIEST OF ALL.

This new breed of shrub roses have become world famous for their unprecedented disease resistance and free-flowering habit, making them among the easiest roses you could grow, especially if you wish to avoid spraying in your garden. 'Flower Carpet' roses have a low spreading habit. They can be grown in pots, and even hanging baskets. In the garden they look fabulous either as single plants among a cottage-style flower border or mass planted as a hedge or groundcover. They reach about a metre in height but can be kept lower with trimming. They make stunning weeping standards for the garden or containers. In a mild climate they retain their leaves all year round and established plants have been known to flower for 10 months of the year. Like any rose they thrive with lots of fertiliser and plenty of water. The more you give them the more they will bloom with a dense covering of rich green foliage. They ask for only the occasional trim to keep growth compact. No fuss here either. The hedge trimmers will do. 'Flower Carpet' will grow in sun or semi-shade, but flowers better in full sun.

THE BEST ROSES

There are so many roses (at least half a dozen new ones released on the market each year) that choosing between them can be daunting. The other problem for those who fall hopelessly in love with roses is restricting your collection to a number you realistically have room for — which ones not to have?

Roses are susceptible to disease, and if you are to have more than a few, it will be hard to get away from spraying to keep them looking good. Some roses, however, are a lot more susceptible and generally a lot weaker growing than others. It is important to choose varieties that are robust and free flowering, the overall health and vigour of the plant being just as important as the beauty of the individual flower — more important really. The following selection includes current top performers in each colour group.

Use the table on this page and page 96 to find the best roses for your garden. Once you have your shortlists go to pages 97–101 for descriptions.

(f) = fragrant

MODERN BUSH ROSES	CLIMBING ROSES	OLD-FASHIONED STYLE — LARGE FLOWERS	OLD-FASHIONED STYLE — SMALL FLOWERS
WHITE & CREAM	*WHITE & CREAM*	*WHITE & CREAM*	*WHITE & CREAM*
Iceberg	Iceberg	Proud Titania (f)	Flower Carpet White (f)
Margaret Merrill (f)	Albéric Barbier (f)	Fair Bianca (f)	Seafoam
Auckland Metro (f)	Mme Alfred Carrière (f)	Grus an Aachen (f)	Wedding Day (f)
	Wedding Day	Mme Alfred Carrière (f)	*R. banksia* 'The Pearl'
	R. banksia 'The Pearl'	White Sparrieshoop	Patio Cloud
PINK	*PINK*	*PINK*	*PINK*
West Coast	Compassion (f)	Heritage (f)	Flower Carpet Pink
Sexy Rexy	New Dawn (f)	Mary Rose (f)	Fl. Carpet Apple Blossom
Aotearoa (f)	City of London (f)	Gertrude Jekyll (f)	Rosy Cushion
Strawberry Ice	Albertine (f)	Abraham Derby (f)	The Fairy
Carolyn (f)	Bantry Bay		Cécile Brünner (f)
			Kapiti
PURPLE	*PURPLE*	*PURPLE*	*PURPLE*
Big Purple (f)	Veilchenblau	Lavender Lassie (f)	Lavender Dream
Moody Blues		Old Port (f)	
Super Bowl (f)			
Old Port (f)			
RED	*RED*	*RED*	*RED*
Deep Secret (f)	Dublin Bay (f)	L. D. Braithwaite (f)	Flower Carpet Red
Ingrid Bergman		Phantom	Eye-opener
Paddy Stevens		Colour Break	
Candella			
Trumpeter			
Colour Break			
YELLOW	*YELLOW*	*YELLOW*	*YELLOW*
Friesia (f)	Graham Thomas (f)	Graham Thomas (f)	*R. banksia* 'Lutea'
Gold Medal	Golden Showers (f)	English Garden (f)	Fairy Moon
Elina (f)	*R. banksia* 'Lutea'	Yellow Button (f)	Buff Beauty (f)
	Buff Beauty (f)	Golden Wings	
ORANGE & APRICOT	*ORANGE & APRICOT*	*ORANGE & APRICOT*	*ORANGE & APRICOT*
Just Joey (f)	Westerland (f)	Abraham Darby (f)	Penelope (f)
Spek's Centennial (f)	Cornelia (f)	Charles Austin (f)	Cornelia (f)
City of Auckland (f)	Buff Beauty (f)	English Garden (f)	Buff Beauty (f)
Lantern (f)		Ambridge Rose (f)	

'Rosy Cushion'.

'Seafoam'.

THE BEST ROSES

STANDARD ROSES

WHITE & CREAM
Iceberg
Margaret Merrill (f)
Flower Carpet White (f)
Patio Cloud (mini standard)
Seafoam
White Bells

PINK
Flower Carpet Pink
Fl. Carpet Apple Blossom
The Fairy
Pink Bells
Kapiti
Sexy Rexy
Strawberry Ice
Enchantment

PURPLE
Old Port (f)

RED
Eye-opener
Trumpeter
Trinity
Wanaka (mini standard)
Colour Break

YELLOW
Friesia (f)
Fairy Moon

ORANGE & APRICOT
Spek's Centennial (f)

ROSES FOR POTS

WHITE & CREAM
Flower Carpet White (f)
Whiteout
Patio Cloud

PINK
Flower Carpet Pink
Fl. Carpet Apple Blossom
Tinkerbell
The Fairy
Enchantment
Kapiti
Rexy's Baby
Little Opal

PURPLE
Lavender Jewel

RED
Flower Carpet Red
Patio Jewel
Trinity
Wanaka

YELLOW
Rise'n'shine
Dorola

ORANGE & APRICOT
Sweet Dream
Patio Gem

LOW MAINTENANCE SHRUB ROSES

WHITE & CREAM
Flower Carpet White (f)
Seafoam

PINK
Flower Carpet Pink
Fl. Carpet Apple Blossom
Rosy Cushion
The Fairy
Kapiti

PURPLE
Lavender Dream

RED
Phantom
Eye-opener
Flower Carpet Red

YELLOW
Fairy Moon

BEST PICKING ROSES

WHITE & CREAM
Auckland Metro (f)
Iceberg
Margaret Merrill (f)

PINK
Aotearoa (f)
Carolyn (fr)
Compassion (f)
City of London (f)

PURPLE
Big Purple (f)
Moody Blues
Super Bowl (f)

RED
Deep Secret (f)
Ingrid Bergman
Paddy Stevens
Candella

YELLOW
Gold Medal
Elina (f)
Just Joey (f)

ORANGE & APRICOT
City of Auckland (f)
Lantern (f)

'Candella'.

THE BEST VARIETIES

'Abraham Darby'
DAVID AUSTIN

This rose has huge beautiful apricot-yellow flowers with a delicious fragrance. It is a disease-resistant variety that repeat flowers easily. It is capable of growing to 2.4 m with support.

'Albéric Barbier'
OLD-FASHIONED RAMBLER

Albéric Barbier is a very pretty, vigorous-growing climber that grows well in all climates. Its soft lemon buds open to cream flowers with a light, delicate fragrance. It looks wonderful grown over a wall and has exceptionally glossy, dark green foliage.

'Albertine'
OLD-FASHIONED RAMBLER

The large apricot-pink flowers are a beautiful sight, with enormous volumes of blooms in early summer and rich green glossy foliage for the rest of the season. It loves to ramble over trees and shrubs and has a superb rich fragrance.

'Ambridge Rose'
DAVID AUSTIN

Apricot, medium-sized blooms with a beautifully double, old-fashioned form and a lovely fragrance, it flowers throughout the season. An average-sized, neat bush fitting easily into any garden.

'Aotearoa'
SAM MCGREDY, HYBRID TEA

Aotearoa was the official rose to mark New Zealand's sesquicentennial in 1990. It has the classic hybrid tea form with large creamy-pink flowers on long stems. Its fragrance is truly magnificent and it is remarkably disease resistant.

'Auckland Metro'
SAM MCGREDY, HYBRID TEA

This Sam McGredy rose is arguably the best white rose you could grow for both picking and garden display. It has large, beautifully formed creamy-white flowers with a powerful fragrance. This is an extremely healthy plant well worth having in the garden.

R. banksia 'Lutea'
OLD-FASHIONED CLIMBER

This thornless climber flourishes in warmer climates. Though scentless, the pretty pale yellow double flowers cascade in late spring — a magnificent sight. Pruning is necessary only to keep size under control; this is best done straight after flowering.

R. banksia 'The Pearl'
OLD-FASHIONED CLIMBER

A thornless, not too rampant climber ideal for a warm climate or a warm wall in a cold climate. It flowers continuously all summer with lots of lovely, smallish double white flowers.

'Bantry Bay'
SAM MCGREDY CLIMBER

This long-flowering climber is perfect for growing over fences, walls, posts and the like. Its large double flowers are a glorious pink colour and have a delicate 'wild rose' fragrance.

'Big Purple'
HYBRID TEA

A hybrid tea rose with huge deep purple blooms. The flowers have a powerful, heady fragrance. It has deep green matt foliage and is a vigorous and bushy grower.

'Buff Beauty'
HYBRID MUSK, CLIMBER

Large trusses of buff-yellow flowers fade to primrose. This is a vigorous grower with a delicious fragrance and it flowers continuously.

'Candella'
SAM MCGREDY, HYBRID TEA

An award-winning picking rose with straight long stems topped with large formal-shaped roses in rich velvet red with a silvery reverse. The bush is robust and healthy producing lots of flowers throughout summer.

'Carolyn'
SAM MCGREDY, HYBRID TEA

Warm salmon-pink, extremely fragrant picking roses of classic form are produced in great numbers through spring, summer and autumn on a strong healthy bush.

'Cécile Brünner'
OLD-FASHIONED CLIMBER

Cécile Brunner is an easily accommodated, moderate-growing climber with well-formed daintily shaped flowers of pink. Its lightly fragrant flowers are abundant in early summer, complementing the small dark green leaves. An old favourite with good disease resistance.

'Charles Austin'
DAVID AUSTIN

This rose has large, double, cupped apricot and yellow blooms. It has a beautiful fruity scent and flowers repeatedly throughout the season on straight tall stems.

'City of Auckland'
SAM MCGREDY, HYBRID TEA

The strongly fragrant blooms of this hybrid tea rose are a stunning colour of deep gold and tangerine. These flowers are produced all summer long on a strong bushy plant with dark glossy foliage.

'City of London'
CLIMBER

This is one of the sweetest-perfumed climbers to be found. In cooler climates it is bushy and low growing, making it ideal for smaller areas; in warmer conditions it grows upwards and outwards. The delicate pink-coloured blooms are part of its charm.

'Colour Break'
FLORIBUNDA

'Colour Break' has uniquely coloured brown-red double flowers. Its many-petalled blooms give it an old-fashioned quartered look. It is a very showy, free-flowering rose, especially good for mass planting.

'Compassion'
CLIMBER

This sweetly perfumed climber has lovely blooms of salmon pink shaded apricot orange. The large double flowers make for perfect cutting. It flowers repeatedly and is a vigorous and healthy grower.

'Cornelia'
HYBRID MUSK

Best grown as a moderate climber on a post or a wall, old-fashioned 'Cornelia' has the sweetest fragrance. The rich apricot-pink flowers are small, double in form and produced in clusters well into late autumn in a mild climate.

'Deep Secret'
HYBRID TEA

This is a beautiful deep, dark, black-red rose. Its floral fragrance and longish stems ensure excellent cutting. This healthy bush bears dark foliage with an attractive silvery sheen.

'Dorola'
SAM McGREDY, PATIO

This sturdy little bush is covered with small yellow-gold blooms throughout the season.

'Dublin Bay'
SAM McGREDY, CLIMBER

One of the most popular climbing roses of all and the most outstanding red-flowered climbing rose you will find, 'Dublin Bay' is lightly scented and flowers continuously throughout the summer. Its blood-red-coloured blooms look stunning climbing over pillars or walls.

'Elina'
HYBRID TEA

Large perfectly formed blooms of pale creamy-yellow adorn this hybrid tea. Single flowers are borne on each stem and sit well against its dense dark green foliage.

'Enchantment'
FLORIBUNDA, PATIO

A compact and bushy shrub, 'Enchantment' has beautiful pale peachy-pink flowers with a delicate refreshing scent. These are produced *en masse* on large clusters and are a beautiful sight.

'English Garden'
DAVID AUSTIN

This rose has large soft apricot-yellow flowers. Its beautiful fragrance makes 'English Garden' perfect for picking or planting near paths or seating areas. Large growing.

'Eye-opener'
GROUNDCOVER

Eye-opener can best be described as a flowering groundcover shrub. It is basically maintenance free, requiring only a light trim to keep it in shape once in a while. In full bloom it is covered with small, single form, red flowers displayed on a background of shiny green foliage. It is stunning as a standard, also in a large barrel with white flowers such as verbena.

'Fair Bianca'
DAVID AUSTIN

This rose flowers right through the season and has a beautifully powerful fragrance. A David Austin rose of usefully small proportions, it has open double white flowers with a slightly pink centre.

'Fairy Moon'
GROUNDCOVER

This spreading shrub rose is covered in clusters of small creamy-yellow flowers on shiny healthy foliage.

'Felicia'
HYBRID MUSK

'Felicia' has clusters of double flowers in the palest apricot and has a delicious sweet scent. It flowers throughout the season and grows to a strong bushy plant.

'Flower Carpet Apple Blossom'
SHRUB

Masses of soft pink and white flowers with a light fragrance on this latest of the 'Flower Carpet' series, another evergreen, disease-free rose.

'Flower Carpet Pink'
SHRUB

The 'Flower Carpet' series of roses are probably the easiest roses you will grow. This, the first of the series, is adorned with clusters of bright pink flowers for months on end.

'Flower Carpet White'
SHRUB

White 'Flower Carpet' is scented. It produces mass upon mass of informal creamy-white flowers on very dark green foliage. An unbeatable low-growing white rose for mass planting.

'Friesia'
FLORIBUNDA

With its clusters of clear yellow flowers, healthy bright green foliage and sweet fragrance, this is a beautiful display rose. Its compact and bushy growth makes it an ideal garden plant.

'Golden Showers'
CLIMBER

This delightfully scented climber has pointed buds that open to yellow blooms fading to cream. It flowers continuously and freely in masses of trusses. It works well as a shorter climber or growing over a pillar.

'Golden Wings'
OLD-FASHIONED SHRUB

'Golden Wings' is an old-fashioned rose producing large single yellow blooms continuously through the season. It grows extremely well and has large flat and leathery foliage of deep green.

'Enchantment'.

'Gold Medal'
HYBRID TEA

'Gold Medal' is quite simply spectacular. Its flowers have unique colourings of deep gold with red-orange tints and pretty light green foliage. The bush grows vigorously and is particularly disease resistant. The flowers are borne on long stems and bloom continuously all season.

'Graham Thomas'
DAVID AUSTIN, CLIMBER

'Graham Thomas' is the most popular David Austin rose. It is a very large plant which in New Zealand is best grown as a climber. It has large rich-yellow flowers, glossy green foliage and a heavenly fragrance. It flowers in clusters on stems long enough for cutting. Quite simply it is magnificent!

'Grus an Aachen'
OLD-FASHIONED SHRUB

You could be forgiven for calling this a David Austin rose. It is of the same style. The creamy-white to soft pink, many-petalled flowers are very fragrant and repeatedly produced on a neat low-growing bush, accommodated in the smallest garden.

'Heritage'
DAVID AUSTIN

Layers and layers of large pink petals form perfect blooms produced in clusters on large deep green foliage. A lax, rather open bush that needs support to look its best. Its scent is delightful.

'Iceberg'
FLORIBUNDA

This is the most popular white rose in the world, and so it deserves to be. Although 'Iceberg' is a floribunda, it grows and behaves more like a shrub rose. It flowers heavily in spring and again in autumn, producing shell-pink buds that open to large white flowers with a pleasant scent. It grows into a vigorous bush with light green foliage.

'Iceberg' — Climbing
CLIMBER

This rose flowers profusely producing long sprays of white flowers and crisp green foliage. Its flowers are perfect for cutting and it has few thorns.

'Ingrid Bergman'
HYBRID TEA

This hybrid tea rose produces long-lasting and exquisitely formed deep red blooms with a hint of fragrance. The long-stemmed flowers, combined with lovely dark glossy foliage, make it an ideal picking rose. It is particularly hardy: sturdy and highly resistant to disease.

'Just Joey'
HYBRID TEA

This rose is something else. Large, frilled coppery-orange petals and a powerful fragrance gives this rose real garden appeal. The flowers of this hybrid tea sit on attractive dark green leathery foliage.

'Kapiti'
SAM MCGREDY, SHRUB

Kapiti is a delightful spreading groundcover shrub. Huge clusters of deep rose-pink semi-double blooms are produced throughout the season and often into autumn. The healthy foliage is coloured deep green. It looks lovely spilling out of a large container or as a weeping standard.

'Lantern'
SAM MCGREDY, HYBRID TEA

'Lantern' has shining high-centred blooms in a blend of yellow, orange and salmon with a delightful perfume. The blooms are freely produced on a strong upright plant.

'Lavender Dream'
SHRUB

Clouds of small lavender-pink flowers smother this charming old-fashioned rose throughout the summer. 'Lavender Dream' is a smaller-growing shrub rose perfect for warmer climates, and exceptionally easy to grow. There are attractive red hips in autumn.

'Lavender Jewel'
PATIO

This delightful Patio Rose has small lavender-pink buds that open to beautifully formed double flowers of deep lavender. These contrast well with the healthy and particularly deep green foliage.

'Lavender Lassie'
OLD-FASHIONED SHRUB

The flowers of this rose are exquisite: huge sprays of lavender-pink with a beautiful scent. It repeat flowers through the season and has plenty of bright green, disease-resistant foliage.

'L. D. Braithwaite'
DAVID AUSTIN

Bright crimson fragrant flowers are slow to fade on a bush that is relatively low and spreading for an Austin rose. It is seldom without a flower.

'Little Opal'
PATIO

A perfectly formed mini rose of clear pastel pink, 'Little Opal' is a vigorous healthy bush producing huge crops of blooms good for picking. It has an upright habit.

'Margaret Merrill'
FLORIBUNDA

This very fragrant rose is truly beautiful, combining the charm of both old and modern roses. High-centred buds open to delicate white blooms with a hint of satin pink. The foliage is healthy matt dark green with bushy, leafy growth.

'Mary Rose'
DAVID AUSTIN

This rose has bright rich pink flowers sitting on a background of deep green, disease-resistant foliage. Large double blooms have the delicious fragrance of the old damask roses.

'Mme Alfred Carrière'
OLD-FASHIONED CLIMBER

This climbing rose is a must for every New Zealand garden. Its large sweet-scented white flowers bloom continually throughout the season with flushes in early spring and again in autumn. It is one of the most popular old climbers around.

'Moody Blues'
HYBRID TEA

The flowers of this rose are a most exquisite shade of soft lilac. The blooms sit well against the attractive light grey-green colour of its leaves. A strong grower that flowers profusely throughout the season.

'New Dawn'.

'Moonlight'
HYBRID MUSK, CLIMBER

Small white scented flowers are produced in clusters on this rambling hybrid musk. It is a vigorous and healthy grower and flowers continuously throughout the season.

'New Dawn'
CLIMBER

This is a notable repeat-flowering climber. Beautifully scented blooms of the softest blush-pink sit on a background of dark green and glossy foliage. It grows well over arches or pergolas and looks stunning simply tumbling over a bank.

'Old Port'
FLORIBUNDA

'Old Port' is a modern rose with old-fashioned flowers. The beautifully scented blooms are very full and a rich burgundy-purple colour. The plant flowers freely and is well clothed in medium green, disease-resistant foliage.

'Paddy Stevens'
HYBRID TEA

This is a beautiful recent release of outstanding quality. The large blooms of warm coral-orange and salmon contrast well with the dark green and glossy foliage.

'Patio Cloud'
PATIO

Known elsewhere in the world as 'Fluffy', this patio rose is a delight. Showers of small, double, white flowers cover the plant all summer long. Its musky scent and deep green foliage make it well worth having in your garden or a container.

'Patio Gem'
PATIO

Small deep coral-pink and double-petalled flowers clothe this bushy little plant. It is particularly free flowering, delicately scented and has healthy deep green foliage.

'Patio Jewel'
PATIO

This is a larger-than-normal patio rose, growing to about 90 cm tall. Its hybrid tea-style flowers of bright crimson-scarlet complimented by bushy and shiny green foliage make it perfect for prominent positions in either the garden or a pot.

'Pearl Drift'
FLORIBUNDA

Masses of pearly pinky-white flowers drip from the glossy green foliage of this very healthy rose. It is a vigorous bushy grower and flowers freely throughout the season, flowering right into winter in a mild climate.

'Penelope'
HYBRID MUSK

'Penelope' is clustered with semi-double, creamy-pink flowers that bloom through summer and well into autumn. The flowers have a delicate musky fragrance. It is a vigorous, bushy grower and clad in matt dark green foliage often tinged with red.

'Phantom'
SAM McGREDY, SHRUB

In full bloom, 'Phantom' is an arresting sight. This groundcover shrub has huge tresses of single to semi-double scarlet-red flowers with rich golden stamens. The foliage is healthy, darkest green and particularly disease resistant.

'Proud Titania'
DAVID AUSTIN

'Proud Titania' has perfectly formed buds of the palest peach, which open to rich creamy-coloured, scented blooms. It is a vigorous grower and can reach 1.3 m.

'Rexy's Baby'
PATIO

'Rexy's Baby' is perfect for massed planting, edging and containers. Its delicate rose-pink buds open to double pink flowers with salmon-tinged centres. It flowers profusely in even-spaced clusters and looks wonderful in a vase.

'Rise'n'shine'
PATIO

Clear golden-yellow flowers are borne freely on this lovely bushy plant. The foliage is shiny bright green and reliably disease free. It is an excellent cutting rose and is easily the best yellow patio rose.

'Rosy Cushion'
SHRUB

Delicate pinky blooms cover the polished dark green foliage of this shrub rose. Clusters of flowers are freely produced on this vigorous grower and repeat over the summer. All in all, it's an extremely versatile shrub for the garden.

'Trinity'.

'Seafoam'
SHRUB

'Seafoam' is an unusual and very beautiful shrub rose. Clusters of small creamy-white very double flowers cover its glossy disease-free foliage continuously throughout the season. It can be used as a groundcover or can be trained like a rambler, and makes one of the best weeping standard roses.

'Sexy Rexy'
SAM MCGREDY, FLORIBUNDA

This is a world-famous rose. In full bloom it is smothered with trusses of beautiful salmon-pink flowers. The dark green foliage is disease resistant and the plant has a lovely growth habit.

'Spek's Centennial'
SAM MCGREDY, FLORIBUNDA

'Spek's Centennial' has a strong spicy fragrance and superbly coloured blooms of coppery-bronze to amber — a floral artist's dream. It flowers continuously and is a vigorous and bushy grower.

'Strawberry Ice'
FLORIBUNDA

Attractive cup-shaped flowers of translucent white have rose-cerise petal margins. This is a vigorous and healthy grower with large, glossy bright green leaves.

'Super Bowl'
SAM MCGREDY, HYBRID TEA

Soft silvery-lavender flowers have a powerful sweet perfume. There are long stems perfect for cutting and few thorns.

'The Fairy'
GROUNDCOVER

Dainty sprays of tiny soft-pink rosette-shaped flowers and medium green foliage mean this shrub is perfect for cutting and display. It begins flowering later than most, in mid-summer, but continues with flush after flush of blooms until early winter. And it's perfect for pots and hanging baskets.

'Tinkerbell'
PATIO

A fragrant miniature rose in sweet clear pink, 'Tinkerbell' is very free flowering and healthy. The flowers are good for picking.

'Trinity'
SAM MCGREDY, PATIO

Perfect formal roses in miniature are produced in great profusion on a bush reaching about a metre tall.

'Trumpeter'
FLORIBUNDA

The brilliant orange-scarlet colour and profusion of blooms make this an excellent rose for a splash of hot colour, blooming continuously through the summer. It is a compact and healthy plant with glossy disease-resistant foliage.

'Veilchenblau'
OLD-FASHIONED CLIMBER

An almost thornless climber, 'Veilchenblau' has small cup-shaped blooms of purplish-blue with a cream centre and yellow stamens. Sweetly scented, it will do well even in a shady position.

'Wanaka'
SAM MCGREDY, PATIO

Profusions of bright orange-red blooms cover the plant all summer long. The blooms are small but packed with petals and sit against a background of semi-glossy deep green and disease-resistant foliage.

'Wedding Day'
OLD-FASHIONED RAMBLER

'Wedding Day' is a rampant climber and a wonderful sight in full bloom. Yellow buds open to creamy-white with bright orange-yellow stamens. It flowers only once and has a wonderfully delicate scent.

'West Coast'
HYBRID TEA

This big, strong hybrid tea has masses of large well-shaped pink blooms. It is densely covered in large glossy deep green leaves. Perfect for cutting and perfect too in the garden, 'West Coast' is a healthy disease-free plant.

'Westerland'
CLIMBER

Flower colour varies from bronze to salmon-apricot on this climber. It produces sweetly scented blooms and large glossy-green foliage. 'Westerland' is a vigorous and healthy grower.

'White Out'
SAM MCGREDY, PATIO

Small clusters of pinky buds reveal white blooms of double formal shape. 'White Out' is a particularly easy patio rose to grow with compact and healthy growing habits.

'White Sparrieshoop'
OLD-FASHIONED SHRUB-CLIMBER

This large shrub rose is best employed as a moderate-sized climber or 'pillar' rose, ideal for growing on a pergola or verandah post where it will not take over the whole structure. The flowers are gorgeous creamy-white, single with yellow stamens and have a pleasant fragrance.

'Yellow Button'
DAVID AUSTIN

A low spreading bush with arching branches and delightful small to medium flowers. They are rosette form with reflexing petals in shades of soft to yolk-yellow and have a strong fruity fragrance.

Perennials

Strictly speaking, 'perennial' means any plant that lives on to flower season after season (i.e., any plant that isn't an annual). In everyday gardening language this broad definition has been usefully narrowed down to mean all those non-woody plants that survive in the garden for a number of years.

What is perennial to a cool-climate gardener may be an annual to a warm-climate gardener, and vice versa. Often when perennials are grown in a climate opposite to that of their natural habitat, they will either be killed by frost or flower poorly in the second season through lack of winter chilling. In many cases it is a lot easier simply to enjoy the plant as an annual, rather than to go to all the trouble of altering the conditions to suit.

Perennials are more permanent than annuals but less permanent than trees and shrubs. They generally need lifting and dividing every few years. Most need to be cut back after flowering.

Some of the most spectacular foliage plants are perennials. Plants like *Hosta*, *Heuchera* and *Gunnera* do produce flowers, but it is the leaves that are the main attraction. Other perennials, like *Agapanthus*, *Bergenia* and Chatham Island forget-me-not have beautiful flowers as well as being grown for their foliage. Those that retain their foliage over winter are especially valuable.

Often referred to as perennials are annuals that regenerate themselves from seed so easily that they behave like perennials, returning to flower every year, albeit not always in exactly the same place. All we need to do is to avoid disturbing the young progeny with over-rigorous weeding.

Shasta daisy with perennial wallflower.

LOW PERENNIALS

. . . for the front of the flower border, groundcovers under trees and shrubs,
for cascading over walls, spilling out over path edges, for pots,
window boxes or hanging baskets.

Agapanthus dwarf cultivars
50 cm or less
One of the best plants you could have in your garden, agapanthus puts up with any soil in sun or shade. Its lush green, strappy foliage is present all year round and the lovely long-stemmed flowers are a bonus in spring and summer. Agapanthus will stand light frosts, but in the English climate it is considered a tender blue-flowered treasure, so we should count ourselves lucky that we can grow agapanthus throughout most of New Zealand with such ease. The dwarf forms are particularly charming and make magnificent permanent edging plants. Among the best are: 'Streamline', with masses of pale blue flowers and abundant soft foliage, 'Snowball', a white-flowered form, and 'Peter Pan', a rich blue. All perform well on the coast, in clay or sandy soils, tolerating periods of drought or wet soils. The flowers are lovely for picking.

Alchemilla mollis
LADY'S MANTLE
30 cm
An old-fashioned perennial, much loved as an edging plant with very attractively shaped, soft-textured leaves and soft yellow summer flowers. It has a nice bushy habit, kept in good condition by cutting back to about 3 cm above the ground each autumn. Plant in average, well-drained soil in semi-shade. Plants can be lifted and divided in spring or autumn. A good companion for spring bulbs.

Anthemis punctata subsp. cupaniana
Under 30 cm
A delightful low-spreading perennial with lacy grey foliage and lots of fifty-cent-piece-sized yellow-centred daisy flowers in spring and early summer. Great in pots or flanking pathways, for picking, dry soils and for coastal gardens. It will not thrive without good drainage in sun or part shade. Trim after flowering.

Arctotis acaulis (syn. A. scapigera) hybrids
Large, eye-catching daisy flowers in bright colour blends of pinks, hot oranges and reds, deep purples, yellows and white. They make a good groundcover, thriving in hot dry locations and are good for coastal gardens, tolerating light frosts. They flower for a long summer season, after which they should be cut back hard to encourage fresh growth from the base. This perennial is comparatively short lived, but new plants of arctotis are easily produced from cuttings.

Argyranthemum frutescens dwarf hybrids
DWARF MARGUERITE
40 cm
The marguerite daisies are well known for their quick growth and generous flowering performance. They seem to flower continuously, asking only to be cut back once a year to keep them compact. The latest developments are the dwarf forms, such as the excellent 'Elfin Series', which are ideally suited to containers and remain as bushy compact plants in the garden. Give them full sun and average, well-drained soil and they are sure to please. Like all marguerite daisies they will tolerate periods of drought once established. There are pink, white and yellow varieties to choose from.

Armeria spp. & cultivars
THRIFT
Under 30 cm
Low-tufted foliage sends up hundreds of sweet little pompom flowers at the ends of straight stems in spring and summer. They come in shades of pink or white and are an old cottage-garden favourite, ideal for edges and rockeries. Easy to grow, resisting drought and coastal conditions, a free-draining soil in full sun is their favourite position. If you find your soil is too heavy, try them in a pot.

Arthropodium cirratum
RENGARENGA, NEW ZEALAND ROCK LILY
60 cm
Soft green, strappy foliage is attractive

Argyranthemum frutescens 'Elfin' hybrids.

all year round, and in summer is adorned with sprays of white flowers. At its loveliest mass planted around deciduous trees, this is a superb perennial for shade or semi-shade. It thrives on the coast and tolerates dry conditions once established. One of the best native groundcovers.

Bergenia cordifolia cultivars
ELEPHANT'S EARS
Height 30 cm
Lovely big leaves giving striking textural contrast make this an excellent perennial for mass planting as a groundcover. The flowers appear in early spring and are red, pink, lavender or white depending on variety. Bergenias tolerate dry shade once established, growing in sun or shade but flowering best with some sun.

Brachyscome multifida 'Break O' Day'
SWAN RIVER DAISY
30 cm
This low mounding plant with its fine ferny foliage is sprinkled for most of the year with appealing little daisy flowers of lavender blue. It looks wonderful spilling over walls or pathways and works well in pots. Give this long-flowering perennial a warm sunny spot and well-drained soil. A trim once a year will keep it compact and bushy.

Campanula
BELLFLOWER

There are hundreds of different campanulas, all with characteristic bell-shaped flowers but varying widely in form. *C. portenschlagiana* has small heart-shaped leaves, forming low mounding mats about 10 cm high. The flowers are violet-blue bells on short erect stems, appearing in spring. An excellent small-area groundcover, it prefers part shade in a warm climate, otherwise full sun. A similar low campanula for part shade is *C. poscharskyana*. It sends out sprays of blue flowers from late spring into summer and is more vigorous than *C. portenschlagiana*, and not quite so compact. Both are good in containers, as edging plants or on walls.

Cerastium tomentosum
SNOW-IN-SUMMER
Under 10 cm

A very easy perennial with ground-hugging silver foliage (see photo below) and a smothering of little white flowers in summer. A well-drained position in full sun is best, but semi-shade will suffice. Good also in pots.

Cerastium tomentosum.

Convolvulus sabatius (syn. C. mauritanicus)
BINDWEED

A very useful blue-flowering perennial with a low spreading habit and myriads of blue cup-shaped flowers in summer. Wonderful cascading out of pots, baskets or paving. It is tolerant of dry or coastal conditions and grows best in well-drained soil with full sun. Trim after flowering.

Corydalis flexuosa 'Blue Panda'
40 cm

Sky-blue flowers present themselves in good numbers through autumn, winter and spring. The fern-like foliage is reason alone to grow this plant, contrasting beautifully with large-leaved plants like hostas. A moist, well-drained soil enriched with compost in semi-shade is where it thrives. 'Blue Panda' is compact growing, suitable as a border plant. This is an easy-to-grow plant whose exquisite looks belie its hardiness. A must for blue-flower addicts.

Dianthus cultivars
Border Pink
20 cm

These are the low-growing cousins of carnations. The tight grey-green foliage hugs the ground year round and over a long season have a covering of fragrant blooms. There are many varieties. Two of the best are the long-flowering 'Far Cry' (pink flowers) and 'Far North' (white flowers). Border pinks are good coastal plants, good in pots and tolerating periods of dryness once established. They need full sun and perfect drainage but are otherwise very easy to grow, flowering mainly in summer and autumn.

Diascia 'Ruby Field'
25 cm

Dainty salmon-pink flowers are produced in great profusion for a long summer period. This is an excellent perennial for a well-drained soil in full sun or semi-shade. It is long flowering and likes to be kept well watered.

Erigeron speciosus cultivars
FLEABANE
30 cm

Low-clumping, very free-flowering daisy plants ideal for the edge of the flower border, flowering in spring and summer. Flowers measure about 5 cm across in shades of pink or lavender with cheerful yellow centres. Very easy, they ask only for an average garden soil and full sun. Keep plants tidy and prolific by lifting and dividing every few years. The well-known, much-loved relative *E. karvinskianus* with its small pinky-white daisies is very pretty but unfortunately seeds rather too freely and should be kept

well away from native bush, where it has become a serious problem.

Euphorbia amygdaloides var. robbiae
SPURGE
45 cm

An easy plant to light up shady corners and where the soil is prone to dryness, this *Euphorbia* is an excellent filler for covering the ground under deciduous trees. It will also grow in sun. The foliage is bright green with yellow bracts in spring. With spreading roots, it requires space, but is not difficult to keep under control.

Euphorbia polychroma
CUSHION SPURGE
30 cm

Euphorbias produce some of the finest foliage colour for winter and early spring. *E. polychroma* is a neat mounding plant, attractive all year round with bright green new growth, topped with yellow bracts in early spring. Provide full sun and a well-drained soil and prune after flowering.

Felicia amelloides
BLUE MARGUERITE
50 cm

Bright blue daisies with yellow centres will carry on right through spring, summer and autumn. This is a good perennial for a pot and does well in coastal gardens. Give it a well-drained soil in full sun.

Gazania hybrids
AFRICAN DAISY
Height under 30 cm

Bright summer yellows, oranges, reds and pinks lasting for a very long time and thriving in hot, well-drained conditions. An ideal coastal or container plant, perfect for cascading over clay banks or binding crumbling soils. Flowers are more prolific in poor soil. Protect from frost.

Geranium spp. & cultivars
CRANE'S BILL GERANIUMS
50 cm

There are many different crane's bill geraniums. Among the favourites is 'Johnson's Blue', a bright blue-flowered treasure that flowers through spring and summer on attractive lacy foliage. *G. endressii* has soft pink flowers and attractive foliage that makes dense clumps. 'Russell

Pritchard' is a compact grower with deep pink flowers and grey-green foliage, a very easy, very long-flowering plant. Full sun or partial shade, and a well-drained soil is all they ask for.

Helianthemum cultivars
Sun Rose
Small grey-green leaves clothe low-mounding plants that become smothered in delightful rose-like flowers in spring and summer. These are dry-tolerant plants ideal for pots, baskets and beach gardens, or walls, needing good drainage and full sun. Flowers are pink, white, red, yellow or orange. Long flowering but not long lived, so don't be sad if your plant turns up its toes after a couple of seasons' profuse flowering.

Helichrysum argyrophyllum
EVERLASTING DAISY
20 cm
With spreading silver-grey foliage and masses of little yellow paper daisies in autumn, this is another dry-loving plant for coastal gardens, pots and walls, needing good drainage and full sun. Flowers last forever when dried.

Helipterum anthemoides 'Paper Cascade'
PAPER DAISY
30 cm
White paper daisies (see photo above) are produced in great profusion on grey foliage. This popular pot or basket plant is also suitable for a well-drained place in the garden. It is very pretty and very long flowering, requiring full sun.

Helleborus 'White Magic'
WINTER ROSE
50 cm
There are lots of different hellebores, all excellent for winter or early spring flowers in shady locations. The flowers are distinctive: five petals with prominent stamens in shades of green, pink, purple or white. Double forms also exist. 'White Magic' stands out because it has upward-facing flowers ideal for picking. The foliage is an attractive year-round feature. Hellebores like a moist, compost-rich soil in semi-shade or shade. They perform best in a cool climate but are still easy and worthwhile in mild climates. Keep them well watered in dry weather.

Heuchera cultivars
CORAL BELLS
Up to 50 cm
Heucheras are grown mainly for their handsome foliage, but most have attractive flowers as a bonus. They are reliable and easy, making an excellent groundcover for semi-shade and tolerating periods of dryness. They are good as year-round edging plants or planted for foliage contrast. 'Chocolate Ruffles' has large ruffled leaves, dark green aging to chocolate brown, with burgundy underneath. 'Palace Purple' has large deep purple-bronze leaves. 'Lace Ruffles' has large frilly green leaves marbled with white. The old-fashioned species *H. sanguinea* has smaller green leaves and delicate stems of pink flowers in summer. Heucheras will grow in full sun but the foliage is at its best in part shade.

Hosta culltivars
PLAINTAIN LILY
Under 50 cm
Hostas are hard to go past for shady spots in want of dramatic foliage. They are so loved that a great many cultivars have been developed, each with its own special leaf pattern. A mixture of mass-planted hostas, or even one variety mass planted, is an eye-catching sight. You must, however, be prepared for bare winter soil as they go completely dormant. In spring you will need to be ready with the slug and snail bait to protect the newly emerging leaves. Hostas must have shade and moist well-drained soil.

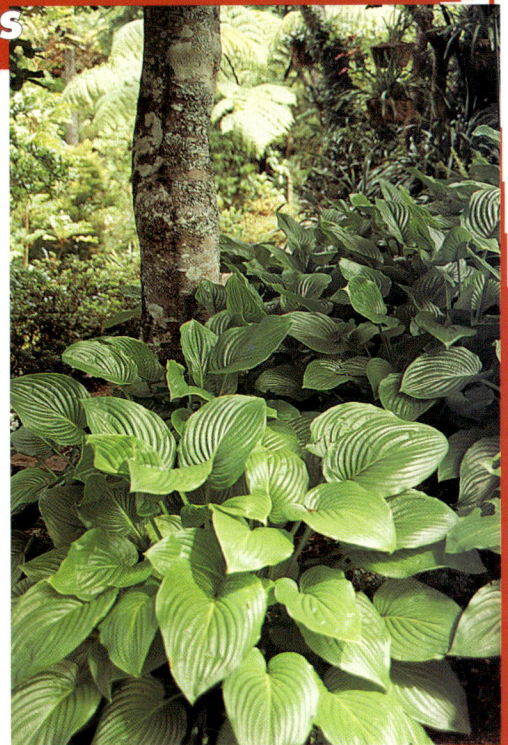

Hosta.

They look good in a pot and in spring produce purple or white flowers on spikes above the foliage.

Iberis sempervirens
CANDYTUFT
25 cm
This low spreading plant becomes completely covered in snowy-white flowers in early spring. It needs sun and a well-drained, ideally sandy, soil.

Impatiens New Guinea hybrids
These subtropical perennials are treated as annuals in a cold climate. They are excellent for both garden and container with attractive glossy foliage and boldly coloured flowers in bright shades of pink, red or orange. Grow them in full or part shade in well-drained soil.

Leucanthemum xsuperbum 'Snow Lady'
SHASTA DAISY
30 cm
Long stems and large snow-white daisy flowers with yellow centres are fantastic for picking and easy to grow. Flowers appear over summer on clump-forming plants that are easily divided in winter or early spring for more plants around the garden. There are a number of different varieties growing up to a metre tall. 'Snow Lady' is a compact form for the front of a border. Average well-drained soil and full sun is what they like.

Liriope muscari
TURF LILY
Under 45 cm
Grassy dark green clumps sport blue, grape-hyacinth-style flower spikes in autumn. Great as a border or mass-planted under trees, where it will cope with dry soil as well as shade. Clumps are divided and transplanted in winter or spring.

Mazus radicans
SWAMP MUSK
Under 10 cm
A delightful little New Zealand native thriving in good moist soil and partial shade, but flowering best in sun. Forms a good mat of small mottled leaves with dainty lobelia-like flowers, white with touches of purple and yellow.

Myosotidium hortensia
CHATHAM ISLAND FORGET-ME-NOT
50 cm
A native perennial with stunning glossy, deeply veined leaves and blue flowers in summer. They are much coveted but to grow them well you need a frost-free climate and a moist, well-drained, compost-enriched soil in semi-shade. To thrive, plants need lots of fertiliser, care that they never dry out, and protection from slugs and snails. Well worth growing.

Nepeta xfaassenii
CATMINT
30 cm
A purple-blue haze of mass-planted catmint makes a stunning border to summer-flowering roses. Small blue flowers cover small grey-green leaves on a low spreading plant. It grows best in full sun in a well-drained soil and tolerates periods of dryness or coastal conditions. Catmint flowers for ages, over summer and autumn. Cats love to roll in it, so plant enough to keep everyone happy. 'Six Hill's Giant' is a larger-growing variety with brighter blue flowers.

Osteospermum cultivars
AFRICAN DAISY
Under 30 cm
Another spreading daisy, fantastic as a bank cover, but cold hardier than the gazanias, withstanding light frost. The flowers cover the plant in spring and summer, most often seen in shades of pink and purple, also white and yellow. Some forms are bushy, others spreading. Full sun and good drainage are essential.

Pelargonium xhortorum cultivars
ZONAL PELARGONIUMS, GERANIUMS
Under 50 cm
The common geranium is not really a geranium at all, but a type of pelargonium. All pelargoniums are easy to grow in warm well-drained conditions. They make excellent coastal plants, enjoying the sandy soil, but will be knocked by anything more than a light frost. They all love growing in pots because of the warm and well-drained conditions. Pruning prevents plants from becoming leggy and unattractive. Cut back stems throughout the flowering season as the flowers die down. In early autumn prune plants back hard. Feed at three-monthly intervals with a balanced fertiliser .Pelargoniums are some of the easiest plants to propagate from cuttings. Because they grow and age quickly, it's best to propagate new plants every two or three years. Cuttings are made in autumn from new green growth — a good way to use your prunings. They should be at least 10 cm long with the bottom cut at a leaf node and the tips left intact. Remove all but the four top leaves and plant into well-drained mix. Zonal geraniums will flower from October to February. As well as traditional scarlet, geraniums come in bright orange, apricot, crimson, and all shades of pink, purple and white.

Pelargonium xdomesticum cultivars
REGAL PELARGONIUMS
Under 50 cm
The azalea-flowered regal pelargoniums come in a huge range of rich colours, available as named cultivars in the spring and summer. The flowers are very showy, usually blotched or veined and have a velvety texture. The plants are more open in habit than the common geranium, with woody stems. Regal pelargoniums are effective if a mixture of complementary varieties are used together or mixed with annuals in large containers.

Pelargonium peltatum cultivars
IVY GERANIUM
Ivy geraniums are indispensable for window boxes and hanging baskets. Colours are bright reds and pinks, soft pink or white. The ivy-shaped leaves are light glossy green, densely covering the vigorous clambering branches. Flowers are present for a long time in summer.

Pelargonium tomentosum
PEPPERMINT GERANIUM
This pelargonium is grown for its leaves, which have an irresistible velvet texture and an unmistakable peppermint fragrance. It makes an appealing groundcover for a shady spot. Good drainage is required.

Phlox subulata hybrids
PROSTRATE PHLOX
Under 10 cm
A mass of colour with flowers totally covering the foliage in spring or summer, in shades of bright pink, lavender blue, soft pink, or white. Good in pots, in rock gardens, on banks or retainer walls, with bulbs and other perennials, they need a warm sunny spot in well-drained soil. They will tolerate dry, exposed conditions, and do well in coastal gardens in any climate. Plant a variety for a colourful tapestry effect.

Pulmonaria cultivars
LUNGWORT
30 cm
Tough and easy lungworts are evergreen groundcover perennials suitable for dryish soil and shade. Small but pretty, early spring flowers of deep blue, pink or white are nestled amongst the attractive speckled foliage, which forms a compact, dense mound.

Scabiosa 'Blue Butterfly'
PINCUSHION FLOWER
30 cm
One among many attractive perennial scabiosas, 'Blue Butterfly' is very neat of habit and very long flowering. It has very densely packed foliage and mauve-blue flowers on stems long enough to pick but short enough to allow the flowers to sit neatly upright above their green carpet. From spring through to autumn it is hardly without flower, as long as it has reasonable drainage and plenty of sun.

Tradescantia xandersonii.

Stachys byzantina
LAMB'S EARS
Under 20 cm

Unmistakable soft downy leaves in silver grey. There are pale lavender flower spikes but these are best removed for it is the foliage that is the real feature. Lamb's ears is the perfect edging plant, spreading quickly into a weed-stopping mat. It will grow in any average soil, but looks sad in cold wet winter conditions. It prefers full sun or light shade. Easily lifted and divided.

Sutera cordata
BACOPA SNOWFLAKE
Under 10 cm

A mat-forming creeper with lush green foliage and lots of little white flowers through the year. A great edging, or for mass planting under roses, in the front of a flower border and in pots or hanging baskets. Feed and water regularly and provide a well-drained soil in sun or part shade.

Thymus spp. and cultivars
THYME
Under 20 cm

A must for a herb garden, it should be remembered that thyme is a fantastic flowering perennial. The many different varieties are easy to grow with both foliage and flower colour — prime candidates for the front of the flower garden or in pots. Thyme must have full sun and a well-drained soil to grow well.

More about thyme: Go to page 168.

Tradescantia virginiana hybrids
SPIDERWORT
Under 50 cm

Bright purple, pink or white flowers with an interesting three-petal form lie amongst spiky leaves all through summer into autumn. This is an easy perennial for moist soil in light shade.

Verbena cultivars
VERBENA

Verbenas are low sprawling plants producing masses of flowers throughout spring and summer. They are excellent in pots and hanging baskets, enjoying well-drained, warm conditions. They are good for picking, ranging in colour from white through pinks, reds, to purples. Verbenas grow well in coastal gardens but in humid climates summer mildew can be a problem for some varieties. Two recently developed disease-resistant, frost-tolerant cultivars are 'Scarlet Fire' and 'Purple Passion'. Both are ground-hugging with dense foliage spreading to about 50 cm, but only 5 cm high, with a spring to autumn covering of colourful flowers. Verbenas like full sun or part shade and a well-drained soil. Trim lightly after flowering and feed regularly for the very best results.

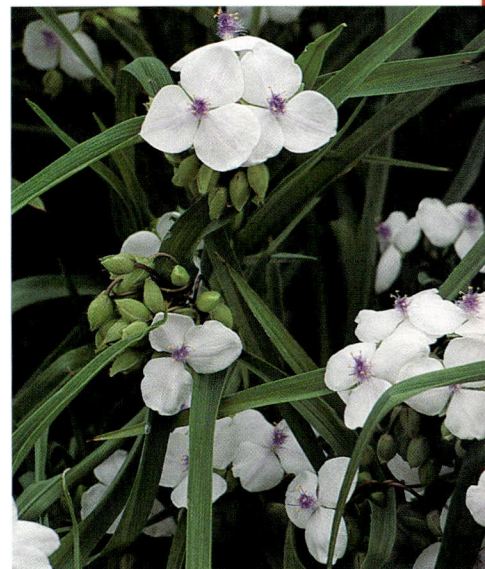

TALLER PERENNIALS
. . . flowers for picking, for filling under and around trees and shrubs, for cottage garden colour, for the middle and background of the flower border, for fragrance.

Acanthus mollis
BEAR'S BREECHES
1 m

A great filler for dry shade, *Acanthus mollis* is as much a shrub as it is a perennial, being strong growing, deep rooting and permanent, too vigorous for the average flower border. It is a native of the Mediterranean with large glossy leaves and striking upright spikes of purple and white flowers in summer and autumn. A strong accent plant, tolerant of clay soils, sun or shade.

Achillea cultivars
YARROW
60 cm

Lots of little flowers grouped together to form plate-like heads of colour on top of long sweeping stems, good for picking and many of them produced continuously over a long spring and summer season. They are also good as dried flowers. The 'Galaxy' hybrids come in shades of pink, red and apricot, very easy to grow in any average soil. 'Anthea' is a charming yellow-flowered form with silver foliage. Achilleas enjoy warm well-drained conditions and full sun. They tolerate dry soils and coastal conditions. The mass of uniquely shaped flower heads *en masse* makes good contrast among other flowers.

Achillea ptarmica 'The Pearl'
YARROW
60 cm

'The Pearl' is a vigorous-growing perennial, different from other achilleas with white flowers that look like giant gypsophila, perfect for picking. Flowers appear in late summer, continuing through autumn. Very easy to grow in any well-drained soil in full sun, tolerating dry conditions. Underground roots spread quickly but are not difficult to keep in check.

Achillea 'Galaxy' hybrid.

Agapanthus orientalis cultivars
AFRICAN LILY
1 m
Agapanthus is easy to grow in any soil, in sun or shade, and is indispensable for mass planting of banks or dry shady areas under trees, or lining driveways. The lush green strappy foliage is present all year round and the lovely long-stemmed flowers, lovely for picking, are a bonus in spring and summer. There are both blue- and white-flowered forms. All perform well on the coast, in clay or sandy soils, tolerating periods of drought or wet soils.

Ageratum houstonianum
FLOSS FLOWER
50 cm
One of the longest-flowering, easiest perennials for warm-climate gardens. In cold climates it can be grown as an annual. Flowers are bright blue, in fuzzy clusters at the end of long stems. They keep on coming right through the warm half of the year, providing valuable late autumn colour. Any reasonably drained soil in full sun will do. Cut back hard in winter.

Anemone xhybrida
JAPANESE ANEMONE, WINDFLOWER
Up to 90 cm
Easy to grow and useful for filling shady areas, Japanese anemone forms a dense weed-stopping cover of foliage and in autumn sends up long stems of charming pink or white flowers with yellow centres. This plant tolerates heavy soils, enjoying damp conditions. Good in wild or woodland gardens, or around deciduous trees, they will grow in sun or shade. Cut back spent flower stems and old foliage after flowering and the fresh new growth will soon appear.

Anthemis tinctoria
GOLDEN MARGUERITE
50 cm
A mounding plant spreading to about a metre with masses of bright yellow daisies over a long spring and summer period. Drought tolerant and excellent for coastal gardens, it tolerates dry soils. A relatively new variety, 'Sauce Hollandaise', has soft cream flowers with yellow centres. It grows taller, to 80 cm. Plant in full sun and trim after flowering.

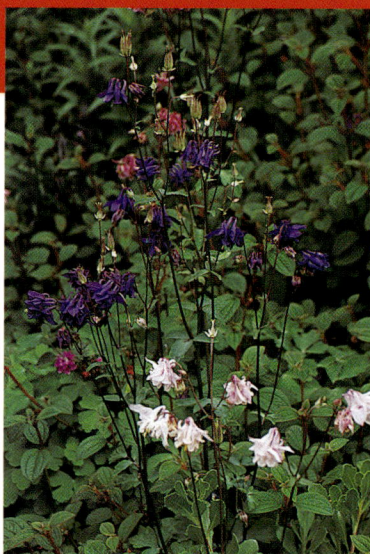

Aquilegia hybrids.

Aquilegia hybrids
GRANNY'S BONNET
50 cm
Foliage resembles a maidenhair fern and is an attractive year-round feature, especially in combination with bolder-leaved plants. The delicate airy flowers are produced freely in spring in a wide range of colours: purple, pink, yellow, and white. Most varieties set seed quite readily, but in general these are not long-lived perennials, needing replacing every few years. Cut plants back after flowering, leaving a few to develop seed pods for self-seeding. Full sun or part shade and reasonable drainage are required.

Argyranthemum frutescens cultivars
MARGUERITE DAISY
Up to 1 m
Quick, easy fillers and ideal for poor soils or coastal conditions, the marguerite daisies are well known for their easy cultivation. They grow and spread quickly into quite large woody plants, so give them space and cut them back hard, at least once a year after flowering. Prunings can be used to propagate new plants. Marguerites are generous plants, producing huge volumes of flowers almost all year round. Be prepared to replace them after a few years if they become untidy or too large. For small spaces or containers, plant the dwarf varieties such as the 'Elfin' hybrids. Plant in full sun or part shade and any reasonably drained soil.

Asclepias physocarpa
SWAN PLANT
1 m
Your first encounter with this plant was probably when you learned about the

life cycle of the Monarch butterfly. And that is why you would grow it now. You may need more than one plant to survive the population of caterpillars you will attract. Though perennial, a swan plant doesn't usually make it past the first year.

Asclepias tuberosa
BUTTERFLY BUSH
75 cm
This plant will also attract swarms of butterflies, but it is valued for its colourful flowers too. The bright orange flowers are produced in flattish heads on tall leafy plants during summer and autumn. Not always available as a growing plant, this one is best grown from seed, requiring good drainage and full sun. It is dormant in winter.

Aster novi-belgii cultivars
MICHAELMAS DAISY
Lots of small pink, blue, white or purple daisy flowers are crowded on to long stems perfect for picking. Michaelmas daisies are tough survivors, easy to grow in almost any soil, in sun or semi-shade. They will grow unattended, but with a little care will reward with better colours and flower forms. Those left to their own devices will revert to smaller, less-interesting forms. To look after them, give them plenty of space, lift and divide every year or two, and feed them occasionally.

Astilbe hybrids
FALSE SPIRAEA
20–90 cm
Feathery flower spikes and ferny foliage make a stunning show when this perennial is planted *en masse*. Astilbe is a moisture-loving perennial, perfect for the surround of ponds, enjoying semi-shade and any soil that does not dry out. There are many cultivars of various heights and colours; in shades of pink, lavender, red, cream or white.

Campanula
BELL FLOWER
Up to 2 m
Of the many tall-growing campanulas, *C. lactiflora* forms stand out among the easiest. They stand periods of drought and will even grow in dry shade. There are blue, pink and white

forms, growing up to 2 m with branching stems packed with starry bells. Plant in semi-shade and cut back after the spring flowering to encourage an autumn flush. Flowers are excellent for picking. Around a metre tall are the forms of *C. persicifolia*, in shades of blue, pink or white. From a leafy base it sends up straight pickable flower spikes reaching about a metre in height. The flowers are cup-shaped on unbranched stems. They enjoy sun or part shade, may need staking and should be lifted and divided every three or four years.

Canna cultivars
CANNA, INDIAN SHOT
1 m
Bold foliage and bright flowers are the hallmark of the ever-easy cannas. In northern parts they enjoy the warm climate and quickly form large clumps, ideal for low-maintenance mass planting in difficult soils. The colours are warm to hot: pinks, reds, oranges, yellows, making a continuous display from summer to autumn. Modern dwarf forms remain around a metre in height, but there are taller varieties up to 2 m or more. Cannas will die down if subjected to frost, but in cold climates the tubers can be lifted and stored over winter, just like a dahlia. In mild frosts the roots will stay dormant in the ground, sending up fresh foliage in spring. Mulching will give extra protection against the cold. For best flowering provide a warm location in full sun, summer watering and occasional fertiliser. A new canna grown especially for its foliage and making a dramatic statement in gardens or containers is 'Tropic Glow'. The foliage is brightly striped in red and orange tones. Orange flowers

Canna 'Tropic Glow'.

appear in summer, but can be removed to allow the foliage the limelight it deserves.

Clivia miniata
CLIVIA
50 cm
Among the most beautiful plants for dry shade, clivia has lush, dark green, strappy foliage and round heads of bright orange flowers. They appear in winter and are valuable for picking. Clivias never seem to have an untidy stage, remaining robust and healthy year round. In a warm climate they are grown to perfection in clumps under deciduous trees. The requirements are shade, frost protection and good drainage. In frosty climates they are best grown in containers. Dry conditions are best for flower production. Too much water over autumn may inhibit flowering.

Coreopsis verticillata 'Moonbeam'
TICKSEED, CALLIOPSIS
40 cm
Far too pretty to deserve such an uninspiring common name, this yellow-flowered perennial is a top performer and is extremely easy to grow. It is drought resistant, good for coastal gardens, and flowers from spring through to autumn. The flowers are daisy-like, yellow with darker centres. The foliage is light and airy. Different cultivars are in varying shades of yellow. 'Moonbeam' is a deserving favourite, very prolific with lemon-yellow flowers, but all are easy to grow. Coreopsis looks good in combination with other perennials and enjoys full sun.

Cynara scolymus
GLOBE ARTICHOKE
1.5 m
Even if you have yet to discover the culinary delights of the globe artichoke, it makes a wonderfully striking feature for the garden, whether it be among herbs, vegetables or flowering perennials. These giant Scotch thistles have huge silver leaves and never go unnoticed. Grow them as a centrepiece to lower-growing plants rather than mixed with tall perennials, and give them plenty of space. They grow at least as wide as they are tall. The purple flowers appear in summer, unless you eat

them first. Full sun and a well-drained soil are required.

Diascia rigescens
TWINSPUR
50 cm
Rich pink tubular flowers are densely packed on to the end of upward-arching stems, providing months of colour through summer and autumn. A short-lived perennial that needs replacing every two or three years, but easily grown from cuttings in autumn. It grows best in a sunny position in well-drained soil with plenty of moisture.

Echinacea purpurea
CONE FLOWER
1 m
Lovely rose-purple, long-lasting daisy flowers on long stems appear above coarse-textured leaves in summer and autumn. There is also a white form. As long as they have good drainage, echinaceas will thrive, resisting dry conditions and impoverished soils. The flowers are good for picking and blend well with other perennials in a mixed border. Plant in full sun.

Echium candicans (syn. E. fastuosum)
PRIDE OF MADEIRA
1.2 m
For poor dry soils and coastal climates, echiums are not to be overlooked. The biennial species grow very tall indeed, 3 or 4 m with huge single flower spikes above giant rosettes of foliage. This is a perennial form, a branching shrubby plant with lots of flower spikes, closely packed with deep lavender-blue flowers in late spring. Sun and a well-drained soil are essential. Echiums despise wet feet.

Euphorbia charachias
SPURGE
1 m
This is a shrubby perennial ideal for mass planting in dry locations and providing attractive winter flowers, good for picking. The blue-green leaves are crowded on to reddish stems with terminal flowerheads of bright lime green. After flowering, cut back the stems to the base and fresh growth will sprout ready for next winter's flowerheads. A sunny position is best.

Euphorbia 'Jade Dragon'
SPURGE
80 cm
An exciting new euphorbia with distinctive blue-green foliage and a compact habit. The large lime-green flowers emerge from attractive winter buds in spring. Give 'Jade Dragon' a well-drained soil and full sun.

Gaura lindheimeri 'Whirling Butterflies'
75 cm
Right through summer and autumn, masses of airy pink-and-white flowers on long stems sway in the breeze. This pretty perennial is very easy to grow, tolerating dry soil. It is a good background plant to lower-growing perennials and annuals and is useful for picking.

Helianthus salicifolius 'Golden Pyramid'
AUTUMN GLORY
This is one of the sunflower family. Though nowhere near as large as the common sunflower, the flowers of autumn glory are produced in such masses that they are just as eye-catching. They appear in late summer and autumn, generally on quite tall plants. 'Golden Pyramid' is a compact form, suited to most situations. Plant in well-drained soil in full sun.

Heliotropium arborescens
CHERRY PIE
50 cm to 1 m
It is the sweet chocolatey fragrance that makes this plant so highly desirable in the summer garden, but it is good to look at too. The flowers are violet blue, the foliage green with purple overtones, colours varying slightly between cultivars. Cherry pie fits well in mixed flower borders and can be grown in containers. It is treated as an annual in frosty climates. It grows well in any average soil with reasonable drainage and enjoys humidity. Mature plants become woody and shrub-like. Cut back by at least half in autumn. Plant in full sun or semi-shade for very hot areas.

Hemerocallis cultivars
DAY LILY
50 cm to1 m
Each flower only lasts a day, but the next day there will be one to replace it and there are plenty on display at a time. With their flaxy foliage and continuous crops of flowers through summer and autumn, day lilies provide both texture and colour. They look wonderful mass planted or in a mixed flower border, performing well with a minimum of attention. There is a range of colours, plenty for hot colour themes and pastels too. They will tolerate heavy soils and grow happily in part shade, although they flower better in full sun. Some are evergreen, others are deciduous and go dormant in winter. They range in height from about 50 cm to 1 m. Among the best are:
'Aztec Gold', large golden yellow, evergreen.
'Green Flutter', greenish-yellow flowers, deciduous.
'Moon Goddess', soft lemon with ruffled edges, evergreen.
'Rose Tapestry', cream flushed pink, deciduous.
'Russian Rhapsody', lavender, evergreen.
'Seventh Symphony', large deep red with gold centre, deciduous.
'Stella d'Oro', golden yellow flowers, deciduous.
'Taylormade', bright burnt orange, evergreen.

Kniphofia cultivars
RED HOT POKER
1.5 m
Grassy foliage and upright stems of flame-coloured flower spikes. There are a number of species, with orange or yellow flowers. Red hot pokers flower for a long time over summer and autumn and do well in coastal gardens. Good planted in groups, and appealing in unison with equally easy blue-flowered agapanthus. Plant in full sun and almost any soil.

Lavandula spp. and cultivars
LAVENDER
Up to 1 m
Shrubs really but listed here to remind you to include them in your flower garden. They are ideal companions for flowering perennials and roses.

More about lavenders: Go to page 41.

Lavatera thuringiaca 'Barnsley'
MALLOW
2 m
This perennial grows quickly to fill a sizeable space, and the long spring-into-summer smothering of soft pink flowers with darker centres is a stunning sight. A very 'cottagey' perennial. It is easy to grow in average well-drained soil in full sun. Prune hard after flowering or in early spring.

Lobelia xspeciosa 'Queen Victoria'
90 cm
Dark foliage is set against scarlet flowers in summer and autumn. A damp soil and a position with some afternoon shade is best.

Lupinus Russell hybrids
RUSSELL LUPIN
1.5 m
Stunning Russell lupins with their long pickable spikes of colourful flowers thrive in cold climates. In a warm climate they are short lived, best treated as annuals, with fewer flower spikes per plant. They love full sun, a dry sandy or pumice-based soil and acid conditions, and require lifting and dividing every few years.

Lychnis coronaria
ROSE CAMPION
With grey foliage and summer flowers of white or pink, this is a popular perennial for cottage gardens. It is happiest in well-drained soil and full sun and performs well in coastal gardens.

Pelargonium citrosum
REPELARGONIUM, LEMON-SCENTED PELARGONIUM
The lemon fragrance of the foliage is pleasant to humans but repels insects such as mosquitoes. Repelargonium is a large and fast grower, with small pink summer flowers. Easily trimmed to control size.

Penstemon cultivars
PENSTEMON
Up to 1 m
Penstemons are easy-to-grow, summer-flowering perennials, very free flowering and good for picking. They have attractive rich green foliage and tall stems with colourful trumpet flowers. Give them full sun and an

average garden soil. The range of cultivars is huge. Some of the best are: 'Snowstorm' (cream flowers, 70 cm tall), 'Alice Hindley' (pale lilac with a white throat, 90 cm tall), 'Susan' (soft pink, 90 cm tall), and 'Firebird' (deep red, 90 cm tall).

Phygelius aequalis 'Yellow Trumpet'
CAPE FIGWORT
1 m

Tubular trumpet flowers are soft creamy-yellow, hanging in clusters from long leafy stems and continuing to flower from summer into winter. This is a shrubby perennial good for the back of the flower border. Flowers are useful for picking. Grow 'Yellow Trumpet' in sun or part shade in a well-drained soil. Prune in spring.**

Primula spp.
CANDELABRA PRIMULA, BOG PRIMULA
Up to 1 m

Bog primulas flower in early summer and provide colour to water gardens. They produce tall stems with flowers arranged in tiers. Colours are wide ranging: reds, yellows, blues, pinks, purples, orange. A pond edge is a favourite position. They thrive in deep rich soil that never dries out in part shade. Plants are dormant in winter, except for the species *P. prolifera* (syn. *P. heladoxa*), the easiest of the bog primulas, which is evergreen. It has very tall 1 m stems of bright yellow flowers and grows well in a warm climate.

Rudbeckia fulgida 'Goldsturm'
CONE FLOWER, BLACK-EYED SUSAN
70 cm

This autumn-flowering perennial is a sunflower relative. The brilliant gold flowers have distinguishing black centres. They are easy to grow in full sun and well-drained soil. Flowers are good for picking and look fabulous mass planted in the middle or at the back of a perennial border.

Salvia leucantha
MEXICAN BUSH SAGE
1 m

This one-among-many sages has bright violet flowers at the end of long branches densely clothed in silvery-green leaves. It is a wonderful plant for autumn flowering, continuing on into winter. Flowers are good for picking.

As with most salvias, full sun and a well-drained soil is needed. Sandy soils are ideal and it likes coastal conditions.

Salvia madrensis
MEXICAN SAGE
1.8 m

An impressive yellow-flowered sage with a shrubby habit and large plumes of flowers on long stems for picking. It flowers from late summer into winter. Provide a well-drained soil and full sun.

Salvia uliginosa
BOG SAGE
2 m

A preference for heavy soils is an endearing feature of this very pretty blue-flowered perennial. It flowers on and on through summer and autumn with its sky-blue flowers set upon long straight stems. Plant in full sun or light shade in moist soil.

Sedum spectabile cultivars
STONECROP
60 cm

Stonecrop is a succulent perennial, ideal for hot dry places but growing easily in any average garden soil, thriving in heavy soils, which is unusual for a succulent. The fleshy light green foliage makes an interesting textural contrast and is further enhanced with the onset of the flattened flowerheads of bright red, pink, yellow or purple. This is a long-flowering perennial for full sun or part shade, easily increased from cuttings and just needing a cut back after flowering.

Sidalcea hybrids
PRAIRIE MALLOW
1 m

Close relatives of hollyhocks but not as tall, sidalceas are splendid cottage-garden perennials. One plant produces many spikes of saucer-shaped flowers in shades of pink. They prefer full sun and a moist, well-drained soil. Like hollyhocks they are susceptible to rust in a warm climate but are otherwise easy to grow.

Sisyrinchium striatum
SATIN FLOWER
60 cm

Wonderful tall creamy-yellow flowers with spiky foliage are easy to grow in light soil in sun or part shade. They look great mass planted and are good for picking.

ABOVE: *Sedum spectabile.*
LEFT: *Rudbeckia* 'Goldsturm'.

Zantedeschia aethiopica 'Little Child'
DWARF ARUM LILY
60 cm

The easy-care arum lily grows wild in northern parts, but is too lovely to be called a weed. The large lush leaves and stunning white spring flowers are valuable contributors to shady areas of a garden. The flowers are great for picking. This dwarf form has downscaled flowers and foliage but is otherwise the same, and just as easy to grow. A moist composty soil in part shade is ideal.

Bulbs

Bulbs are responsible for some of the most spectacular seasonal flower displays. Such beauty is remarkably easy to create, for bulbs come complete with a ready-to-use growth support system. Between flowering seasons bulbs store their energy in various kinds of specialised root or stem tissue, all of which are popularly referred to as bulbs. As well as true bulbs, there are also corms, tubers, and tuberous roots. All are perennial in their native habitat, but if the prevailing climate or soil type doesn't suit, bulbs cannot regenerate sufficiently for a repeat performance the following season. In such cases they are best treated as annuals. For example, tulips are best treated as annuals in a warm climate, and freesias are best as annuals or container plants in a cold climate.

Ranunculus.

GETTING THE BEST FROM YOUR BULBS

PLANTING FOR IMPACT

If you have only a few bulbs, perhaps a dozen tulips, it is best to plant them all in one group rather than scatter them throughout the garden.

COMPANION PLANTS

Bulbs are very effective flowering in unison with annuals. The best effects are the simple ones. For example, tulips look terrific rising above a sea of forget-me-nots; bright yellow daffodils look great with blue or purple flowers. Try them with violas or pansies.

When extra colour is required in autumn and winter while the bulbs get ready to flower, annuals such as primulas or pansies can be planted over the bulbs. Pansies will flower from bulb planting time right through to lifting time. Bulbs that have an untidy post-flowering stage can be surrounded by annuals or perennials that have a growth spurt in early summer and will flop over the fading bulb foliage and steal the show with their flowers.

NATURALISING BULBS

For a natural look and a minimum of fuss, some bulbs can be planted in permanent position to flower year after year. Ideally they'll multiply to produce an ever-increasing number of spring blooms. Daffodils are a classic example. Depending on climate, many other bulbs can be grown in this way.

Bulbs for naturalising in the north include snowflakes, Spanish bluebells, and many of the South African natives. Crocus, bluebells, snowdrops and even tulips are suitable for naturalising where winters are cold.

How to Grow Bulbs

Sun or shade?

Most bulbs require good light to flower well. A position in full sun is generally best but in warmer areas the cool-climate bulbs such as tulips and hyacinths will enjoy a position in part shade. Few bulbs will grow in dense shade, but the light shade of a deciduous tree can be ideal. Shade lovers for naturalising under deciduous trees include erythroniums and bluebells. Beware of planting bulbs near trees if the soil is dry during the bulb's autumn–spring growing season. Extra feeding may be necessary to make up for the competition from tree roots. Use lots of compost as a soil conditioner and mulch.

The soil

Good drainage is essential. Improve heavy soils by adding generous quantities of well-matured compost, peat or coarse materials such as sand or pumice. These need to be dug into the soil to a depth of at least 50 cm, well below the planting depth of the bulbs. If in doubt, the safest and easiest way is to plant the bulbs in containers or raised beds. Sandy soils require more frequent watering and feeding. It is a good idea to improve the water-holding capacity of sandy soils with the addition of compost. The lighter the soil, the deeper the bulbs should be planted.

More about soils:
Go to page 3.

More about compost:
Go to page 196.

Planting time

Spring-flowering bulbs are planted in autumn. Summer- and autumn-flowering bulbs are planted in spring. To a certain extent planting time is dictated by climate. In a warm climate, those from a cold climate (such as tulips) are planted later, often as late as early winter. In a cold climate, frost-tender spring bulbs can planted in spring for summer flowering. For full details see the chart on the next page.

Planting depth

A general rule is to plant bulbs twice as deep as their width. The larger the bulb, the deeper they are planted. In warm areas, cool-climate bulbs are planted deeper, where the soil is cooler, up to 20 cm deep. In cool climates, tender bulbs will receive some protection from frost if planted deeply. Also, the lighter the soil, the deeper one should plant. If in doubt, err on the shallow side. Many bulbs have contractile roots, which pull them deeper into the soil until they find their optimum depth.

Spacing

There is no exact spacing for bulbs. It is a matter of balancing the space needed to multiply with what is best for a good display. The closer the bulbs are planted, the more they will compete for light, nutrients and water — but the better the effect.

Bulbs grown in pots or those lifted each year can be planted more densely than those left in the ground to multiply. Those that don't tend to multiply, such as tulips in a warm climate, can be planted closest of all.

Bulbs that are grown permanently in the ground are best given some room to multiply. The closer they are planted, the sooner they will become overcrowded and will require lifting and dividing.

BULB CALENDAR

WARM CLIMATE (Auckland, Northland, Bay of Plenty)

PLANT

	Summer D	J	F	Autumn M	A	M	Winter J	J	A	Spring S	O	N
Allium				•	•	•						
Anemone			•	•	•	•						
Babiana				•	•	•						
Brodiaea				•	•	•						
Crocus					•	•						
Erythronium			•	•								
Freesia			•	•		•						
Gladiolus nanus			•	•	•							
Hyacinthus					•	•						
Ipheion			•	•		•						
Iris				•	•	•						
Ixia			•	•		•						
Lachenalia			•	•		•						
Muscari				•	•	•	•					
Narcissus				•	•	•						
Ranunculus			•	•		•						
Sparaxis			•	•		•						
Tritonia			•	•		•						
Tulipa					•	•						
Watsonia			•	•		•						

IN FLOWER

	Summer D	J	F	Autumn M	A	M	Winter J	J	A	Spring S	O	N
Allium	•	•									•	•
Anemone								•	•	•	•	
Babiana									•		•	
Brodiaea	•	•										•
Crocus								•	•		•	
Erythronium								•	•	•	•	•
Freesia								•	•	•	•	•
Gladiolus nanus									•		•	
Hyacinthus								•		•	•	
Ipheion									•	•	•	
Iris								•	•	•	•	•
Ixia	•								•	•	•	•
Lachenalia								•	•		•	
Muscari									•	•	•	
Narcissus							•	•	•	•	•	
Ranunculus									•	•	•	•
Sparaxis	•									•	•	•
Tritonia	•									•	•	•
Tulipa									•	•	•	
Watsonia	•									•	•	

COLD CLIMATE (Central North Island and south)

PLANT

= plant in pots

	Summer D	J	F	Autumn M	A	M	Winter J	J	A	Spring S	O	N
Allium				•	•	•						
Anemone			#	#	#	#						
Babiana				#	#	#				•	•	
Brodiaea				•	•	•						
Crocus				•	•	•						
Erythronium			•	•								
Freesia				#	#	#				•	•	
Gladiolus nanus			#	#	#							
Hyacinthus				•	•	•						
Ipheion			#	#	#							
Iris				•	•	•						
Ixia			#	#						•	•	
Lachenalia			#	#								
Muscari				•	•	•						
Narcissus			•	•	•							
Ranunculus			#	#	#							
Sparaxis			#	#						•	•	
Tritonia			#	#						•	•	
Tulipa				•	•	•						

IN FLOWER

	Summer D	J	F	Autumn M	A	M	Winter J	J	A	Spring S	O	N
Allium	•	•										•
Anemone										•	•	•
Babiana										•	•	•
Brodiaea	•	•										
Crocus								•	•	•		
Erythronium										•	•	•
Freesia										•	•	
Gladiolus nanus	•											
Hyacinthus										•	•	•
Ipheion											•	•
Iris										•	•	•
Ixia	•	•										
Lachenalia											•	
Muscari										•	•	•
Narcissus									•	•	•	•
Ranunculus										•	•	
Sparaxis	•	•										•
Tritonia	•	•										•
Tulipa									•		•	•

WATERING

Bulbs should be kept evenly moist from planting time until the leaves turn yellow. Over-watering is a more common problem than under-watering. Few bulbs will last long in a waterlogged soil. While dormant most bulbs will tolerate drought conditions; some absolutely require a dry rest in summer.

FEEDING

Bulbs you buy come with their own packed lunch. Without fertiliser they will probably still flower in the first year, though flower size and quality may suffer. Also, the following season's bulbs will not develop to their full potential. Bulbs like daffodils need feeding during the growing season in order to perform well the following year. Bulbs in pots need feeding more often than those in the ground.

When planting in the garden, use a bulb food at the rate of 200 g per square metre, spread evenly over the surface or mixed in thoroughly to about the depth the bulbs will be planted. Do not add fertiliser directly to each planting hole. At the same time top-dress bulbs already in the ground from last year. Ideally make another application, at the rate of 100 g per square metre, directly after flowering.

In pots, use a balanced slow-release fertiliser. Mix it into the potting mix at planting time and follow up with a fast-acting liquid fertiliser, such as Phostrogen®, once the shoots appear.

Never use fresh animal manures with bulbs. These will cause burning and increase the likelihood of disease.

More about watering:
Go to page 202.

More about fertilisers:
Go to page 200.

Ipheion.

More about mulching:
Go to page 204.

MULCHING

Mulching helps keep the soil cool in warm climates and provides some frost protection in cold climates. It discourages weed growth and contributes to the overall well-being of the soil. A 5–10 cm layer of fine bark, peat, well-rotted compost or straw is the most effective. A mulch spread too thickly may inhibit flowering by blocking out too much light.

BULB PESTS

As pests and diseases often occur in warm weather, winter-growing spring bulbs escape many of the problems experienced by warm-weather growers. However, from time to time, some of the following will make their presence felt.

SLUGS AND SNAILS:

Slugs and snails are the most universally damaging bulb pests. They relish the young shoots of emerging bulbs so be ready with snail bait. Hyacinths are particularly vulnerable.

Dutch iris.

BULB FLY:

Narcissus flies are the most troublesome enemies of daffodils. They also attack other bulbs such as tulips, hyacinths, snowflakes and snowdrops. Flowers from infected bulbs will be poor or non-existent. Infected bulbs will feel soft and light, most noticeably around the neck. If unsure, cut some open for inspection. The maggot can be seen inside the bulb. Avoid planting infected bulbs. Any that become infected should be dug up and burned. For some measure of protection, mound and compact the soil surrounding the base of the leaves as they die down after flowering. This hinders the entrance of the fly. A sprinkling of diazinon granules (Soil Insect Killer) can also be worked into the soil.

APHIDS:

Bulbs do not always escape the ravages of these common garden pests. Particularly vulnerable are tulips, irises, and ranunculus when the weather starts to warm up. Aphids suck the sap and disfigure the flowers. They are also capable of spreading tulip and iris viruses, for which there is no cure. Viruses generally weaken plants and cause markings (such as white stripes) on the petals. Virus-infected bulbs should be destroyed.

Fortunately, aphids are fat-bodied creatures fond of crowds, so they are easily seen and can be controlled before the damage is done.

More about pests and diseases: Go to page 215.

THRIPS:

Thrips attack in hot, dry weather. They are well known for their affect on summer-flowering gladioli and dahlias, rasping the foliage and distorting the flowers.

DISEASES

Diseases may affect the actual bulbs or the growing bulb plants. Storage conditions for bulbs should be dry, well ventilated and cool. Downy mildew occurs in cool wet weather. The first sign of attack is a white downy growth on the foliage. Spray at first sight with a fungicide such as Fungus and Mildew Spray®.

Powdery mildew is most common during summer. It appears as a white powder on leaves and buds. Ranunculus and anemones that are in leaf in late summer and autumn are susceptible to powdery mildew.

LIFTING BULBS

The main reasons for lifting bulbs are to protect them from unfavourable soil conditions in their dormant season and to divide the clumps. Dividing is necessary to prevent overcrowding (which inhibits flowering) and is an easy way to propagate new plants.

Some bulbs, such as ranunculus, deteriorate to the extent that it is not worth the effort to lift them. They are thus usually treated as annuals with new bulbs purchased each autumn. This has certain advantages. New planting schemes can be experimented with each year. Bold displays can be made by planting bulbs close together as there is no need to allow space for them to multiply.

Other bulbs are lifted and replanted the following autumn. Many will not thrive in soil that is watered over summer. Bulbs in irrigated flower gardens are therefore best lifted once the foliage has died down. The gap can be filled with summer-flowering annuals until the bulbs are replanted.

In a well-drained soil, many are happy to be left in the ground to 'naturalise'. Daffodils are a classic example, but if your daffodils seem to be flowering less prolifically than in the past, the problem may simply be that it is time to lift and separate them.

For easy lifting and to minimise the disturbance to other plants in the garden it is best to plant bulbs in good-sized groups. Furthermore, the job of lifting is made a lot easier by planting bulbs in special plastic baskets, which are buried under the soil. Sometimes contractile roots will pull bulbs deep into the soil so that they are hard to find when lifting. Baskets are the ideal way to get around this problem.

Spring-flowering bulbs are lifted in late spring or summer. This should be done as soon as convenient after the foliage has turned yellow. The longer they are left in the ground, the more susceptible they will become to pest and disease problems. Place markers next to clumps to be lifted before the foliage has gone completely.

Loosen each clump with a spade and lift it with a fork. Separate the bulbs and discard any that are soft or damaged. Small bulbs that are not wanted for growing on can also be discarded, saving the biggest, healthiest specimens for next season's flowers.

STORING BULBS

Bulbs in storage must be kept dry. Any moisture will encourage diseases to attack. Bulbs should be dried completely in flat trays before being put into containers. Net or paper bags are best. Plastic bags should be avoided. A cool well-ventilated shed is ideal. Cool-climate bulbs, such as tulips, grown in warm climates should be stored in the fridge for six to eight weeks prior to planting. This is essential for such bulbs to flower well. Do not store warm-climate bulbs such as freesias in the fridge.

Bulbs in pots

Containers extend the possibilities in even the largest of gardens. This is especially true of bulbs.

Bulbs become immediately more noticeable in containers than they would in the garden. Even a few bulbs will stand out in a well-placed pot. In the garden, you generally need to plant more to make the same impact.

Drainage is the overriding requirement for successful bulb culture. Unsuitable soils can be improved or raised beds can be built, but the easiest way to ensure good drainage is to grow bulbs in pots in a well-drained potting mix. In summer the very porous nature of terracotta can be a nuisance, but for spring bulbs that grow through the wet winter the extra drainage is an advantage.

Grown in pots, warm-climate bulbs can be enjoyed in cold climates. The cool-climate bulbs are more easily managed in warm climates. Pots can be kept in a cool shady place until they flower, moved into pride of place for flowering and out of sight again once flowering has finished.

Bulbs in pots look best if planted generously so that the pots look full. They can be planted so that they are almost touching. It is generally best to lift and repot them each year. In deep pots bulbs can be planted in two or three layers. This allows more bulbs per pot and also extends the flowering season, the deepest bulbs flowering slightly later.

Bulbs in pots need more feeding than those in the ground. It is better to feed a small amount often than a lot at once. Monthly feeds with a balanced liquid fertiliser will supplement the slow-release nutrients already in the potting mix. Liquid feeding can begin as soon as the first shoots appear and continue until the leaves start to turn yellow.

It is important that the potting mix doesn't dry out during the growing season. Special care is needed to prevent summer-planted bulbs, such as anemones and ranunculus, from drying out.

Use your best, freshly purchased bulbs for pots. They can be planted in the garden the following year.

PROBLEM SHOOTING — WHY BULBS FAIL TO FLOWER

Bulbs are not difficult to grow but sometimes things go wrong.
If your bulbs failed to flower, it will most likely be for one of the following reasons:

1. **TOO WET.** There is nothing bulbs hate more than poor drainage. Root growth will suffer, flowering will be poor and bulbs will rot. If soil drainage is beyond help, grow your bulbs in pots or raised beds in potting mix. Ensure pots have adequate drainage.

2. **TOO DRY.** Don't allow the soil or potting mix to dry out from the time they are planted until flowering has finished and the leaves start to fade. The most vulnerable are bulbs such as anemones planted in summer while the weather is still dry.

3. **TOO WARM.** Bulbs from cold climates need a certain period of cold temperatures in order to flower properly. Tulip or hyacinth bulbs planted too early, while the soil is still warm, may fail to flower.

4. **TOO COLD.** Bulbs that come from warm climates need protection from frosts in order to do well in a cold climate.

5. **TOO SHADY.** Although cold-climate bulbs enjoy a cold shady spot while they develop roots and shoots, with a few exceptions most bulbs must have good light in order to flower. Erythroniums are among the few that prefer shade. Cold-climate bulbs enjoy some shade in a hot climate and will flower on the southern side of the house where there is plenty of reflected (but indirect) light.

6. **TOO DEEP.** In a warm climate deep planting is recommended for cool-climate bulbs, but below about 25 cm the soil temperatures remain constant so there is no advantage in planting deeper than this. If bulbs are planted too deeply shoots may not be able to push their way to the surface and at best the result may be short stems.

7. **TOO SHALLOW.** If planted too shallow, bulbs can be susceptible to drying out or damage during cultivation of the soil surface. They may also receive too much light for healthy root and shoot development. Bulbs grown in pots for indoors are often planted with their tips exposed. In this case it is necessary to keep bulbs away from light until the shoot has emerged.

8. **PESTS AND DISEASES** (see pages 116–17).

Often bulbs will flower in their first year after planting but not in the following year.
The reason could be any of the above but more likely one or more of the following:

1. **FOLIAGE REMOVED TOO EARLY**. The foliage should be allowed to die down naturally to allow new bulbs to be produced for the next year's flowering. Where daffodils are grown in lawn, the lawn must be left unmown for about six weeks after flowering. In the garden it is best to disguise the leaves by planting perennials and annuals and avoid the temptation to cut or tie the fading foliage.

2. **BULBS ROTTED.** Most bulbs prefer a warm dry summer if they are to be left in the ground to multiply. Too much warmth and moisture renders bulbs susceptible to disease.

3. **WRONG CLIMATE.** In a warm climate many cold-climate bulbs will simply refuse to reproduce successfully. They need cool temperatures to produce healthy new bulbs and to initiate next season's flower buds. Bulbs such as tulips will not last long if left in the ground permanently.

Allium

Allium is a large genus, which includes onions, garlic, and chives, garden enemies such as onion weed, as well as some very lovely ornamentals. The two ornamentals most freely available in New Zealand are *A. moly* and *A. christophii* (syn. *A. albopilosum*). They are easy to grow in all but the hottest subtropical gardens, remaining in the ground for years without the need for lifting.

A. moly (golden garlic) is a low-growing plant with delightful star-like, bright yellow flowers, which are excellent for picking. It enjoys sun or part shade and looks good with herbs or perennials, in pots or naturalised under deciduous trees where it increases easily by bulb offsets.

A. christophii (star of Persia) will add late spring drama to any garden. The huge, metallic violet flowerheads appear quite futuristic on their long stems. The flowers last a very long time and even look great sitting in the garden once they've dried out. As dried flowers for indoor arrangements they are superb.

Anemone

Anemone coronaria is the brightly coloured 'poppy anemone'. The flowers are especially good for picking, being long lasting and strong stemmed. They are valuable for both garden and vase from early winter when other flowers are not in plentiful supply.

There are two main strains: the double-flowered St Brigid hybrids and the single-flowered De Caens hybrids. The small globular tubers can be planted as soon as they are available in late summer, but if planting while the weather is still dry be sure to keep the soil well watered and, ideally, apply a mulch. By planting tubers at two- or three-weekly intervals from February to May you will have continuous flowering from mid-winter through spring.

Choose a warm sunny position in a well-drained soil. Soaking the tubers in water for a few hours prior to planting helps them to establish quickly. Tubers are planted with the flat side facing upwards (and the pointed side downwards), but because of the knobbly shape of the tuber it is sometimes difficult to tell which side is which. If you are not sure, plant the tubers on their sides and the roots will soon pull them the right way up.

The poppy anemones originate from relatively warm climates. Pots are the best way to grow them in frosty climates. After their first season of heavy flowering, any anemone tubers that have survived are likely to be weak and susceptible to disease. It's not worth trying to keep them for a second season's flowering. Instead, plant fresh tubers each autumn. Fortunately, they are cheap enough to be treated as annuals.

A. blanda is less flamboyant than its poppy-flowered cousins, but just as desirable and better suited to a cooler climate. It looks especially superb when grown in a low pot. The short-stemmed daisy-like flowers are in shades of blue, pink or white and the lacy foliage makes a dark green carpet. The plant grows about 15 cm tall. *A. blanda* is frost hardy. It likes sun or part shade and suits mass planting under deciduous trees.

Babiana

Babiana or 'Baboon flower' is native to South Africa. Like its freesia relatives, it thrives in warm parts of the country where it is extremely easy to grow in most soils and can be left in the ground for years. The funnel-shaped flowers are clustered on spikes 30 cm tall. 'Blue Star' is a deservedly popular form with large flowers in rich shades of blue and violet. In frosty climates babianas can be grown in pots under shelter. Plant in autumn in a well-drained garden soil in full sun. Lifting is only necessary every few years to prevent overcrowding, or if the soil is wet over summer.

Brodiaea

Brodiaea laxa (syn. *Triteleia laxa*) is an attractive Californian native. It flowers over a long period from late spring into summer and is easy to grow throughout New Zealand. It can be left in the ground to naturalise.

The stunning blue flowers, looking not unlike a miniature agapanthus, are long stemmed and excellent for cutting. The cultivar 'Queen Fabiola' is especially handsome. It is very effective in perennial borders, especially with silver-foliaged plants.

Brodiaeas are best planted in groups. Plant the bulbs in autumn in well-drained soil and full sun. In frosty areas protect the bulbs with a mulch 10 cm thick.

Crocus

Winter-flowering crocus are native to the northern hemisphere where they flower in great droves, magnificent against the snow in scenes that warm-climate gardeners can only marvel at.

In New Zealand they'll thrive and multiply in most South Island gardens but in mild climates do not regenerate so easily. In their first year bulbs will flower well, but in northern regions it is best to treat them as annuals and plant new bulbs each year.

Make the most of them by planting in pots so that they can be appreciated at close quarters. They can be planted close together for a truly brilliant display. Plant in autumn and keep them as cool as possible. When shoots appear move pots into a sunny spot to flower. This may be a bright room indoors.

Erythronium

Erythroniums or 'trout lilies' hail from evergreen forest regions of North America. The flowers resemble small nodding lilies and are among the few bulbs that revel in a shady position. They thrive in a rich, moist, well-drained soil. During the winter–spring growing season plenty of moisture is required, but in summer they enjoy the relative dryness created by the surrounding roots of trees and shrubs. Unlike most other bulbous plants, the fleshy corms of the trout lily will not survive if allowed to dry out completely and must not be left out of the ground for too long.

Buy corms early, ensuring that they have been appropriately packaged to prevent drying out. Plant them straight away in late summer or early autumn.

Trout lilies look spectacular flowering in large drifts under deciduous trees where they will happily multiply. They dislike being disturbed and should only be lifted and divided every few years to prevent overcrowding.

Although they come from cold climates and do very well in our coldest regions, trout lilies are less fussy in warm climates than many other cool-climate bulbs, especially as they flower in the shade. In cold climates more sun will be tolerated.

E. tuolumnense has dainty, bright yellow flowers held above the leaves on a delicate 20–30 cm stem. *E.* 'Pagoda' is a stunning large-flowered hybrid with creamy-yellow flowers and large marbled leaves. It reaches about 45 cm tall in flower. *E.* 'White Beauty' has large white flowers and green-brown mottled leaves.

Freesia

Fragrant freesias are easy to grow. They have a long flowering season with lots of flowers on each stem. Perfect as cut flowers, freesias come in a wide range of beautiful colours, and they are well suited to growing in pots.

In all but the very coldest New Zealand climates, freesias thrive and multiply easily. In areas with severe or prolonged frosts they can be grown in pots or planted after the last frost to flower in summer. Good drainage and a sunny position are required. Freesias are not fond of being overcrowded by other plants so are best given their own pockets of soil and planted in groups.

As long as they are in a well-drained soil, freesias do not need to be lifted every summer but can be left in the ground to multiply. The foliage should be allowed to die down naturally if flowering is going to be as good the following year. Freesias grown in the ground in frosty climates should be lifted in autumn once the foliage has faded and stored in a dark dry place until planted the following spring.

By raising in pots for indoors, flowers can be had from June until Christmas — even in a cold climate. Plant some in late summer for winter flowering, and another potful each month through to August. Water gently after planting and place in a cool shady position until shoots appear, when they can be brought indoors. Flowers appear about eight weeks after planting and flowering continues for up to eight weeks. Before planting, store corms in a dark, well-ventilated shed or room, and not in plastic bags.

Gladiolus

There are a number of gladioli that grow through winter to flower in the spring. Of these, two of the loveliest are the Nanus hybrids and *G. tristis*. The Nanus hybrids or 'miniature gladioli', are smaller versions of their summer-flowering cousins, with softer-coloured flowers. 'The Bride' has pure white flowers with a green-tinged throat. 'Nymph' is pure white with a rose flare. 'Guernsey Glory' is soft purple with red petal margins and white markings. There are many more. *G. tristis* has soft creamy-yellow flowers, which are superbly scented at night. The long leaves are fine and rush-like. Ideally, the corms of spring-flowering gladioli are lifted in summer once the foliage has died down and stored in a dry place until they are planted again in autumn. In a well-drained soil they can be left in the ground with varying success, but are best when the soil is dry in summer.

Hyacinthoides (Bluebells)

The bluebell most easily grown throughout New Zealand is the Spanish bluebell, *H. hispanica* (syn. *Scilla hispanica* and *Endymion campanulata*). They will cope with warm climates as well as frost and even tolerate quite heavy soils. Spanish bluebells naturalise happily in semi-shade. There are pink- and white-flowered forms as well as blue. The English bluebell, *H. non-scriptus* (syn. *Scilla non-scripta* and *Endymion non-scriptus*), does best in a cold climate. The flowers are smaller than those of Spanish bluebells.

Bluebells both look and perform best when planted in groups beneath deciduous trees and shrubs in the more informal parts of the garden. Dappled shade and a cool soil rich in humus is what they love best. They also enjoy a good mulch.

Ipheion

A dainty and very pretty warm-climate bulb that thrives in most New Zealand regions but can be grown indoors in

Gladioli Nanus cultivar.

pots in cold climates. Star-shaped blue flowers smother the attractive strappy leaves. It forms a dense, weed-stopping carpet less than 15 cm high that can be left undisturbed for years. The leaves are present for most of the year with only a short dormant period in mid-summer. 'Wisley Blue' is an excellent cultivar. Ipheion looks good in a low pot. Bulbs can be kept in pots for a couple of flowering seasons, after which they are best transferred to the garden or separated and replanted in pots. When growing in pots stop watering as the leaves fade and store the pot in a dry dark place until the following autumn when watering is restarted.

Iris

The most popular bulbous irises are the closely related Dutch, Spanish and English irises. They are superb cut flowers with long strong stems and a long vase life.

Dutch irises are the first of the group to flower, usually in early spring. They make up the largest and best-known group with an ever-increasing list of cultivars. In shades of blue, yellow, purple or white with numerous multicoloured forms in between, they are characterised by a golden blotch on each fall.

Spanish irises flower two or three weeks later than the Dutch irises. They are very similar to Dutch irises but with slightly smaller flowers.

The English irises are early-

Hyacinthus

Hyacinths are close to perfection in form, but it is their incredible perfume that is treasured the most. The colours range from deep purple through clear blues, creamy white and soft yellow to many shades of pink. Well suited to growing in containers, these winter- and spring-flowering bulbs can be enjoyed indoors or out — placed where their fragrance will be fully appreciated. Hyacinths are cold-climate bulbs. In Christchurch growing hyacinths is relatively straightforward. In Auckland a bit of trickery can work wonders.

In their first season newly purchased bulbs will rarely fail to flower, regardless of the climate into which they are introduced. It is the quality of flowering (the stem length in particular) and future season's flowerings that will be greatly enhanced if some basic temperature requirements are taken care of.

The trick to growing really beautiful hyacinths is to establish a good crop of healthy roots before the flower stems start to grow. To develop their full potential the roots need a good 10 weeks at below 11°C. This means delaying planting until the soil is cool enough. This can be as late as June.

GROWING HYACINTHS IN POTS
Choose firm plump bulbs, the larger the better. Make sure your pot has adequate drainage and choose a well-drained potting mix. Plant the bulbs so that they are just covered with potting mix. The more bulbs per pot, the better they look. Bulbs can be placed so that they are almost touching. Low, bowl-shaped pots tend to look best.

Once the bulbs are planted, place pots in a cool shady place. Keep the potting mix constantly moist but never waterlogged. Lay snail bait! When shoots are about 8 cm long pots can be moved to a sunny deck or a bright indoor room where the warmer temperatures will quickly lead to flowering. Potted hyacinths need two to three months of cool temperatures before being brought indoors to flower. If brought into a warm room too soon, the stems are likely to be short and the flowers will be hidden by the leaves.

When flowering is finished and the leaves start to turn yellow, trim off the flower stem, stop watering and allow the potting mix to dry out. Once the leaves have died down, lift and store the bulbs in a dry place until replanting.

It's best to buy new bulbs for pots each season, planting last year's potted bulbs in the garden.

GROWING HYACINTHS IN WATER
Special narrow-neck vases provide a fun way to grow hyacinths. Fill the vase up to its neck with water, with the optional addition of a piece of charcoal to keep the water fresh. Sit a good-sized bulb in the top of the vase so its base just touches the water. Keep the vase in a cool dark cupboard until the roots fill the vase. The shoot as this stage should be just starting to appear. The flower spike will develop rapidly once the bulb is brought out into the light. Always use new bulbs for growing hyacinths this way.

GROWING HYACINTHS IN THE GARDEN
In the garden, hyacinths are best mass planted in generous groups of one colour. Raised beds are ideal.

Choose a sunny well-drained position and plant them 10–15 cm apart and up to 15 cm deep. The warmer the climate, the deeper the bulbs should be planted. The young shoots are relished by slugs and snails so be ready with the snail bait.

Hyacinths grown in cool climates can be left in the ground successfully as long as the soil remains relatively dry over summer, but in general they are best lifted once the leaves have died down and stored in a dry place until next planting season.

The lifted bulbs will generally be smaller than the ones you planted. The flowers they produce the following year will be smaller but will have no less fragrance or colour than the first season's flowers.

---

summer flowering, usually in December. They have the largest flowers with more rounded petals. Both the leaves and flowers appear later than Dutch or Spanish irises and bulbs can be planted later — in autumn or in winter.

To grow irises a well-drained soil is essential. They enjoy the fertile conditions created by digging in lots of compost prior to planting. Apply fertiliser when the first shoots appear.

Irises grow well in pots and can be a lot more manageable when grown in this way. Stop watering once the leaves start turning yellow and put the pots aside in a dry place until the following autumn.

Although irises will generally multiply more successfully in a cooler climate they will flower successfully in most parts of New Zealand given a well-drained sunny position. Bulbs deteriorate quickly if left over summer in a damp soil and are therefore best lifted and stored over summer in a dry place. When lifting it is best to dust bulbs with a fungicide to prevent the foliage diseases that can be a problem with irises. Take extra care when lifting English irises as the bulbs are larger and softer and so more easily damaged.

Ixia
Ixias, also known as corn lilies, are great survivors, naturalising easily in some of the poorest soils. Star-shaped flowers are borne in long heads at the ends of very fine but strong stems that are excellent for picking. Ixias like a warm climate with a long hot summer and a fairly open position. They do not fare well in damp summers, as the bulbs to rot. They need protection from frosts in the coldest regions.

Ixias enjoy the well-drained warm conditions of a pot. Alternatively, they can be planted in spring after the frosts for summer flowering.

Lachenalia

Colourful lachenalias light up a garden in winter. The flowers, like miniature hanging lanterns, are in glowing blends of red and gold. They are generously packed on to compact stems 20–30 cm tall. The leaves, two per bulb, are attractively mottled. *L. aloides* 'Pearsonii' is a New Zealand-raised cultivar and one of the best.

Spectacular in pots, window boxes and hanging baskets, lachenalias look best in gardens if planted in large groups. In a well-drained soil that remains relatively dry in summer, they can be left in the ground from year to year and will multiply by bulb offsets.

If soil drainage is a problem, pots are the answer. When grown in pots, the bulbs can either be lifted after the foliage has died down or left dry in their pots over summer. After two seasons' flowering in pots, it will be best to lift and divide the bulbs and replant them into fresh potting mix or in the garden.

Lachenalias enjoy full sun. They will fail to thrive in very cold, excessively wet conditions. Although they will tolerate light infrequent frosts, in very frosty climates they are best grown in pots with protection.

Leucojum (Snowflakes)

Snowflakes are the warm-climate gardener's answer to snowdrops (*Galanthus*). The most commonly grown snowflake is *L. aestivum*. The white bell-shaped flowers are very pretty, dotted with green at the tip of each petal. They hang daintily from their stems above a mass of rich green foliage.

Snowflakes are at their best naturalised in large drifts. They will grow easily in combination with grass and, like daffodils, do not appeal to the tastebuds of livestock. Moist rich soil in shade or part shade is where snowflakes grow best. They can be left in the ground for years without lifting and, unlike other spring bulbs, enjoy summer moisture.

Muscari

The charming little grape hyacinth is an easily grown, long-lived bulb that grows almost anywhere in New Zealand. The flowers are fragrant and true blue. There is also a white form. The strappy foliage forms a dense shaggy carpet upon which the grape-like bunches of tiny urn-shaped flowers sit. Muscari can be planted permanently as a carpet in front of shrubs and are attractive under shrubs such as magnolias or azaleas, which flower at the same time.

The blue flowers contrast beautifully with daffodils and, like daffodils, muscari will survive in the ground for a number of years without lifting.

Plant in autumn in sun or part shade. In warmer climates part shade is beneficial.

Narcissus (Daffodil)

Most daffodils will grow well in most parts of New Zealand. They can be left in the ground to flower year after year without the need for summer lifting. The rate at which they multiply varies with different varieties, but narcissi are among the most successful spring bulbs for naturalising. They are widely planted in paddocks in combination with deciduous trees.

A similar effect is achieved on a smaller scale by growing bulbs in the lawn. The only problem here is that for bulbs to produce flower buds and store enough food for the following season the leaves must be left to die down naturally. This means that lawns containing daffodils should not be mown until about six weeks after flowering. Planting earlier-flowering forms helps a little by at least allowing mowing earlier in the spring. The best forms for naturalising are the vigorous-growing, least-expensive ones, such as 'Erlicheer' or 'King Alfred'.

Planted in garden beds, daffodils can still benefit from the foil of a bright green lawn but won't get in the way of the lawn mower. The post-flowering foliage can be somewhat disguised by companion planting. Perennials that put on a growth spurt or flower in mid-spring as the daffodils start to fade are very useful. Pots are the most convenient way to grow daffodils as they can be hidden away when the post-flowering stage begins.

A sunny position is preferred. Most daffodils will flower in part shade, especially in a warmer climate, but steer clear of the shadiest parts of the garden. Daffodils under trees may find themselves in competition with tree roots for food and water, in which case extra attention to feeding and watering will be needed.

Daffodils thrive on plenty of water during their winter growing season but must have a well-drained soil. Heavy soils can be improved by adding coarse materials, such as sand or potting mix, and this is especially important underneath the bulbs. Low-lying, boggy sites should be avoided. If drainage is poor, raised beds or pots are the best alternative.

Early-autumn planting is recommended for daffodils to allow the roots as much time as possible to develop before flowering.

Although daffodils will continue to flower and multiply in the ground for a number of years, lifting every few years will allow the bulbs more space. Lift in summer as soon as possible after the leaves have died down. Dispose of any soft bulbs likely to be infected with narcissus bulb fly.

More about bulb fly: Go to page 117.

The genus *Narcissus* includes many different species and cultivars in all different shapes and sizes. Flowering time also varies between cultivars. Planting a range of early, mid and late season daffodils will extend your flowering season.

Ranunculus

Ranunculus are members of the same plant family as anemones and have been perfected to the same extent as cut flowers. The flowers of the modern cultivars have a formal camellia-like shape and are very vibrantly coloured. The mixed colours look fabulous together in a vase and in the garden put on a dramatic show of colour during the cooler months. Ranunculus are also readily available as separate colours, which gives greater scope for creative planting. With their long stems, bright colours and striking form, a mass planting can give a similar but much less-expensive effect as a mass planting of tulips.

Though not frost hardy, ranunculus will grow well throughout the country. In frost-free climates the claw-like root tubers can be planted from late summer through to winter for a continuous winter and spring display. In cold areas spring planting after frosts gives spring and summer flowering.

The most important requirements are full sun and a well-drained soil. Poor drainage will result in inferior blooms and a shorter flowering time. Add plenty of compost to the soil to give your ranunculus the richly fertile conditions in which they thrive. Combine this with liquid feeding during the growing season and the flowers will reach their maximum potential.

It helps to soak tubers in water for a few hours before planting. Plant with the claws facing downwards. Early plantings should be mulched to protect them from hot sun and watered if the weather is dry. Water directly after planting and keep the soil moist throughout the growing period but take care not to over-water. Over-wet soil before the roots emerge can cause bulbs to rot. Watch out for powdery mildew in hot dry weather.

Ranunculus bulbs are relatively inexpensive and if given the right growing conditions will produce many flowers per bulb, which makes up for the fact that they are best treated as an annual with fresh bulbs planted every year.

Sparaxis

Sparaxis are related to freesias and ixias, the South African bulbs highly suited to growing in our warmer climates. They are flamboyantly colourful flowers, in various bright colours with contrasting dark blotches. They will naturalise easily in the most difficult soils as long as they receive moisture during the winter growing period and relative dryness in summer. They make a wonderful spring show around evergreen shrubs and along hedgerows.

There are some attractive individual species, but they hybridise freely and are most commonly available as hybrid mixes. It is possible to develop patches of separate colour groups in your own garden by marking plants as they flower and either culling or shifting corms to a new place the following autumn.

Relatively inexpensively priced, sparaxis represent extra value for money because they will last in the ground for years in the right climate. They will flower for a long time and are great for picking.

Sparaxis will withstand a brief frost to -5°C, but in colder areas they are best grown in pots in a warm greenhouse or conservatory until frosts are over.

Tritonia

Another easy-to-grow relative of freesias, these charming flowers are well suited to the warmer regions of New Zealand where cool-climate bulbs are more challenging to grow. Flowering in late spring and early summer they provide excellent cut flowers after most other spring bulbs have finished flowering. They are very like freesias in growth habit and appearance with grassy foliage and many flowers per stem.

The corms can be lifted after the leaves wither and replanted in autumn or, in a well-drained soil, left in the ground to naturalise.

All tritonias will multiply freely in the right conditions, but modern hybrids should not be confused with their invasive cousin, the orange-flowered montbretia (*Crocosmia crocosmiiflora*). However, even montbretia has its place, for example, it is excellent on dry banks.

Although unable to sustain long periods of freezing temperatures, tritonias will tolerate the occasional frost of -5°C or lower. In very cold climates they could either be grown in pots or planted in spring for late-summer flowering. They are popular bulbs for containers in any climate.

Traditionally, mainly orange shades of tritonia have been available but more recently pinks and whites have become readily available separately.

Tulipa

Tulips have a special beauty all of their own and have been favourite flowers for centuries. They come from high-altitude regions of the northern hemisphere where they experience very cold winters and hot dry summers. To thrive and prosper they need to be given such conditions, by artificial means where nature doesn't oblige.

The good thing, as with most bulbs, is that tulips will always flower in their first year. In any climate they are happy to grow as annuals, new bulbs being purchased each year. To ensure the best long-stemmed flowers are produced, all that is required is some chilling prior to planting if natural conditions aren't cold enough. In warm climates they need to be refrigerated for at least two months prior to planting and planted no earlier than May.

In warm climates, if lifted, bulbs may produce flowers in subsequent years but they are usually of dwindling number and quality. In a cool climate tulip bulbs will last longer but in order to survive indefinitely, producing flowers year after year, they must still be lifted at the end of each season. Warm damp conditions in summer cause the dormant bulbs to rot. Bulbs are lifted about six weeks after flowering when the foliage has died down. They should be dried thoroughly and stored in a dry place at 18–21°C, the temperature required to allow new flowers to be initiated.

Tulips are superb in pots. They can be planted quite closely, approximately 10 to a 30 cm diameter pot, 10–20 cm deep. Lift bulbs once the leaves have died down and transplant to the garden the following year, using new bulbs for pots.

There is a huge range of cultivars to choose from. Planting a range of varieties will give an extended flowering time.

Tulips.

124

Canna

Canna lilies have bold foliage and bold flowers. Don't let the fact that they exist as weeds in some climates put you off. These are attractive easily-grown plants with a multitude of different-coloured varieties. They can be confined to pots or grown towards the back of a flower border where they will provide strong form and contrast. Both dwarf (approximately 1 m) and tall (up to 2 m) forms are available. Some, such as the recently introduced C. 'Tropicana', are valued primarily for their beautifully coloured foliage.

Cannas do best where summers are consistently warm, and enjoy full sun. Where frosts do not reach below -16° they can be left in the ground to naturalise. Otherwise, the tubers can be lifted and stored just like dahlias. Introduce cannas to your garden by purchasing tubers in spring or potted plants at any time of the year. Otherwise, lift and divide existing plants.

Dahlia

Lots and lots of flowers, over a very long season, and in most soils and climates, dahlias are truly generous plants. Growing from tubers, they flower right through summer in return for a minimum of fuss and bother. For bold, bright colour when the spring bloomers have finished, these Mexican beauties are unbeatable. The variety of flower form, size and colour is huge. They come in dwarf forms for pots or large, long-stemmed forms that are fantastic for picking.

To start dahlias in your garden, buy tubers in spring, about August. In a well-drained soil they can be planted and left *in situ*, but they are generally better lifted in autumn for replanting in spring, especially in cold climates or when the soil is not very well drained. Store over winter in sawdust or sand in a dark, frost-free place. At lifting time they can be divided to make new plants. Plants should be divided at least every three years, even in a warm climate, as overcrowding will affect flowering performance. Always leave a part of the old stem on divided tubers. Alternatively dahlias are easily propagated from cuttings taken from new growth in spring.

Dahlias need full sun, summer

Dahlias.

moisture, and shelter from strong winds. A compost-rich soil is beneficial. Feed with liquid fertiliser every few weeks and remove spent flower heads to encourage continuous flowering. Stake tall varieties to prevent wind damage. Fungal diseases, especially powdery mildew, can cause problems in warm moist climates. Insects such as thrips, caterpillars and earwigs can also attack. Since these occur mainly towards the end of the flowering season, spraying is not always necessary.

Planting pests and diseases: Go to page 116–17.

Gladiolus

Good old glads. So lovely for picking and so easy to grow. The corms of summer-flowering gladioli are planted in spring for flowering in summer. Planting to flowering is roughly 100 days so for a succession of flowers for picking you can plant a few corms every week or two. There are so many colours and flower forms that there is something to suit every taste, from pastels to brights. Gladioli like a well-drained soil with plenty of compost and a sunny location, sheltered from wind. Staking may be necessary to prevent blooms from falling over. Thrips can be a problem, rasping away on the leaves and damaging the flowers in summer. Thrips thrive in hot dry weather, so you may escape the worst damage by planting early, depending on the weather. Blooms should be cut just as the bottom flowers are opening. For corms to flower the following year it is important to leave plants undisturbed until the foliage turns brown a month or two after flowering. Then corms can be lifted for storing in a cool shady place over winter.

Lilium

Most lilies are not difficult to grow as long as you have a rich, very well-drained soil (such as a volcanic loam). Otherwise they are best grown in pots or raised beds. There are three basic types commonly grown: the Asiastic hybrids, oriental hybrids, and trumpet lilies.

The trumpet lilies comprise a range of different species and hybrids. Two of the best known and most easily grown are *L. regale* and *L. longifolium*, the Christmas lily. Both have fragrant, trumpet-shaped flowers. *L. regale* is perhaps the best beginners' lily. It grows to about 1.5 m tall with elegant wiry stems topped with clusters of gorgeous funnel-shaped flowers. The petals are wine coloured on the outside, white on the inside, with a warm yellow centre. *L. longifolium* and its various cultivars are pure white all over. Unlike most lily varieties, it lasts very well as a perennial in warm, subtropical climates.

The Asiatic lilies are compact, no more than 1 metre tall, and very free flowering. They are relatively easy to grow, but lack the flower size and fragrance of the other groups. A new strain to be developed from these is the LA hybrid lilies. These are a cross between Asiatic lilies and the trumpet lily *L. longifolium* and have the best attributes of each: larger, slightly scented flowers, earlier flowering, greater disease resistance, and rapid multiplication. They come in a range of colours.

The oriental hybrids have enormous, fragrant flowers, stunningly proportioned and speckled with contrasting colours. They flower in mid-summer and will grow well in warmer regions but need protection from the hottest afternoon sun.

Lilies need excellent drainage and plenty of water. Sandy soils answer the drainage requirements but will need ample compost added for water retention. Lilies growing in potting mix need frequent watering (daily in dry periods). The pot needs to be large (e.g., three bulbs to a 40 cm diameter terracotta pot) and water-saving devices like paint-on sealer (e.g., Terraseal) and wetting agents (e.g., Saturaid) are almost essential. Mulching is a very good idea. Feed with a balanced liquid fertiliser in spring and summer.

Bulbs are available from garden centres in May. Since they deteriorate rapidly if allowed to dry out, you should buy them as soon as they become available and plant without delay. Check that the bulbs you buy are packaged properly to prevent drying out. Planting depth is usually around 15 to 20 cm, but this can vary with the variety so check the recommendation on the packet. Unlike other bulbs that are lifted between flowering seasons, lilies prefer to be left undisturbed for as long as possible, even if they are in a pot. You will need to lift and divide them to prevent overcrowding every few years, depending on the variety.

Zantedeschia

Calla lilies go beyond the faithful old-fashioned arum lily (*Z. aethiopica*). There are a number of smaller-flowered, different-coloured hybrids, which are grown from rhizomes available for planting in early spring. Potted flowering plants are often available in summer. These hybrids are deciduous, disappearing completely from view in winter. Callas are long-lasting cut flowers of exceptional charm and gutsy form, adding strength to floral arrangements. They also look good as a mass display in the garden. Grow them in any reasonably well-drained, average garden soil, and feed regularly with liquid fertiliser in spring and summer. They like plenty of compost and prefer full sun or light shade. Callas can be left in the ground as perennials in mild climates but will flower best if lifted and divided every few winters. Where frosts reach below -12°C, they must be lifted in autumn and stored over winter. However, the rhizomes must not be allowed to dry out.

Annuals

nnuals are the seasonal highlights of the garden. They are short-term plants that you throw away at the end of their flowering life (usually in early spring and again in late summer) to replace with the next season's bloomers.

Annuals are those plants that grow, flower and set seed within a year. Those that take longer (up to two years), growing one year and flowering the next, are called biennials. Some are so good at setting seed that they will come up in your garden season after season of their own accord if you let them (tidy gardeners may be too good with their weeding to allow this). Cottage gardeners are among those who rely on the ability of certain annuals to self-sow.

Most of the plants in the following list are true annuals. A few are actually perennials commonly grown as annuals. All are plants for colourful flower displays, easy to grow from seed or seedlings, freshly planted each new season. There are tall annuals and low-growing annuals, some for each season. They are easy to grow with quick results.

Annuals can be purchased as seedlings in punnets, or you can grow your own from seed, but the fastest and easiest way to have annuals flowering in your garden is to buy advanced plants that are already flowering. Such plants are often called 'potted colour' in garden-centre jargon. Though a higher price is paid per seedling, the roots are well developed and, being in their own pot, suffer little disturbance at planting time. This means that a 'potted colour' plant is far less likely to die of transplanting shock than one of half a dozen little seedlings sharing a punnet. The other advantages are instant gratification and the chance to see the exact flower colour as you buy. Especially for things like pansies planted in late autumn, when the ground is getting cold and damp, and snails are still out in force, potted colour is a good way to go.

Annuals do not always complete their life cycle at the most convenient time for the gardener, creating a messy patch or a gap in the garden while you get around to replacing them. A good way to get around this is to save annuals for containers that can be moved out of sight at the end of the season until you have time to deal with them.

As long as you restrict your areas of annuals to what you have time for, they are very rewarding plants, smothering themselves with showy flowers for months on end. The fact that annuals need planting with each change of season means that you have the opportunity to create a new look each year. Because they are relatively inexpensive, they are ideal for experimenting with.

California poppy, *Eschscholzia californica.*

Growing from seed: Go to page 209.

ALYSSUM
Lobularia maritima
10 to 20 cm
One of the prettiest and easiest annuals of all, alyssum will flower all year round in a mild climate, self-sowing to renew its fragrant clumps in seemingly all the right places. It is perfect for growing in and around paving. Alyssum grows in full sun or part shade and survives periods of drought and poor soil, but doesn't take kindly to cold wet conditions, so clay soils in winter can pose problems. Flowers are white, cream, pink, purple, red or apricot shades. Good for pots and hanging baskets, especially as a border to other flowering plants.

Alyssum.

BEGONIA
Begonia Semperflorens-Cultorum hybrids
15 cm
As easy as pie. Begonias put on a long summer and autumn show of pink, reds or white flowers against glossy bronze or green foliage. They are very free flowering, perfect for creating carpets of colour, standing up to dry weather, summer heat in full sun to light shade, in most soils, but avoid overwatering.

BUSY LIZZIE
Impatiens walleriana
under 25 cm
Busy lizzies are a first choice for shady spots in summer, either in pots or in the garden. They start flowering in spring and go on looking fabulous right through summer. In a frost-free climate they will survive the winter to flower again the following summer, though the best displays tend to be from first-year plants. Impatiens, as they are just as often called, come in an ever-increasing range of varieties, in just about every shade except true blue or yellow. They are exceptionally easy to grow, preferring filtered sun rather than dense shade.

CALENDULA
Calendula officinalis
40 cm
Bright yellow or orange, these many-petalled daisy flowers are a welcome sight in winter, popping up via self-sown seed from last winter's flowers, but easily removed if they are not where you want them. Among the easiest of annuals to grow, calendulas are popular for herb and vegetable gardens, where they repel insect pests and add a splash of colour amongst the green. The petals are edible and look wonderful sprinkled on cakes or salads. They will grow in any soil, enjoying full sun.

CALIFORNIAN POPPY
Eschscholzia californica
20 cm
Bright orange is the most well-known colour, but there are also softer shades of cream or lemon as well as pink and purple shades. These poppies flower for a long time over spring, summer and autumn with lacy foliage, a low spreading habit and myriads of satin-textured poppy flowers. They will grow in poor soil and tolerate dry conditions. Very easy to grow with self-seeding as a bonus, a must for cottage gardens.

CINERARIA
Senecio xhybridus (syn. *Pericallis xhybrida*)
The common tall-growing cineraria grows wild in old gardens of warmer climates. The dwarf forms have larger flowers on compact plants, just perfect for mass planting as a colourful carpet in shady sites or for pots. The colours are electric blues, rich glowing pinks, purples, as well as pastel pinks, creams, yellow or white. There are also attractive bicoloured forms. Easy to grow, for cool season flowering, planted in autumn or early spring.

CLEOME
Cleome spinosa
1 m
Sometimes called spider flower after the long anthers protruding from the flowers like daddy-long-legs. The flowers are produced in big rounded clusters on top of long stems, quite an interesting feature for the spring or summer garden. Plant in spring in a sunny location. Good at the back of flower borders.

CORNFLOWER
Centaurea cyanus
up to 60 cm
Lovely cornflowers are favourites for picking and drying and for their intense blue colour. There are also pink and white varieties. Usually tall, dwarf and medium height forms are now available. Easy to grow in full sun, cornflowers are sown or planted from autumn to early spring. They do not perform well in hot weather.

COSMOS
Cosmos bipinnatus
up to 1 m
Easy-to-grow cosmos comes in white, pink, purple or yellow. The main type is tall, but lower-growing varieties have also been developed. Great for picking and for long summer garden display, these cottage gardeners' dream flowers will self-sow and can be cut back after a spring flowering for a second show in summer. Related to dahlias, they are superb flowers for late summer and autumn. Cosmos tolerates poor soils, requires good drainage and full sun, and does not take kindly to overwatering.

FAIRY PRIMROSE
Primula malacoides
under 20 cm
Indispensable for planting with bulbs and for creating drifts of airy colour in winter and early spring. The lacy flowers sit above soft green leaves in shades of pink, cerise, purple and the favourite of all, white. At its best as a companion carpet for bolder flowers, fairy primrose is an easy-to-grow annual for pots or the garden. Plant in autumn or winter. Plant in volume — one punnet will never be enough!

FORGET-ME-NOT
Myosotis sylvatica
under 30 cm

Another perfect companion for bulbs, forget-me-nots are especially good for covering spare ground under trees and shrubs or filling spaces between other flowers. The dainty flowers make a pretty blue haze right through spring, setting seed for the following year, so that once you have it in your garden you will never need to plant it again. As well as blue, there are pink and white forms. Forget-me-not grows in sun or shade. Sow directly into the ground or plant seedlings any time.

FOXGLOVE
Digitalis purpurea
1 m

Foxgloves make a statement in the garden in spring or early summer. They are about the easiest to grow of the tall stately flowers, producing their elegant spikes of bell flowers in shades of purple, pink, apricot, cream or white. The fact that they are considered weeds in rural areas pays credence to how easy they are to grow. They will self-seed in the garden but are not difficult to control. In any case, few would complain at the sight of a mass of foxgloves in flower. They enjoy sun and tolerate a range of soils. Foxgloves are biennial, so you will have to wait a year before your seedlings come into bloom. Sow seeds or plant seedlings in spring or autumn.

Foxglove.

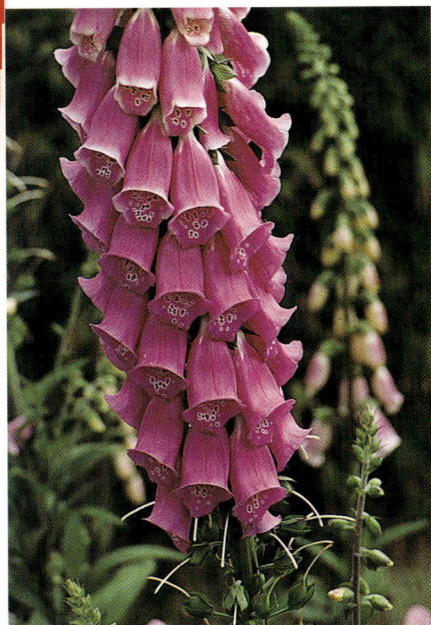

HOLLYHOCK
Alcea rosea
up to 2 m

Hollyhocks are very tall with stunning saucer-shaped flowers on stately stems. These old-fashioned charmers are easy to grow and worthy of a place in any garden but have the unfortunate susceptibility to rust in warm climates. For this reason, they are really only grown on a large scale in cool climates. There are many colours, both double and single-flowered forms. Hollyhocks flower in summer and need a sunny sheltered spot. Staking may be necessary. Seed may be sown directly into the ground or seedlings transplanted in summer or autumn. Like foxgloves, they are biennial and will self-sow readily.

HONESTY
Lunaria annua

Honesty is as much grown for its round papery seedheads as it is for its flowers, but it makes an ideal groundcover in part shade under trees, where it will self-sow quite happily. The foliage is dense, dark green and attractive, with pretty variegated forms sometimes available. The most common colour is violet, but there is also a white form. Honesty is very easy to grow in most soils, flowering in spring and summer with seedheads maturing in late summer. Sow seeds directly into the garden or transplant seedlings in spring.

ICELAND POPPY
Papaver nudicaule
up to 60 cm

The delicate, cup-shaped flowers have a texture like crumpled silk, in delicious shades of salmon, orange, pink, cream, and yellow. They are held on slender stems and are just perfect for picking. The stems and flower buds are covered in silky hairs which along with the flowers glisten in the late winter sun. Sow in trays in summer or autumn and transplant only good-sized seedlings in autumn in compost-rich, well-drained soil and full sun. They will grow in any climate but are at their best in a cool climate. In very cold climates plant in spring for summer flowering. To prolong flowering, remove spent blooms or pick for indoors. Pick flowers in the early morning and dip the stems in boiling water for 30 seconds.

LARKSPUR
Consolida spp.
up to 2 m

Smaller cousins of delphiniums but a lot easier to grow, longer flowering and less fussy of climate. The flowers are much prized for picking and drying. They also make a wonderful garden display in spring and early summer, particularly good with old-style roses. The flowers are pink, white, blue or purple, clustered on tall stems. Plant in spring or autumn, avoiding the hot summer. Flowering is impaired once the weather gets too hot.

LIVINGSTONE DAISY
Dorotheanthus bellidiformis
10 cm

A carpet of colour for late winter and spring, livingstone daisies are succulent plants with close-packed daisy flowers in iridescent pinks, purples and yellows. They insist on full sun but do not like hot summer weather. They need good drainage, other wise standing up to poor soils and periods of dryness. Plant in autumn or winter or sow seeds in trays in late summer. A good annual for seaside gardens.

LOBELIA
Lobelia erinus
up to 20 cm

Indispensable for hanging baskets or pots, where they are top performers on their own or as a border to larger flowers. Teaming masses of small blue, white, purple, pink, or red flowers are produced on plants that vary from cascading to mounding to upright. For baskets make sure you buy a cascading variety. Lobelias flower from spring right through to the end of autumn, enjoying full sun and a well-drained soil. They are quick growing and very easy, among the very best of the blues. Sow seeds in autumn or plant seedlings in spring.

LOVE-IN-A-MIST
Nigella damascena

Airy flowers and foliage for a soft romantic touch, especially in cottage gardens. The tall-stemmed flowers are blue, pink or white. They appear in spring followed by attractive seedheads in summer, which can be picked and dried for winter use indoors. Love-in-a-mist self-sows easily and is very easy to grow. Sow seed directly into the ground in autumn or plant seedlings in autumn or spring.

MARIGOLD
Tagetes hybrids
up to 70 cm
Not many flowering annuals have the heat and drought tolerance of marigolds. They come in a whole host of flower forms and growth habits from the little French marigolds to tall, large-flowered hybrids. They are long flowering and flamboyant. Yellow is the predominant colour, but there are also orange- and red-toned varieties. Dwarf marigolds are good for pots. Full sun and good drainage is required for these summer annuals. Sow seed or plant seedlings in spring or early summer, avoiding cold soil.

NASTURTIUM
Tropaeolum majus
under 20 cm
A trailing annual with brilliant red, orange or yellow flowers. Good for pots, window boxes or hanging baskets where it won't get away on you. Flowers are decorative and edible. Nasturtium is an attractive feature in the herb or potager garden, easy to grow and drought tolerant. Sun loving and summer flowering, it is best started in spring, from directly sown seed or transplanted seedlings.

PANSY
Viola xwittrockiana
If you were allowed only one annual, pansies would be a likely choice. They flower and flower, starting in autumn, continuing through winter and spring and into summer. Traditionally not for hot weather, there are now more and more heat-tolerant strains being developed. Pansies come in just about every colour, even black. They are fantastic in pots, hanging baskets, window boxes or garden borders and good with bulbs. They will grow in sun or semi-shade, most rewarding in a well-drained soil with fertiliser. Protect from snails. If autumn-planted pansies get tatty over winter, trim them back and feed them with liquid fertiliser and a fresh crop of flowers will appear in no time.

PETUNIA
Petunia xhybrida
The queens of the hot weather annuals, petunias come in lots of colours, lots of flower forms and on plants ranging from compact and upright to cascading and spreading. They make an excellent choice for summer pots or hanging baskets and tolerate dry conditions. They do not like wet conditions and the larger-flowered varieties do not stand up well to relentless rain. Small-flowered versions called 'multiflora' (lots of flowers) petunias are making their presence felt with markedly improved weather resistance and prolific flowering. Plant from early summer. Petunias will continue flowering right through till the winter temperatures arrive, especially if you remove spent blooms regularly.

POLYANTHUS
Primula vulgaris
There is an astonishing array of polyanthus to choose from, not just plain clear colours, but all sorts of multicoloured varieties with amazing patterns as if the petals had been painted by hand. The plain colours — red, orange, yellow, blue, purple or white, with their yellow centres — are great for colour scheming. All look lovely in containers. There are longer-stemmed varieties for picking or short-stemmed ones best for mass planting effects. Polyanthus are winter- and early spring-flowering, excellent with bulbs and around dormant rose bushes. Plant seedlings from autumn to spring.

SALVIA
Salvia splendens
20c m
Glowing candles of scarlet that thrive in the hot summer sun, salvia is the most famous and reddest of red annuals for mass display in gardens or containers. There are also purple, white and salmon forms of this annual. There are numerous perennial salvias, all quite different. Plant easy-to-grow *Salvia splendens* in spring into compost-rich, well-drained soil in full sun and it will flower from early summer until the first frost.

SCABIOSA
Scabiosa atropurpurea
75 cm
Also known as pincushion flowers,

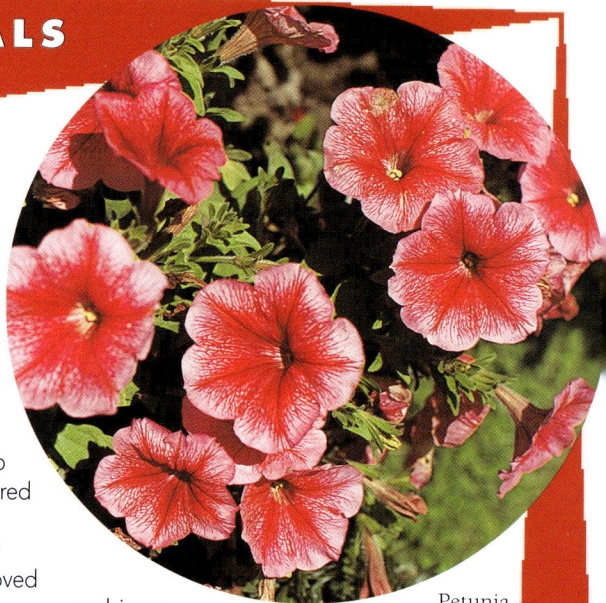

Petunia.

scabiosas exist in both perennial and annual forms. The annual, *Scabiosa atropurpurea*, is tall, wiry stemmed, and good for picking. The flowers are in many colours: deep burgundy, purple, pink, and white, generally available as a mixture. They are very easy to grow in well-drained soil, fed for best results. Sow straight into the garden or transplant seedlings in spring for summer flowering.

SHIRLEY POPPY
Papaver rhoeas
80 cm
Shirley poppies flower in summer, providing lovely cut flowers in shades of pink and red. They can be grown from seed sown directly or planted as seedlings in spring and summer. They like a well-drained soil and full sun.

SNAPDRAGON
Antirrhinum majus
up to 75 cm
Snapdragons make their flowers on straight tapering spikes ranging in height from 15 to 75 cm. Colours cover most of the spectrum and are available separately, ideal for colour theming the spring garden. They are wonderful planted in large drifts of colour. In a warm climate, plant snapdragons in autumn to flower in winter and spring before the hottest weather arrives. In cold climates, plant in spring for spring and summer flowering. Snapdragons are good for picking. The dwarf varieties do well in a pot.

STATICE
Limonium sinuatum
up to 75 cm
Statice is an excellent dried flower

because it holds its colour so well. For garden display it makes a colourful show, but is not the shapeliest of plants and needs staking. It is, however, an excellent plant for seaside gardens, tolerating heat, drought and salt spray. Flowers are yellow, white, pink or purple. Plant in a sunny location in well-drained soil, watering only when dry. Statice is best sown or planted in spring for summer flowering.

STOCK
Matthiola incana
up to 60 cm
Fragrance to drool over is what stock is most memorable for, but they look beautiful too. Believe it or not, they are related to cabbages. The fragrance is best at night or on overcast days. Stocks are cool-season flowers for early spring, in attractive shades of pink, purple, red, white or cream. The flowers are clustered on upright stems ideal for picking and drying. There are tall and dwarf cultivars, and single- and double-flowered forms, but a batch of double-flowered seeds never produces 100 per cent doubles. Plant seedlings from autumn to early spring in a well-drained fertile soil. Find a cool location: semi-shade in a warm climate or sun in a cold climate.

SUNFLOWER
Helianthus annuus
Up to 3 m
Sunflowers grow so quickly that they outgrow nursery containers too quickly for many of them to be sold as growing plants. The way to grow them is from seed sown directly into the soil. This is easy. Wait till frosts are over and sow into light, well-prepared soil. Alternatively, sow seeds into peat pots indoors a month or so early to get a head start in cold climates. Flowers appear two to three months after sowing, depending on variety. There is an increasing number of different sunflower cultivars becoming available in this country. They are fun and easy to grow. Position them in full sun and provide support for the tallest varieties. Foliage can be straggly, so they are best planted at the back of the garden with other flowers in front.

SWEET PEA
Lathyrus odoratus
climber
The only difficulties in growing sweet peas is you have to remember to plant them and they need something to climb on. A tepee of sticks or stakes is as elaborate as they need, but any sort of support will do as long as it is in full sun.

Sweet peas can be planted in autumn or spring to flower in summer. They are available as seedlings but possibly best grown from seed sown directly into well-prepared ground. Give them a well-drained composty soil and feed them generously with liquid fertiliser once they start to grow. A mulch is a good idea to keep roots cool. They will flower 12 to 15 weeks after sowing. As soil-borne diseases can affect sweet peas, avoid planting in the same place two years in a row.

Old-fashioned sweet peas are exquisitely fragrant. Many of the modern hybrids, while stunningly beautiful to look at, have lost much of this scent. Check this out when choosing your varieties.

There is nothing to compare with a vase of sweet peas freshly picked from the garden. Every child should have a go at growing them. If you were deprived as a youngster, it's not too late.

Sunflower.

SWEET WILLIAM
Dianthus barbatus
45 cm
Sweetly scented pink and white flowers are crowded on compact plants in summer. This old-fashioned favourite is easy to grow in any well-drained soil. It declines in hot weather so is best planted as early as possible in spring or in the autumn. Light shade is a good idea in warm climates, but otherwise it will grow in full sun. Good for picking.

TOBACCO
Nicotiana hybrids
25 cm
Nicotianas are traditionally tall fragrant perennials. Relatively new are dwarf strains grown as summer annuals. They rival the petunias in their hot weather tolerance and long flowering, coming in a range of lovely colours: pinks, red, white, cream and lime green. Suitable for any garden — cottage to formal — they require average garden soil with reasonable drainage and full sun to light shade.

VIOLA
Viola cornuta
under 20 cm
Violas are baby pansies. What they lack in size their flowers more than make up for in volume, smothering the plants from early spring. As they are low growing with a tidy compact habit, they are the perfect border in containers or in the garden. They are ideal for planting with bulbs. Violas are easy to grow in sun or semi-shade, from autumn to summer. They will perform best in a well-drained, compost-rich soil with occasional liquid feeding.

VISCARIA
Lychnis viscaria
30 cm
Masses of quaint lavender-blue or pink flowers cover compact plants in spring and summer. Lovely *en masse* as garden fillers or in pots, viscarias need full sun and a well-drained soil. They tolerate dry conditions and will flower for a long time. Sow or plant in spring.

WHITE FLOWERS

	SPRING	SUMMER	AUTUMN	WINTER
ANNUALS	Alyssum	Love-in-a-mist	Alyssum	Alyssum
	Cineraria	Honesty	Pansy	Pansy
	Fairy primrose	Lobelia	Lobelia	Fairy primrose
	Forget-me-not	Cosmos	Viola	Polyanthus
	Foxglove	Busy Lizzie	Snapdragon	
	Larkspur	Hollyhock	Cosmos	
	Lobelia	Petunia		
	Love-in-a-mist	Salvia		
	Pansy	Sweet pea		
	Polyanthus	Foxglove		
	Snapdragon	Larkspur		
	Stock			
	Viola			
PERENNIALS	*Agapanthus*	*Achillea ptarmica*	*Anemone xhybrida*	*Bergenia cordifolia*
	Anthemis punctata	*Agapanthus*	*Aster novi-belgii*	*Helleborus* 'White
	Argyranthemum frutescens	*Anthemis punctata*	*Gaura lindheimeri*	Magic'
	Arthropodium cirratum	*Argyranthemum frutescens*	*Tradescantia virginiana*	
	Bergenia cordifolia	*Arthropodium cirratum*		
	Dianthus	*Cerastium tomentosum*		
	Helleborus 'White Magic'	*Dianthus*		
	Osteospermum	*Gaura lindheimeri*		
	Phlox subulata	*Helipterum anthemoides*		
	Zantedeschia aethiopica	*Iberis sempervirens*		
		Lychnis coronaria		
		Osteospermum		
		Penstemon		
		Phlox subulata		
		Tradescantia virginiana		
		Verbena		
BULBS	Anemone	Dahlia		Anemone
	Crocus	Lily		Crocus
	Daffodil			Freesia
	Freesia			Hyacinth
	Grape hyacinth			Narcissus (some)
	Hyacinth			Ranunculus
	Muscari			Snowflake
	Ranunculus			
	Snowflake			
	Tulip			

PINK AND PASTEL FLOWERS

	SPRING	SUMMER	AUTUMN	WINTER
ANNUALS	Alyssum	Busy Lizzie	Alyssum	Alyssum
	Cineraria	Cleome	Cosmos	Fairy primrose
	Cornflower	Cosmos	Pansy	Pansy
	Fairy primrose	Foxglove	Snapdragon	Polyanthus
	Forget-me-not	Hollyhock	Viola	
	Foxglove	Larkspur		
	Larkspur	Lobelia		
	Lobelia	Love-in-a-mist		
	Love-in-a-mist	Petunia		
	Pansy	Statice		
	Polyanthus	Sweet pea		
	Shirley poppy	Sweet William		
	Snapdragon	Viscaria		
	Stock			
	Sweet William			
	Viola			
PERENNIALS	*Achillea*	*Achillea*	*Anemone xhybrida*	*Bergenia cordifolia*
	Aquilegia vulgaris	*Argyranthemum frutescens*	*Aster novi-belgii*	*Helleborus*
	Argyranthemum frutescens	*Astilbe*	*Diascia*	
	Bergenia cordifolia	*Dianthus*	*Scabiosa*	
	Dianthus	*Diascia*		
	Erigeron speciosus	*Erigeron speciosus*		
	Heuchera spp.	*Helianthemum*		
	Impatiens	*Hemerocallis*		
	Lavatera 'Barnsley'	*Lavatera 'Barnsley'*		
	Osteospermum	*Lupinus*		
	Phlox subulata	*Lychnis coronaria*		
	Viola odorata cultivars	*Osteospermum*		
		Penstemon		
		Phlox subulata		
		Scabiosa		
		Sidalcea		
		Verbena		
BULBS	Tulip	Lily		
	Ranunculus	Dahlia		
	Freesia	Gladiolus Nanus hybrids		
	Iris	Tritonia		

Busy Lizzie, *Impatiens*.

BLUE FLOWERS

	SPRING	SUMMER	AUTUMN	WINTER
ANNUALS	Cineraria	Love-in-a-mist	Pansy	Polyanthus
	Cornflower	Honesty	Lobelia	
	Forget-me-not	Lobelia	Viola	
	Larkspur	Petunia	Viscaria	
	Lobelia	Salvia		
	Love-in-a-mist	Sweet pea		
	Polyanthus	Statice		
	Snapdragon	Viscaria		
	Viola			
PERENNIALS	Agapanthus	Agapanthus	Ageratum houstonianum	Corydalis flexuosa
	Ageratum houstonianum	Ageratum houstonianum	Corydalis flexuosa	'Blue Panda'
	Ajuga	Campanula spp.	'Blue Panda'	
	Corydalis flexuosa	Felicia amelloides	Nepeta xfaassenii	
	'Blue Panda'	Convolvulus mauritanicus	Salvia uliginosa	
	Echium candicans	Felicia amelloides	Scabiosa 'Butterfly Blue'	
	Felicia amelloides	Geranium 'Johnson's Blue'	Tradescantia virginiana	
	Geranium 'Johnson's Blue'	Myosotidium hortensia		
	Scabiosa	Nepeta xfaassenii		
	Viola odorata cultivars	Salvia uliginosa		
		Scabiosa 'Butterfly Blue'		
		Tradescantia xvirginiana		
BULBS	Anemone			
	Babiana			
	Grape hyacinth			
	Hyacinth			
	Ipheion			
	Bluebells			
	Iris			

Convolvulus
mauritanicus.

Yellow Flowers

	Spring	Summer	Autumn	Winter
Annuals	Pansy	Cosmos	Californian poppy	Calendula
	Cineraria	Marigold	Cosmos	Polyanthus
	Californian poppy	Nasturtium	Pansy	Pansy
	Viola	Petunia	Snapdragon	
	Iceland poppy	Statice	Viola	
	Snapdragon	Californian poppy		
	Polyanthus	Iceland poppy		
Perennials	*Anthemis tinctoria*	*Achillea*	*Achillea*	*Euphorbia*
	Argyranthemum frutescens	*Alchemilla mollis*	*Coreopsis verticillata*	*charachias*
	Euphorbia spp.	*Anthemis tinctoria*	*Helianthus salicifolius*	
	Primula heladoxa	*Argyranthemum frutescens*	*Helichrysum argyrophyllum*	
		Coreopsis verticillata	*Hemerocallis* cultivars	
		Euphorbia polychroma	*Kniphofia*	
		Helianthemum	*Rudbeckia* spp.	
		Hemerocallis cultivars		
		Primula prolifera		
		Rudbeckia spp.		
		Salvia madrensis		
Bulbs	*Allium moly*	Dahlia		
	Crocus	Lily		
	Daffodil			
	Erythronium			
	Hyacinth			
	Iris			
	Ranunculus			
	Tulip			

Hemerocallis.

HOT COLOURS

	SPRING	SUMMER	AUTUMN	WINTER
ANNUALS	Pansy	Californian poppy	Pansy	Calendula
	Californian poppy	Cosmos	Californian poppy	Polyanthus
	Iceland poppy	Busy Lizzie	Viola	Pansy
	Snapdragon	Hollyhock	Snapdragon	
	Polyanthus	Marigold	Cosmos	
		Nasturtium		
		Petunia		
		Salvia		
		Sweet pea		
		Statice		
		Sunflower		
		Foxglove		
		Larkspur		
		Honesty		
PERENNIALS	*Achillea*	*Achillea*	*Achillea*	*Clivia miniata*
	Anthemis tinctoria	*Anthemis tinctoria*	*Asclepias tuberosa*	*Euphorbia*
	Euphorbia spp.	*Arctotis scapigera*	*Coreopsis verticillata*	*charachias*
	Gazania	*Asclepias tuberosa*	*Helianthus salicifolius*	
	Primula prolifera	*Canna*	*Helichrysum argyrophyllum*	
	Sedum spectabile	*Coreopsis verticillata*	*Hemerocallis* cultivars	
		Euphorbia spp.	*Kniphofia*	
		Gazania	*Lobelia xspeciosa*	
		Helianthemum	*Rudbeckia* spp.	
		Hemerocallis cultivars		
		Kniphofia		
		Lobelia xspeciosa		
		Pelargonium xhortorum cultivars		
		Rudbeckia spp.		
		Sedum spectabile		
		Verbena		
BULBS	Anemone	Dahlia		Anemone
	Freesia	Gladiolus		Freesia
	Ixia	Lily		Ranunculus
	Lachenalia			
	Ranunculus			
	Sparaxis			
	Tulip			

Dahlia.

FLOWERS FOR PICKING

	BOTANICAL NAME	COMMON NAME
ANNUALS	*Antirrhinum majus*	Snapdragon
	Calendula officinalis	Calendula
	Centaurea cyanus	Cornflower
	Consolida cultivars	Larkspur
	Cosmos bipinnatus	Cosmos
	Dianthus barbatus	Sweet William
	Helianthus annuus	Sunflower
	Lathyrus odoratus	Sweet pea
	Limonium sinuatum	Statice
	Matthiola incana	Stock
	Papaver nudicaule	Iceland poppy
	Papaver rhoeas	Shirley poppy
PERENNIALS	*Acanthus mollis*	Bear's breeches
	Achillea cultivars	Yarrow
	Agapanthus cultivars	African lily
	Alchemilla mollis	Lady's mantle
	Anthemis punctata	
	Anthemis tinctoria	Golden marguerite
	Aquilegia vulgaris	Granny's bonnet
	Argyranthemum frutescens	Marguerite daisy
	Aster novi-belgii	Michaelmas daisy
	Astilbe	False spiraea
	Bergenia cordifolia	Elephant's ears
	Coreopsis verticillata	Tickseed
	Echinacea purpurea	Cone flower
	Euphorbia charachias	Spurge
	Euphorbia hybrids	Spurge
	Gaura lindheimeri	
	Heliotropium arborescens	Cherry pie
	Helleborus	Winter rose
	Hemerocallis	Day lily
	Leucanthemum xsuperbum	Shasta daisy
	Lupinus	Russell lupin
	Penstemon	
	Phygelius aequalis	Cape figwort
	Rudbeckia fulgida	Cone flower
	Salvia leucantha	Mexican bush sage
	Salvia madrensis	Mexican sage
	Salvia uliginosa	Bog sage
	Scabiosa	Pincushion flower
	Sedum spectabile	Stonecrop
	Sisyrinchium striatum	Satin flower
	Zantedeschia aethiopica	Dwarf arum lily

Russell lupins and asters.

Cacti, Succulents and other Accent Plants

Plants with spiky sword-like foliage and strong architectural lines add drama and texture to any style of garden. They can be used in containers as focal points or as full-stops to anchor a group of shrubs or perennials.

Many of the most dramatic accent plants come from deserts, succulents and cacti that thrive in dry gardens or in containers. In hot dry locations, whole desert gardens can be centred around succulents and cacti, grown in the ground as well as in pots. They are ideal for exposed coastal gardens.

Subtropical-style gardens suit the dramatic forms of succulents, and where the soil is too rich or the watering requirements of rainforest plants rule out succulents in the garden soil, they can be well utilised in pots.

Large cacti make superb accent plants. Mature cacti of various shapes work well against plain walls or paved surfaces where their dramatic shadows can be cast to best effect.

The main requirement for growing cacti and succulents is excellent drainage and, although many will tolerate surprisingly low temperatures, they will not stand cold damp conditions. In most gardens the best place to grow cacti is in pots. Pots should be moved to sheltered locations in excessively wet winter weather. Outdoor pots are best raised so that the drainage hole is not sitting on the ground. Cold tolerance varies with each variety, so watch out for those that prefer to be indoors during your cold time of year. Sun is important to bring out the best colour in most succulents.

Although they will survive for long periods without water, cacti and succulents do need some water to look their best.

As a guide, water weekly during the spring and summer growing period (some varieties will need less, some more). A little feeding in this period is also beneficial. Use weak solutions of liquid fertiliser or a slow-release fertiliser at repotting time or a side dressing once a year.

During winter, cut out feeding altogether and water very sparingly. Allow plants to dry out between waterings. When repotting or planting new plants, do not water straight away. Allow the soil to dry out first. This way the roots that have been damaged in the repotting process have a chance to recover. Water on an inactive root system will only cause it to rot.

Agave attenuata.

Agave

Agaves are large-growing succulents of amazing geometry. They are simply stunning, especially good for dramatic focal points and are used increasingly in all styles of garden. They must have good drainage, protesting at the slightest excess of water, especially when it is combined with cold.

A. americana (century plant): This is the largest agave, growing up to 2 m in maturity, but can be contained in a large pot. Blue-green leaves are edged with hooked spines. Best where it won't do harm to innocent bystanders. Variegated forms are also available.

A. attenuata: The most popular agave of all, and deservingly so. It is slow growing to 1 m with big, sword-shaped, but spineless leaves produced in wide rosettes.

A. victoriae-reginae is a dwarf form making perfect rosettes with dark green leaves edged with white. This is an excellent long-term container plant growing to about 30 cm tall.

Aloe

With similar bold spiky foliage to the agaves, the aloes come in a huge range of shapes and sizes with brightly coloured flowers like red hot pokers at various times of the year. Aloes are succulents needing dry conditions, but some are adapted to the coldest climates.

A. arborescens (tree aloe) grows to about 3 m with thick trunks topped with tapering blue-green leaves and masses of red flowers on long stalks. *A. barbadensis* (syn. *A. vera*) is the one with the magical healing and beauty-enhancing properties. It is of moderate proportions with 50 cm upright fleshy leaves and yellow flowers on top of stalks up to 1 m. *A. brevifolia* is a low grower, reaching only 30 cm, with clusters of red flowers at any time.

A. polyphylla is almost unreal, 'alien-like' with its round shape and leaves arranged in a perfect spiral. This one will grow in a cold climate.

Astelia chathamica 'Silver Spear'

This is a New Zealand native with silver sword-like leaves and a flax-like form. It is always eye-catching, whether planted *en masse* or on its own. Astelias need good drainage, adequate moisture during dry periods, and protection from frost and strong wind, but are otherwise trouble free.

Cordyline

CABBAGE TREE

As young plants they make a spiky foliage shrub sitting on the ground, developing the straight bare trunks with age. At any stage the New Zealand cabbage trees are an arresting sight. They are not fussy about soil type or climatic extremes and will tolerate wet soils.

The most common species is *C. australis*, which grows to 6 m tall. *C. banksii* is a smaller tree, growing to about 3 m tall, with longer leaves and drooping bunches of white flowers. *C. Green Goddess* remains in a compact clump of close-packed broad green leaves, and has long stems of white flowers.

Juniperus chinensis 'Kaizuka'

HOLLYWOOD JUNIPER

The natural spiralling shape of this interesting conifer is very distinctive but it can be pruned in different ways to create all sorts of interesting shapes from crazy zigzags to neat spiral topiaries. A small tree by proportions, suitable for a large container. Junipers are tough plants tolerating a range of soil types.

Palms and Cycads

Accent plants mainly for warm-climate and subtropical-style gardens.

Palms and Cycads: Go to page 68.

Xeronema callistemon

POOR KNIGHTS LILY

This spectacular native plant has fleshy flax-like foliage and bright red brush-like flowers in summer. It enjoys perfect drainage and restricted roots so a pot is the perfect place for it. Best in full sun, it is an excellent coastal plant.

Yucca

Yuccas are desert succulents with very dramatic, stiffly upright, sword-like leaves. They need well-drained soil and tolerate drought once established. They are ideal coastal or container plants. As a bonus there are wonderful spikes of cream flowers in summer. They need full sun. Some have trunk-like stems (cabbage-tree style). Others are stemless or practically so and sit with the base of their foliage at ground level.

Y. filamentosa (Adam's needle) grows to about 1.5 m, producing flowers when quite young. It has a striped-leaved form as well as plain grey-green. It is best located where its sharp points are out of harm's way. *Y. elephantipes* (giant yucca) is spineless. It forms a bare trunk with dark green leaves and flowers in summer. This is a good container plant. There are many other yuccas.

Aeonium arboreum 'Schwarzkopf'.

Aeonium arboreum 'Schwarzkopf'

A short-lived but easy-to-grow succulent for part shade with very interesting rich purple foliage. It grows to about a metre with leaves arranged in rosettes on upward-reaching stems. There are yellow flowers on mature plants. A dry sandy soil is needed.

Crassula ovata (syn. C. argentea)

JADE PLANT

Resembles a miniature tree with a thick trunk and sturdy branches carrying the fleshy grey-green leaves. Pink flowers in spring.

Echeveria elegans

HEN AND CHICKS

Geometrically perfect blue-green rosettes that look more like flowers than foliage. Pink-and-yellow flowers appear in summer. This plant spreads freely by offshoots. There are a number of other excellent *Echeveria* species.

Kalanchoe hybrids

KALANCHOE

Popular houseplants, kalanchoes are tropical plants that can be grown outdoors in a frost-free location. Bright red, pink or orange flowers appear in winter.

Sedum

STONECROP

This is an enormous group. Some of the top favourites are:
S. floriferum 'Variegatum': Strong growing with trailing pink foliage.
S. morganianum (donkey's tail): Trailing chains of pale green fleshy foliage. It is popular for hanging baskets but also good for tall pots or those elevated on a wall or pedestal.
S. rubrotinctum (pork and beans): A spreading plant with bright green, red and orange foliage.
S. sieboldii (syn. *Hylotelephium sieboldii*): Trailing stems with flat clusters of red flowers.
S. spathulifolium 'Cape Blanco': Small silver leaves and pink stems with yellow flowers. This is a very pretty spreading variety that is great mixed with other succulents.

Sempervivum

HOUSELEEK

Clusters of very small, tightly packed rosettes that are great for foliage colour and textural contrasts. *S. arachnoideum* has tiny grey rosettes joined with silver webs. *S. tectorum* has bright green foliage tipped with reddish brown.

CACTI FOR POTS

Cephalocereus senilis

OLD MAN CACTUS

Potentially quite a tall columner cactus but slow growing. Tufts of long pale grey hair.

Cleistocactus

A tall and slender ribbed cactus, thickly covered in spines with lots of flowers. *C. strausii* branches at soil level to form a cluster of columns with white spines and large dark red flowers in spring or summer. It grows relatively quickly for a cactus and reaches up to 2 m in height.

Mammillaria

A large group of low-growing cacti known also as pincushion cactus. A profusion of brightly coloured flowers appears each year in pinks, reds, purples, yellow and white. There is a diverse range of shapes.

Notocactus spp.

Small ball-shaped cacti with prominent and colourful spines, easy to grow and good for small pots. The bright yellow flowers appear in spring or summer.

Opuntia

PRICKLY PEARS

A large group of cacti with flat, rounded prickled stems all growing out of each other in haphazard arrangement. Mature plants are free flowering with bright colours. A popular dwarf species is *O. microdasys*, commonly known as bunny ears.

Grasses

Most gardens have grass, but not all are graced with the presence of the non-mown kind — those highly underrated, interesting ornamental grasses that move in the breeze, adding an extra dimension of textural and colour contrast to the garden.

Grasses are the epitome of low-maintenance plants, looking after themselves once established. They fit with all kinds of garden styles (e.g., native, cottage, water and Japanese gardens), looking good in combination with tough perennials, shrubs and under trees, where they are excellent in large group plantings. The flowers of grasses are wonderful too. Large-leaved and glossy-foliaged plants are shown to best advantage planted next to the contrasting texture of a grass or grass-like plant. Grasses also combine well with flaxes and other spiky-leaved plants. They are an obvious choice for coastal gardens and make excellent container plants. A group of pots containing a variety of grasses can be quite striking.

EASY GRASSES

Carex spp.
NEW ZEALAND SEDGE
Very tough, the New Zealand sedges tolerate a wide range of soils, coastal conditions and frost. They grow in sun or part shade. They will benefit from deep watering in dry spells and the occasional feed. If plants become untidy, cut them back to 5 cm above the ground and they will come away again with renewed vigour. *C. comans* (20 x 30 cm) is a small compact grass with very dense, blue-green foliage, curled at the ends — an ideal edging or groundcover plant. *C. flagellifera* (40 x 50 cm) is more upright with long, arching, light brown foliage that sways in the wind. *C. testacea* (30 x 40 cm) is an orange-foliaged form.

Carex morrowii 'Evergold'
JAPANESE SEDGE
40 cm x 40 cm
Leaves are slightly wider than a true grass, striped green and cream. This compact plant is a superb feature for garden or container. It prefers semi-shade.

Chionochloa flavicans
SNOW TUSSOCK
1 m x 1.5 m
A very graceful native grass that could be described as a small toetoe, except that it is much finer, weeping in habit, and a lot prettier than the common roadside plant. Feathery cream flowers are at the end of long arching stems. It is good near water, as a garden feature among perennials or other grasses, or in a large container. Grow it in good average soil in sun or part shade. Less common in gardens is *C. rubra* with bronzy-red foliage all year round. All species of *Chionochloa* are hardy and easy to grow in most parts of New Zealand.

Pennisetum setaceum (syn. *P. ruppelii*)
FOUNTAIN GRASS
1 m x 60 cm
A grass from tropical Africa for warm climates. Graceful golden-brown foliage and in summer, long upright stems with coppery-pink flower spikes, fading to cream as they age. The flowers are lovely for picking. Drought but not frost resistant, and dormant in winter.

Hawaiian hibiscus.

Lawns

Groundcovers:
Go to page 56.

Plants for shade:
Go to page 76.

Α n attractively shaped, well-kept sweep of green will set off the garden, even when the rest of it is not at its best. However, it's not usually the part that gets the most attention. More often than not the lawn is the bit left over — the space not taken up by garden beds, paths and patios. It's the part that needs mowing, but to most people's way of thinking, requires a lot less care than a garden that needs weeding.

However, the most maintenance-free gardens have no lawn. The ground is covered with a combination of hard surfaces and easy-care trees, shrubs and groundcovers. Granted, these low-maintenance plants take a little time before they have grown large enough to smother the weeds, but a good lawn, one that adds to the overall attractiveness of a garden, needs plenty of attention. Not just mowing, but feeding, lots of watering, and weeding too.

HOW MUCH LAWN DO YOU REALLY NEED?

It's worth giving some thought to the purpose of your various lawn areas. You may be better off with less than you first imagined.

Lawns have both practical and aesthetic requirements. Small children need lawns to play on, but as they grow older you may consider reducing the amount of lawn in favour of extended deck or patio areas and more low-maintenance plantings.

The reason for a front lawn is often to show off the house to best advantage, even if it serves no practical purpose. It may be used as occasional extra parking space, although no lawn will stand up to constant abuse in this manner.

If you have narrow strips of lawn down the sides of your house, seriously consider alternative options. If it is an accessway, it is probably not standing up too well to the foot traffic and would be better as a hard-surface pathway edged with permanent plantings.

Shady areas are not good candidates for lawn, which needs at least eight hours of sunlight each day to grow well. Some lawn types will tolerate a degree of shade, but the best idea is to delegate the shadiest areas of your garden to the planting of shrubs and perennials that thrive in low-light conditions.

Gently sloping lawns can be most attractive, but steeply sloping lawns are difficult to manage. A slope of greater than 30 degrees should be planted in shrubs and groundcovers rather than lawn. Alternatively (but at greater expense), the sloping site could be terraced into two or more flattish areas separated by retaining walls.

Once you have eliminated the areas that do not need to be in lawn, you will have more time to spend keeping the remaining lawn areas looking great.

Lawn design

The shape of a lawn not only makes a huge impact on the look of the whole garden but it also affects the ease of maintenance. Generally, simple shapes work best in both instances. The number of trees to be mown around should be kept to a minimum, preferably nil. There should be a clearly defined line between a planted area and lawn, while still allowing for the spilling over of plants to soften that line. Generously sweeping curves (not wiggly snakes) look best in an informal garden and are easy to manoeuvre the lawn mower around. For a more formal look, go for rectangles and semicircles. The shape of the lawn is aesthetically much more important than the shape of the garden beds, because the lawn in effect defines the shape of a garden room. The 'left-over bits' should be for the beds, not the other way around. It is the shape of the lawn that you see, not the shape of the three-dimensional garden plantings, unless of course they are viewed from above.

Caring for established lawns

Lawns need looking after. At the very least they require regular mowing. The most attractive of them are routinely fed and watered as well.

It is a wise gardener who keeps their lawn area to a useful minimum so that no time is wasted looking after unnecessary areas of lawn and efforts can be concentrated on the part that counts. Make life easy from the beginning by designing a simple-shaped lawn that is easy to water and mow, and by choosing the right lawn seed for your lifestyle.

Once you see the results of a little 'TLC', your lawn might just take on a whole new meaning. No longer a weekend chore, but your pride and joy. Well, maybe!

MOWING is the main job, and seemingly rather enjoyed by those with a fondness for noisy things with wheels. But there is good mowing and bad mowing.

The biggest fault is to mow too low. Lawns that are constantly scalped never get a chance to produce good root sytstems. Short tops mean short roots and a lawn that has little tolerance of dry periods, turning brown with rapid ease and becoming more susceptible to weed invasion. An ideal height is 2 to 3 cm. The critical time to mow a little higher is through the dry summer months.

Keeping the lawn-mower blade sharp gives a cleaner cut and helps minimise disease. If you have a small lawn you might consider replacing the old rotary mower with a small reel (or push) mower. These make a lovely even cut, especially on fine grasses, and are a lot quieter.

Avoid mowing the lawn straight after heavy rain as this will increase soil compaction, leading to poor water penetration. On the other hand, mowing on a very hot day is also best avoided as it creates greater water stress.

If mown frequently, a lawn can benefit from having the grass clippings left on, reducing the need for watering and feeding. The clippings will break down to return important nutrients and organic matter to the soil. However, large volumes of clippings can lead to disease problems so are best removed and returned to the garden later in the form of compost.

Autumn (March to May) is the very best season to sow lawn seed, while the soil is still warm but after the hot dry weather is over. Spring is the next best time, but weeds will be more of a problem. The warmer the weather, the faster your seed will germinate — a few days in warm weather, and up to three weeks in cool weather.

PREPARATION Whether you are painting your house, laying cobblestones or putting down a new lawn, it's the same boring old story — preparation is the key to success. Short cuts in the beginning will result in time-consuming fix-up jobs later. So, give yourself a good three weeks' lead time before sowing and:

1 *Spray* the desired area including all weeds with Round-up® (or an equivalent glysophate-based spray). Do not rotary hoe until weeds are killed or the worst of them will simply be buried to return later — with renewed gusto. Round-up® takes two to three weeks to do the job. There is no residual spray left in the soil so the new lawn grasses will be safe from harm. Although Round-up® kills a wide range of weeds, it does not kill white clover. If you wish to rid your lawn of clover, spray with Shortcut®. A very fast-acting spray, which leaves no soil residual, Shortcut® is also effective on most grasses.

2 *Remove* all dead grass and weeds and rake out any rubbish or rocks.

3 *Rotary hoe* the soil to a depth of about 8 cm and remove clods and lumps. Do not attempt to do this when the soil is wet. A load of sterilised topsoil will be an advantage at this stage. The idea is to have an even bed of finely textured soil for optimum seed germination.

4 *Level* the soil and compact lightly. Iron out the humps and hollows. If rotary hoeing has made the soil very soft it is a good idea to compact it by heeling systematically across the area to be sown.

5 *Feed* the soil with a dressing of lawn fertiliser applied at the rate recommended on the bag, about a handful for every square metre.

6 *Rake* the top 2 cm just prior to sowing to form the seed bed.

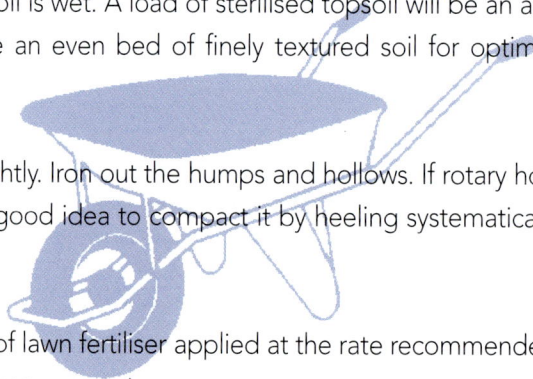

SELECTING THE SEED

The best lawn seed for the job depends largely on what your lawn will be used for. Play areas and lawns subjected to a lot of traffic need hard-wearing grasses, whereas finely textured varieties suit when aesthetics are the main concern. For low maintenance, go for the hard-wearing varieties. The coarser grasses have better heat and drought tolerance. A top-class lawn of fine grasses needs a lot more pampering if it is to stay looking good. Some lawn grasses are slower growing so require less-frequent mowing, others are tolerant of shade. Packaged lawn seeds available from garden centres are blends of two or more different grass varieties, specially formulated for each different use. These are being revised and upgraded all the time.

HOW MUCH SEED?

Seed is applied at the rate of about 30 g per square metre. Most brands will have the coverage area specified on the pack, so it is simply a matter of working out how many square metres you want to cover.

SOWING

Before sowing, the soil should have settled down so that there are no deep footmarks or footprints when it is walked over. Apply the seed as evenly as possible. The best way is to take the total amount of seed you require and divide it into two halves. Broadcast the first half by scattering in a north–south direction as you walk over the whole area. Then scatter the second half in an east–west direction over the same area. Save a little seed for oversowing patches you have missed. Ideally, you should use a roller to firm down the surface after sowing, thus ensuring that the seed is in good contact with the soil.

WATERING

Use a sprinkler or hand-held soft-spray hose attachment to thoroughly water the newly sown area and start the germination process. Keep the lawn moist with daily watering, morning and evenings. Never let it dry out. When the grass is clearly visible, water daily until the first mow.

MOWING

The first mowing should not be until the young seedlings have reached the two-leaf stage (about 3 cm high). At this stage only the top 1 cm is cut off to encourage strong root growth. The height of the cut should remain at 2 cm for the first three months. After this time it can be raised, but never cut lower than 2 cm.

FERTILISER

In addition to the base fertiliser, a second application should be made at the two-leaf stage, after the first mowing. Apply about 20 grams of lawn fertiliser per square metre.

AERATION is a practice commonly carried out on golf courses. It is particularly worthwhile every few years if you have clay soil. The idea is to add air spaces to the soil via holes. These can be made with a garden fork, but need to be 2 to 3 cm apart, so this method would only suit people with exceptionally small lawns or an over-abundance of time. A better way is to rent an aerating machine from a hire service. There are various types. The best time to aerate is in the spring when the grass is actively growing and the weather is damp.

FEEDING can make even the most odd mixtures of nondescript grasses look lush and green. It is best done little and often rather than in heavy infrequent applications. Feed when the grass is actively growing. Start in early spring with repeated applications every five to six weeks until early autumn. The rate of application will depend on the particular fertiliser you are using. Slow-release fertilisers last longer so need applying less often. Follow the instructions on the pack.

Fertiliser should be applied to moist ground and watered in afterwards. Spread the fertiliser as evenly as possible to avoid a patchy look with different tones of green.

A thriving, well-fed lawn is far less vulnerable to invasion by unsightly weeds than one that is struggling to grow.

More about fertilisers:
Go to page 200.

Morte about watering:
Go to page 202.

WATERING is unavoidable if a lawn is to remain green all year round. Fine-textured lawns will need the most watering. The idea is to start watering at the onset of summer, before the lawn turns brown.

On established lawns, a good soaking one or two evenings a week is better than frequent light watering, which only encourages shallow root growth. Allowing the soil to dry out a little between waterings reduces the risk of fungal infections.

If you can afford it, a fixed sprinkler system is the best way to water a lawn. It is not only the most time efficient but a properly designed system is also the most water efficient. Nozzles are positioned to ensure that every inch of lawn receives water, without waste. A timer can be installed to make sure the right amount of water goes on. It is important to make sure that the sprinkler system is set up to suit your water pressure at the time of day it is in use.

Moveable sprinklers are a cheaper and popular alternative. The main problem with these is that it is all too easy to turn them on and forget them. Some areas are under-watered while others receive more water than they need. The watering pattern rarely matches the shape of the lawn.

Hand watering has the drawback of being time-consuming, with the risk of under-watering. The job needs to be done slowly to ensure maximum soakage, but it's a great way to unwind at the end of a hot summer's day, trigger-activated spray wand in one hand, gin and tonic in the other.

Improve soakage and reduce run-off on sloping clay soils by aerating the soil as above.

WEEDS occur most prolifically in undernourished lawns, but will create unsightly blemishes in even the most manicured lawns. The prickly kind are the worst, and bee-attracting weeds, such as clover, are also best avoided. A few weeds in a small lawn can be carefully removed using a trowel, but when things get out of hand, more drastic measures are called for. Fortunately, there are a number of specially devised weedkillers for safe use on lawns.

Onehunga weed is the culprit if you have those small prickles that stick to your feet. It is important to spray it at the right time. Faneron® can be applied in spring and early summer after most of the seeds have germinated but before the plants have gone to seed (i.e., before the flowers appear and turn to prickles). Faneron® is a selective herbicide that does not kill grasses, but it is effective against a number of lawn weeds.

Moss shows up in lawns that are poorly fed or are in shade. It can also be an indicator of poor drainage. Some mosses colonise very dry areas or lawns that are too closely mown. If any of these conditions prevail, weedkillers will only give temporary control.

Check your cutting height is no shorter than 2 cm and try mowing more frequently. Bump up your feeding program, especially in spring and early autumn. For dry areas, try aerating the soil (see above) or checking your watering system. For wet areas, it may simply be a question of ironing out hollows with topsoil and resowing new lawn. For worse cases consider installing drainage or converting the area into a garden for moisture-tolerant plants, improving the soil while you are at it.

For chemical control, first wet the moss thoroughly. Spray with a proprietary spray (for moss in lawns) or ferrous sulphate. Then rake out the dead moss. Large areas will be best resown. Small packs of lawn seed are available for patching-up jobs such as this.

INSECT PESTS lurk beneath lawns just as they do in the garden at large and will attack when they find conditions are favourable. Once you have diagnosed the problem, the treatment is straightforward. The most common insect pests are grass grub and porina caterpillars.

Grass-grub caterpillars give the lawn a general sick, stunted appearance and cause dead brown patches, which tend to be in circular shapes. Lift a square of turf and check for shrimp-shaped, greyish-white grubs feeding on the roots. The adult is a beetle, which flies at dusk between October and December. Caterpillars hatch as soon as three weeks later and are present in the soil from November until the following September. They build up in the soil from low to high levels over 2 to 4 years.

Porina caterpillars surface from the soil at night to chew the grass off at ground level. Look out for unusually short cropping of grass. You may also see the

caterpillars' burrow excavations, small deposits of soil on the grass surface, rather like worm castings. The adult porina is a brown moth about 2.5 cm long, often seen in spring and summer evenings when it is attracted by light. The eggs are broadcast over the soil and the emergent caterpillars soon burrow into the soil. They are mucky green on top with yellowish undersides, reaching up to 7.5 cm long.

Diazinon® controls both these pests, but twice as much is needed for grass grub, so it's worth knowing which particular pest you have (both is possible). Diazinon® goes by various trade names, such as Soil Insect Killer. It should be applied in late summer and autumn. Apply plenty of water to wash it into the soil, and keep children and pets off the area for at least a week.

In hot climates, from Auckland northward, black crickets do considerable damage to lawns when dry conditions prevail. The best deterrent is to keep the lawn well watered.

FUNGAL DISEASES most commonly occurring on lawns are fusarium in cool autumn or spring weather, dollar spot in summer, and red thread at any time of the year. Fungus and mildew spray can be used to control all three, but with attention to maintenance, feeding in particular, you may avoid the need to spray.

Fusarium causes small patches of yellowing grass up to 30 cm across, showing as a greasy slime. Prevent invasion by avoiding nitrogen-rich fertilisers in autumn or winter.

Red thread attacks fine-leaved grasses that are underfed. It shows up as irregular yellowed patches of lawn with pinky-red threads through the leaves. To prevent red thread, feed the lawn every two months in spring and summer and avoid mowing too closely.

Dollar spot causes many small straw-coloured spots with cob-webby growth, which are visible when there is dew on the lawn. Underfed lawns are the most susceptible.

Capsicum *cultivar.*

The food garden

The Vegetable Garden

Neat rows of cabbages, cauliflowers and carrots — and in summer, walls of red tomatoes and tunnels of towering sweetcorn you could run through. It's the back-yard vege patch you might remember from childhood.

Though by no means extinct, the traditional model of a vegetable garden takes more space and more time than most modern gardeners can spare, especially when fresh produce is readily available at affordable prices.

But fresh is never fresher than when it comes from your own garden. This, coupled with a certain 'food renaissance' of late, seems to have rekindled our interest in the art of vegetable growing. There are all sorts of fascinating vegetables that are difficult to come by unless you grow them yourself.

Ideas on how vegetables fit into the overall garden design are also changing. Vegetable gardens are no longer regarded as purely utilitarian, as eyesores to be tucked away at the back of the section. In fact, vegetable plants have gained new status, worthy of rubbing shoulders with the most upper crust of ornamentals.

The simplest scenario is to include a few vegetables amongst the flowers, cottage style. The most elaborate is a French-style potager. Potager gardens are very much in mode, but a well-designed one adapted to its owner's situation can be as practical as it is a fashion statement. The New Zealand version of a potager garden promises to be more than just a passing fad.

Potagers date back to the grand French gardens of the fifteenth and sixteenth centuries where huge vegetable gardens were laid out in formal patterns; decoration was important as food production. Some of the grandest have been restored to their former glory. The potager at the château of Villandry is the most talked-about example. The influence of such gardens on the home garden front has been a renewed focus on the ornamental value of vegetables and greater use of structured, formal layouts.

So, what exactly is the New Zealand potager garden anyway? In fact it's probably not that far removed from our traditional vegetable patch. A variety of vegetables are still grown in deliberate patterns within defined boundaries. The difference is that the patterns are designed to look good as much as for ease of management. The

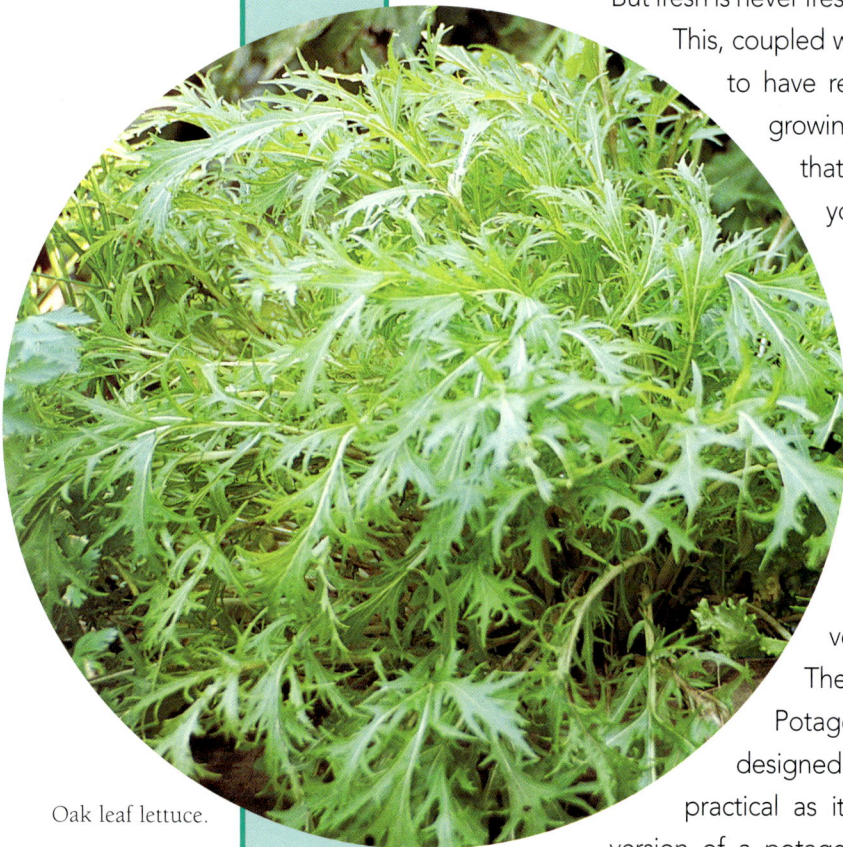

Oak leaf lettuce.

vegetables are grown closer together, are not necessarily in single rows and there are ample paths for easy access. Herbs and flowers are included. All is usually contained within the permanent structure of paving, raised edges and hedges for year-round good looks. The potager can be any size depending on how many vegetables you want to grow, but it will tend to yield more veges per square metre than the traditional widely spaced rows because it is more intensively planted.

Be warned though, the modern potager requires no less work than any other vegetable garden. Close planting means more feeding and more watering. Regular weeding and replanting will be important if the potager is to remain looking its best. Its size should reflect the time you will have to spend on it. The best advice is to start small, restricting yourself to a few favourite vegetables. For example, a tiny potager might simply contain three different lettuces with a border of parsley and chives, and a pot of bright yellow marigolds for colour. Transplant new lettuce seedlings as you harvest and in autumn replace the lettuces with a winter crop of different-coloured beets.

As for the ground plan, the typically symmetrical layout should be modified to suit your situation. It will depend on the area of flat sunny land you have available. Also, presuming that you will be continuously harvesting the veges just as they are looking their best, a more informal layout may be easier to cope with.

The main thing is that the garden is divided up into functional beds and pathways. Main paths should be wide enough for a wheel barrow and you should be able to reach every part of the garden without standing on the soil.

Raised beds are a very good idea, especially if you have heavy clay soil. They are also kinder to your back.

It is easy to imagine that those glorious potagers pictured in books or seen on spring garden tours look this good all of the time. In fact, the biggest challenge, as with any garden, is to keep it looking as good in February or June as it does in November.

So it is important to give the potager some structure with permanent plantings of shrubs and trees. One of the easiest ways is to edge the whole garden with a low evergreen hedge, the best of these being miniature box (*Buxus sempervirens* 'Suffruticosa'). Lavender and rosemary are other possibilities. Small citrus trees, such as Meyer lemon, make an excellent background or centrepiece. They are green all year round and provide colour in winter. Espaliered fruit trees are an especially attractive feature of potager gardens. The effect can be achieved quite easily by planting a row of the poplar-shaped 'Ballerina' apple trees.

It is important, however, not to plant vegetables too close to hedges or trees where they will be in competition for light, food and water.

For bigger gardens, a fixed irrigation system will save hours of watering. It will also save water.

More about soil: Go to page 3.

More about fertilisers: Go to page 200.

More about compost: Go to page 196.

More about citrus trees: Go to page 169.

AUBERGINE

Also known as eggplant, the aubergine is a summer-growing vegetable in the same family as tomatoes, capsicums and potatoes. They can be casseroled, as in the traditional ratatouille, roasted or barbecued. Roasted, skinned and mashed with roasted garlic and lemon juice, they make a delicious spread or dip.

Because aubergines need a good four or five months of warm temperatures from seed to harvest, it is best to buy hot-house raised seedlings for planting as soon as the ground is warm and the frost risk over. Keen gardeners with greenhouses would of course do the seed raising themselves, along with their tomatoes and capsicums.

Aubergines form an attractive small bush, making them well suited to growing in containers. As long as they receive ample watering and feeding they will do well in the well-drained, warm potting-mix environment. A 25 cm terracotta pot would house one aubergine plant. Add a slow-release fertiliser to the potting mix and feed fortnightly with a balanced liquid fertiliser. Plants in the garden should have a well-drained compost-rich soil with a handful of general garden fertiliser per square metre, raked in prior to planting. When the first flowers drop to reveal the tiny new fruit, side dress with another couple of handfuls of general garden fertiliser per square metre, or liquid feed as for potted plants.

Avoid wetting the foliage when watering as this encourages disease problems. Plants may need staking as they become weighted down with fruit.

Harvest aubergines when the skin is smooth and a rich purple colour. Use secateurs to avoid damaging the plant. Picking encourages more fruit to develop.

BEANS

There are all sorts of beans, both annual and perennial.

Perennial beans are known as scarlet runner beans and can really only be grown as perennials in warm climates. In cool climates they are generally treated as annuals. Scarlet runner beans are very attractive with their wall of scarlet flowers, and if space allows are a most worthy occupant for a potager garden, grown on tepees or trellis. Beans are usually the first to be harvested in summer.

Among the annual beans there are dwarf and climbing varieties. Dwarf varieties are the easiest to grow because there is no need to supply supports. They are high yielding for the small amount of space required.

Beans are easy to grow from seed. These are sown directly into a well-prepared soil that has reached warm unfluctuating temperatures of no less than 16°C, night and day. Never sow beans into cold wet soil. Make successive sowings every 3 weeks for a continuous supply. Warm-climate gardeners can sow right through until late summer, while there is still a good 2 or 3 months of warm, frost-free weather to come.

Pick beans frequently while they are young and tender.

BEETROOT

Beetroot is a good-looking plant for the potager with attractive red-veined leaves. It is an easy-to-grow crop that can be eaten raw or cooked. In a warm climate, beetroot can be sown directly into the soil any time from August right through to March, making it an ideal vege for the winter garden. In cold climates beetroot is sown in spring for autumn harvest.

Beetroot needs plenty of food and water. It will not do well over summer unless it is frequently watered. Prepare the soil in plenty of time before sowing with plenty of compost and a couple of handfuls of general garden fertiliser per square metre. To assist germination, soak seed in water for an hour before sowing. Sow directly into the soil and thin to 3 to 5 cm apart when the seedlings are about 5 to 10 cm high. Seed can also be sown in trays for later transplanting or you can purchase seedlings in punnets ready to transplant.

There are round or cylindrically shaped. The round varieties are ready to eat in the shortest time, especially the baby varieties, which are lovely for cooking and serving whole. The cylindrical varieties are best for bottling. Remember bottling?

Some varieties go to seed in prolonged cold weather. Look for non-bolting varieties.

Beware of Club-root!

All brassicas (cabbage, cauliflower and broccoli) are susceptible to this nasty disease, which lurks in the soil, causing the roots to swell and stunting the growth of the affected plants. The best preventative is to practise crop rotation and resist planting any member of the brassica family in soil that was used for a brassica crop the previous growing season. The longer a patch of soil has a rest from brassicas, the safer you will be. Lime is also a good preventative as the disease thrives in acid conditions. Should any plants become infected with club-root, destroy them as quickly as possible. Do not put them on the compost heap.

BROCCOLI

A few plants of sprouting broccoli are useful in winter and early spring, when you can dash out and pick a few heads for a meal any day of the week. They keep producing perfectly edible side shoots long after the central head has been picked. These will keep coming for a long period as long as they are regularly picked.

It is easiest to buy plants in punnets. Plant ideally in spring or autumn into well-drained, rich composty soil. Keep the plants moist and side dress with a general garden fertiliser once the plants get going, and again in a month or so.

CABBAGES

Cabbages come in a wealth of shapes and sizes these days. They look good in the garden and are useful in the kitchen. Chinese cabbages are very quick and easy to grow. There are different cultivars for different seasons, so you can have cabbages in your garden all year round. Cabbages are generally easier to grow than cauliflowers, but they are grown in the same way.

CAPSICUMS AND CHILLI PEPPERS

Vibrantly coloured green, red, yellow or purple capsicums (otherwise known as sweet peppers) are as good to look at as they are to eat. Superb in salads, they take on a whole new delicious flavour when roasted or barbecued. Capsicums need at least three months of warm summer temperatures to ripen, which makes them more challenging, but not impossible, for South Island gardeners.

In warm climates, capsicum growing is a breeze, as long as you don't leave it too late. The best idea is to purchase good-sized seedlings when they become available in garden centres in spring, usually around mid-October. These have been raised in hot houses but should have been given a 'hardening off' period outdoors in the nursery before being offered for sale. If there is still a risk of frost in your area, grow them on in their pots in a warm sheltered position until it is safe to plant. Late plantings may not have time to yield fully ripened fruit before the cool weather arrives. If planted in mid-summer when temperatures are high or the ground is too dry, fruit may not set at all.

Capsicums can be picked at the green stage or left on the plant to ripen to yellow or red (depending on cultivar) three to four weeks later.

Both hot and sweet peppers are derived from the species *Capsicum annuum*, a native of Mexico. There are many different cultivars. The hot chilli cultivars can be used fresh or preserved by pickling or drying.

Plant capsicums or chilli peppers in a warm sunny position in well-drained soil with a handful per square metre of general garden fertiliser. Protect young plants from slugs and snails. When the first fruit appears, feed again by side dressing with general garden fertiliser or applying a balanced liquid fertiliser.

Capsicums are an ideal vegetable for growing in pots. Choose a good-sized pot (at least 25 cm diameter for one plant) and keep it well watered.

CAPSICUMS LOVE:
✓ Warm temperatures
✓ Good drainage
✓ Compost
✓ Water during dry periods

CARROTS

Carrots are grown from seed sown directly into a well-worked, well-drained soil with plenty of organic matter. Because it is the below-ground part of the plant that is of key interest, it makes sense that the soil should be as good as possible, without stones or other obstructions.

The seed is generally sown any time from early August to autumn except in very dry periods. For a continuous supply, seed needs to be sown every few weeks. The seed is very fine and tends to stick together, so mixing with sand prior to sowing is recommended. Alternatively, you can mix carrot seed with radish seed. This speeds up germination and makes thinning easier.

Thinning to a spacing of 2 to 3 cm is necessary once the leaves have grown to about 5 cm. Another thinning when leaves are about 15 cm high will yield delicious baby carrots big enough to eat. Do your best to keep carrot-rust fly out by firming the soil back around the remaining carrots. As the crop matures, prevent the shoulder of the carrots from going green by keeping them covered with soil.

Carrot-rust fly is a big problem where carrots are concerned. The larvae munch on the roots so that even if you salvage some for your own consumption, the carrots will be unattractive and difficult to prepare. Effective control is by way of Diazinon® (Soil Insect Killer), but this defeats one of the main purposes of growing carrots. For most people, the idea of growing carrots is to try and grow them organically. Chemically assisted carrots can be bought cheaply all year round. In warm dry climates the rust fly is practically unavoidable. To start with, choose a fast-maturing variety that has high resistance to carrot-rust fly. It's well worth any extra cost. Eat the carrots when they are young, before the worst damage is done. Never put rust-infected carrots on the compost heap. Plant carrots in a different place each year and always firm dislodged soil around the tops of the carrots after thinning or harvesting. If you don't mind how it looks, a mesh cloth (e.g., Enviromesh) over the crop from sowing onwards will go a long way towards preventing entry of the fly.

CAULIFLOWERS

There is no comparing the taste of a home-grown cauliflower with one from the supermarket. To grow them well you need a deeply dug well-drained soil with compost and lime added.

Prepare the bed in advance, adding the lime. About a fortnight later spread a handful of general garden fertiliser per square metre, rake to mix it in then firm the soil bed. Plant seedlings firmly, disturbing their roots as little as possible and water thoroughly. Seedlings with bent roots or looking sickly are not worth planting.

As the crop grows, make sure the soil remains moist and feed every few weeks with a balanced liquid fertiliser or a light side dressing of general garden fertiliser.

CHICORY

Chicory (or 'witloof') is a salad vegetable rather like a cross between a lettuce and a cabbage. It is good to eat and an excellent crop for winter colour. The red chicory, also known as radicchio, is a particularly attractive vegetable to grow for winter colour in the potager garden. Eaten cooked or fresh it is ready for harvest about 120 days after sowing. Seed can be sown from late spring through to early autumn. The same growing conditions as for lettuce are required.

CRESS

Watercress (*Nasturtium officinale*) is delicious for salads, sandwiches and soups. The good news is that you do not need a stream to grow it in. It does, however, require plenty of moisture and, unlike most vegetables, shade. You can grow it in a pot or in the garden.

For the garden, dig a hole or trench in a shady location and fill it with good compost. Sprinkle the seeds on top and press into the surface. Kept moist, it will germinate in a few days. For pot-grown watercress, stand a large pot in a saucer of water. Fill the pot with good compost and sow the seed. Stand it in a shady place and keep the saucer clean and topped up with water. Feed occasionally with a liquid fertiliser.

Another kind of cress is land cress (*Barbarea praecox*). It has a stronger flavour than watercress. Land cress also likes shade and plenty of water and is grown from seed sown directly into moist soil. Both types are ready to use about 2 months from sowing. Make fortnightly sowings for a continuous supply. Seed can be sown all year round in a mild climate, but spring and autumn are best.

LEEKS

Leeks are an easy-to-grow crop, happy to sit in the garden throughout winter and spring, ready at hand as you need them. If you don't get round to eating them all, they look magnificent when they go to seed. Buy seedlings in punnets in summer or autumn. Otherwise, sow directly into the soil in late summer or autumn, thinning to 15 cm apart. Keep plants well watered, especially in the early stages when the weather can be dry.

For white stems (nice but not essential), mound the soil up around the plants as they grow. Some gardeners go to the bother of growing leeks in lined trenches to keep the leeks free of soil between the leaves.

Plant leeks in well-dug, well-drained soil with general garden fertiliser mixed in prior to planting. Leeks can be eaten quite young and should be ready within 150 days from sowing. There is no need to wait until they reach supermarket thickness (in fact they might not get to that if your soil is a bit on the heavy side).

LETTUCES

There is no substitute for the taste of lettuces picked fresh from the garden. Once you get into the swing of things, it is economical, healthy and very convenient to grow your own summer supply of lettuces. They are number one on the list of indispensable plants for your garden. Modern cultivars are extremely quick and easy to grow. They come in an ever-expanding range of colours and textures, looking as good in the garden as they do in the salad bowl. It would be worthwhile devoting a potager garden to growing lettuces alone. Lettuces can be grown from seedlings purchased at the garden centre in punnets of six to ten plants, or from seed. Growing from seed is more economical if you use a lot of lettuce and offers a wider choice of cultivars. It is arguably more time consuming than purchasing seedlings, but it is also more rewarding. The best idea is to sow a tray of seedlings every few weeks, so that they are ready to transplant into the garden as harvested lettuces vacate the space. You can sow a few different cultivars in the one tray, either from separate packets or by buying a packet of mixed lettuce cultivars. Seed can also be sown directly into the soil. This reduces transplanting shock in hot weather. Take care not to damage roots when transplanting seedlings.

Growing from seed: Go to page 209.

The looseleaf lettuce cultivars can be harvested leaf by leaf if you choose, making them a better candidate for the ornamental kitchen garden than the hearting cultivars, which are harvested all at once. A well-drained, fertile soil with lots of compost will make your lettuces grow faster and healthier. It is best not to add fertiliser to the ground at planting time. General garden fertiliser can be added as a side dressing and watered in two weeks after planting. Liquid fertilisers applied once a week will really get them going. Poor drainage or dry or cold spells can lead to retarded growth, which can make the lettuces taste bitter. So be prepared to water when the rain doesn't do it for you, and seriously consider raised planting beds, which are better for drainage and warmer soil. Generally, lettuces grow best in full sun, but in hot summer climates they often do best with a little shade. Auckland and northern gardeners should consider a position in part shade for the mid-summer lettuces, but full sun for the rest of the year. Lettuces can be grown all year round by careful choice of cultivars.

LETTUCE LOVES:
✓ Good drainage
✓ Compost
✓ A well-fertilised soil
✓ Constant moisture
✓ Quick, even growth

NEW ZEALAND SPINACH

Here is a good alternative to regular spinach for the summer and autumn garden. This sprawling coastal plant is as Australian as it is a New Zealander, but it was discovered here in 1770 by Sir Joseph Banks, who named it New Zealand spinach. And so it has been called since, all over the world (unless you prefer the botanical name, *Tetragonia expansa*).

The plant spreads to a metre or more across, so a single plant or two will suffice. It can be grown from seed, which is best soaked for 24 hours before sowing. New Zealand spinach is a frost-tender plant, but will self-seed in late summer to reappear the following spring if you let it.

New Zealand spinach is very pest resistant and even tolerates dry periods without its flavour being affected. Eat the young leaves.

PARSNIPS

Parsnips are in the same family as carrots and have the same cultural requirements. They are grown from seed (fresh is best) sown directly into warm soil in spring or autumn. They require deeply dug soil, worked to a fine tilth for sowing, and without the recent addition of fertiliser. They are susceptible to carrot-rust fly.

Gourmet lettuces and rocket growing in a pot.

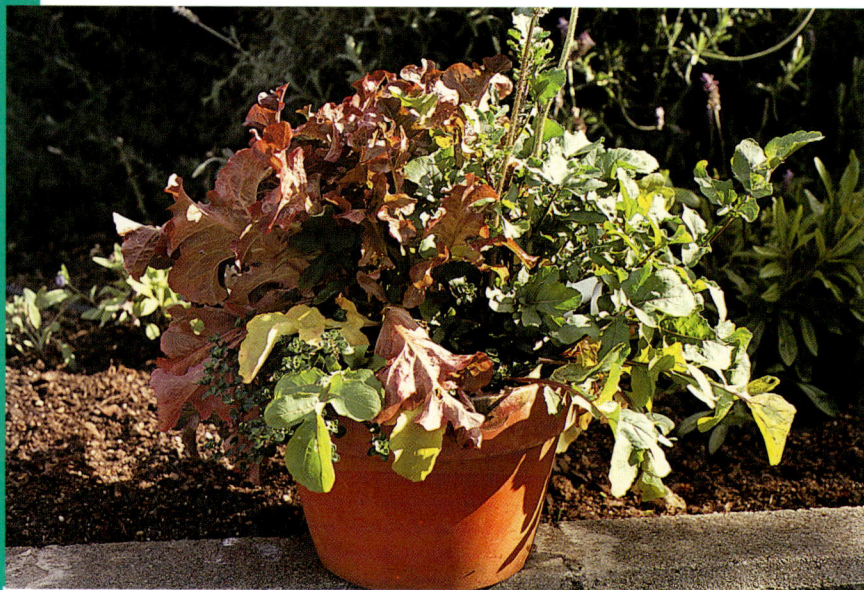

PEAS

Peas are cool-climate vegetables grown from seed sown directly into the soil. They can be grown in any climate, the trick being to avoid flowering in frosty or hot dry weather. Also, the seed likes cool but not heavy wet soil in which to germinate. This means that autumn or winter sowing suits warmer climates, whereas spring sowing suits colder climates. There are different cultivars for different seasons. Always buy fresh seed to avoid disappointment. A well-prepared, well-drained soil bed is important but avoid direct contact with fertilisers. Either plant peas where a well-fertilised crop was grown the previous year or liquid fertilise once the plants are actively growing. Peas, even low-growing cultivars, are best staked to keep them off the ground.

Harvest peas when they are young and tender. Regular harvesting will keep the plants productive. Gardeners with children should have at least one go at growing peas. It's a fun way to discover that peas don't just come frozen in plastic bags, and they taste so good.

PUMPKINS AND SQUASH

If you have the space, pumpkins are easy and fun to grow. There are a number of different cultivars. The ones not to waste space on are the 'self-sown-from-last-year' varieties. More often than not, self-sown pumpkins are not a patch on their predecessors when it comes to taste. This is because the best pumpkins are from specially raised F_1 hybrid seed.

Pumpkins should not be planted until the soil is warm and the risk of frost over. This usually means late October or early November.

Plant in well-drained soil with ample compost and some general garden fertiliser. Most cultivars require a good 4 to 5 months of warm frost-free conditions to reach maturity. In cooler climates look for fast-maturing squash cultivars. There are also bush forms that require less space than large-growing pumpkin vines. Pumpkins and squash are harvested when the vine has shrivelled and before the first frost.

RADISH

If you were a child gardener, radishes were perhaps your first crop. They are good for the beginner's confidence, early to germinate and quick to grow. They can be grown all year round in mild climates. Sow them directly into well-drained soil without freshly added fertiliser. The best soil is one that was well fertilised for a previous crop. Otherwise you can provide fertiliser in liquid form once the radishes have germinated. There are lots of different varieties to try.

SCALLOPINI

Although a different shape altogether, these delightful flying-saucer-shaped vegetables are simply another variety of zucchini, grown in exactly the same way.

SILVERBEET AND CHARD

Silverbeet is the traditional Australasian name for what is elsewhere more commonly known as swiss chard. The red-stemmed form is known as rhubarb chard. There is also a yellow-stemmed variety. With their shiny crumpled leaves these make an attractive show in the potager garden. What's more, they are highly nutritious and very easy to grow. It is possible to have chard in the garden all year round in mild climates, and for at least 6 months in colder climates.

Punnets of seedlings are readily available for plain green silverbeet, but are less common for the coloured forms. Fortunately, all the chards are easily grown from seed, sown directly into the soil or in trays for later transplanting. For a year-round supply, sow seed or plant seedlings in spring and again in autumn. Plant them in a rich well-drained soil with plenty of compost and give plants plenty of room to allow healthy continuous growth. New leaves are produced in the centre of the plant while you pick the outer ones.

Fertilisers that are relatively high in nitrogen, such as liquid blood and bone, are good for silverbeet. Plants may run to seed early if they are allowed to dry out.

As well as the crinkled-leaved cultivars, there is a light green, smooth-leaved silverbeet, sometimes referred to as spinachbeet.

SPINACH

Spinach has smaller smoother leaves than silverbeet, but is just as nutritious and some would say tastier. Spinach is not, however, as reliable as a year-round crop as it has a tendency to run to seed in warm weather. Hence choose a bolt-resistant variety, such as 'Tyee F_1 hybrid', and grow spinach as a cool-season crop. Spinach likes cool roots. If you want to try growing it for summer and autumn harvesting, some shade (e.g., the shade of a taller crop) combined with diligent watering will go some way towards delaying bolting. The tenderest, tastiest spinach is that which has been allowed to grow steadily without set-back, so provide plenty of food and keep the soil moist, but not waterlogged.

Seedlings are available from garden centres at most times of the year. Also, seed can be sown directly into the soil. Plant at three-weekly intervals for a continuous supply. Choose a cultivar to suit your season. Different cultivars have different maturing rates, anywhere from 45 to 80 days after sowing. Harvest whole plants or pick a few leaves at a time. The latter must be done carefully to avoid damaging the plant.

SPINACH LOVES:
- ✓ Cool roots
- ✓ Compost
- ✓ Good drainage
- ✓ Plenty of fertiliser
- ✓ Constant moisture

SWEETCORN

How come a corn cob from the garden tastes sweeter than one from the shop? Simple really. Because they have more sugar in them when there is no delay from plant to plate.

Grow sweetcorn in a sunny sheltered spot in well-drained, well-dug soil. Prior to planting rake through a couple of handfuls per square metre of general garden fertiliser. The best method is to sow seed directly into warm soil. You can also purchase seedlings from a garden centre, but in this case make sure that you disturb the roots as little as possible when planting. Water well after sowing or transplanting.

It is best to plant sweetcorn in blocks rather than rows as pollination (an essential event in the creation of each cob) is via wind. Sweetcorn is a summer crop sown or transplanted from late spring into summer.

TOMATOES

❏ Never put tomato debris on the compost heap.

❏ Buy seed or plants from a reputable supplier. Seed saved from an infected crop can carry over disease to the next crop.

❏ Early planted or early ripening tomatoes have a better chance of avoiding attack if they are harvested before the disease season reaches its peak. Grow disease-resistant varieties or grafted plants. The rootstocks of grafted tomatoes are vigorous, giving rise to strong-growing plants with a better chance of resisting disease. The rootstocks are resistant to soil-borne pests and diseases. Most popular cultivars can be purchased as grafted plants and are worth the extra cost. They do grow very large, so you will need three times more space than for an ungrafted plant. Among the cultivars that are resistant to soil-borne disease (whether they are grafted or not) are: 'Big Beef', 'Gross Lisse', 'Napoli' and 'Roma'.

❏ Avoid watering the foliage.

❏ If diseases have caused problems in previous years or you know they occur in your area it is best to spray with copper hydroxide as a preventative. Spray every 2 weeks from planting. It is important to cover the foliage completely.

Tomatoes require a well-drained warm soil, rich in fertiliser. To ripen successfully they need a warm sheltered position. Grafted plants and tall-growing cultivars need support by way of a fence, trellis or stakes.

Labour weekend is around about the time to start planting tomatoes, but the best determining factor is the weather. The risk of frost should be safely over with established warm temperatures not dropping below 12°C at night. Prepare the soil by digging deeply and adding lots of compost. Spread about 125 g of general garden fertiliser per square metre and mix it in well. Plant seedlings at least 40 cm apart. Grafted plants should be 2 to 3 m apart. Thoroughly water your new plants in their pots or punnet before planting. Plant without disturbing the root system and firm the soil down carefully. Grafted tomatoes should be planted with their graft union (the taped bit) 1 to 2 cm above the soil surface. Individually potted plants will suffer less transplanting shock than those growing together in a punnet.

STAKING AND TRAINING

Position stakes at planting time to avoid damaging the roots later. A grafted tomato plant, unless it has a fence or wall for support, will need three or four stakes. If you do nothing to train your tomatoes, they will still grow and produce some fruit, but for the best possible crop and to keep plants disease free, some training is necessary and easy.

Lateral shoots are the side branches that appear between each leaf and the main stem.

With TALL-GROWING TOMATOES remove these laterals as the plant grows, lightly tying the new top growth to the stake each time. When the plant has a dozen or so good trusses of fruit, cut off the growing tip. This then redirects the plant's energy into the developing fruit.

Home-grown, outdoor tomatoes are by far the tastiest and given 3 months of warm frost-free weather (a New Zealand summer), they are easy to grow. Cherry tomatoes, such as 'Sweet 100', are extremely generous, producing copious quantities of their deliciously sweet tomatoes well into autumn. Children love them and they are the most decorative tomatoes for salads.

The only real obstacle to growing tomatoes is that they tend to be troubled by disease more than other vegetables. Whether you choose to spray or not, take care to prevent disease as much as possible:

❏ Avoid planting tomatoes in the same spot two years running. If you cannot change the location, dig out the top 30 cm of soil and replace it with soil that has not been used for tomatoes (or plants in the same family that are troubled by the same diseases, i.e. potatoes, eggplant, capsicum).

❏ Take care to avoid planting your tomatoes too close together or close to other plants (such as weeds!). This leads to the humid conditions that diseases love. Diseases can overwinter in certain weeds, so cleaning up at the end of the season is essential.

❏ Remove infected or overcrowded lower leaves as plants grow.

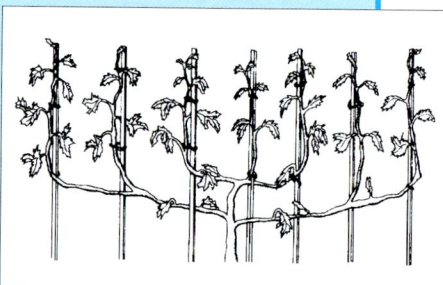

DWARF CULTIVARS only need pruning to prevent overcrowding and disease problems. The less they are pruned the more fruit they will produce.

CHERRY TOMATOES can be staked and pruned as for tall tomatoes or left unpruned. They will cascade from a large hanging basket or tub.

GRAFTED TOMATOES are best pruned by removing the growing tip when the plant has reached 30 cm tall.

This encourages side shoots to grow, and it is these that should be trained, each as if it were an

individual tall plant, but staking and removing the laterals as above. When grown against a wall or trellis they can be supported on strings or wire fixed vertically. If staked instead they will need a row of 2.5 m tall stakes firmly placed at 30 cm intervals.

Remove any foliage that shades the fruit to increase air circulation but do not remove all the leaves.

FEEDING AND WATERING

When a plant does as much growing and produces as much fruit as a tomato does in one very short space of time, it's hardly surprising that it will need frequent feeding and watering. It is important not to let the plants dry out. As plants become loaded with fruit the need for

More about mulches
Go to page 204.

watering will increase. A mulch will help reduce water loss via evaporation.

Once the small fruit appear give the plants a fortnightly feed with a liquid fertiliser such as Phostrogen® Tomato Food. This contains the correct balance of potassium to ensure fruit set. Avoid over-use of nitrogenous fertilisers, which favour leaf growth to the detriment of fruit.

Harvesting before it is fully coloured helps keep the fruit firmer for longer. It also relieves the plant of its load, allowing it to keep on the job of producing more fruit.

TOMATOES LOVE:
✓ Good drainage
✓ Compost
✓ Lots of fertiliser
✓ Constant watering
✓ Warm temperatures

ZUCCHINIS

Among the easiest of vegetables to grow, the thing with zucchinis (courgettes) is to keep up with their enthusiastic productivity. They have a habit of suddenly turning into marrows when your back is turned. The smaller you pick them, the nicer they are to eat. Frequent picking also encourages new fruit to be produced and extends the life of the plant.

Greenhouse-grown seedlings are available from garden centres from spring. Plant these as soon as the risk of frost is over for early crops. Zucchinis can also be grown from seed sown directly into the soil, but ground temperatures need to be warm for successful germination.

Plant zucchinis in well-prepared, well-drained soil, ideally with plenty of compost. A good way to provide favourably warm soil conditions early in the season is to plant them on mounds. Dig a hole and back fill it with good compost. Mix in a handful of general garden fertiliser and then mound the soil back over the top. Plant the seedling on top of the mound. If sowing seeds instead, sow two or three seeds and later remove all but the strongest seedling. Water zucchinis well during dry periods.

Zucchinis are ready for harvest about 8 weeks after seed sowing. For continuous cropping, follow up early spring planting with another 6 to 8 weeks later. Bear in mind that earlier

plantings are less likely to be troubled by powdery mildew, a disease that thrives in hot, humid conditions.

There are a number of different zucchini cultivars, in various shades of green or yellow. Most modern varieties have a bush habit, which takes up less space than the old-fashioned vines without compromising the crop. They do, however, take a relatively large space; about 75 cm between plants is required.

ZUCCHINI LOVE:
✓ Good drainage
✓ Compost
✓ Early and constant picking
✓ Water during dry periods
✓ Warm temperatures

VEGE CALENDER — WARM CLIMATE

	SEPTEMBER	OCTOBER	NOVEMBER	DECEMBER	JANUARY	FEBRUARY
Sow in trays	broccoli	broccoli	broccoli	broccoli	broccoli	broccoli
	cabbage	cabbage	cabbage	cabbage	cabbage	cabbage
	celery	capsicum	capsicum	capsicum	capsicum	cauliflower
	chicory	celery	celery	cauliflower	cauliflower	celery
	leeks	chicory	chicory	celery	celery	chicory
	lettuce	cucumber	cucumber	chicory	chicory	leeks
	silverbeet	eggplant	eggplant	cucumber	cucumber	lettuce
	spinach	leeks	leeks	eggplant	leeks	silverbeet
	spring onions	lettuce	lettuce	leeks	lettuce	spinach
	zucchini	silverbeet	silverbeet	lettuce	silverbeet	spring onions
		spinach	spinach	silverbeet	spinach	
		spring onions	spring onions	spinach	spring onions	
		sweetcorn	sweetcorn	spring onions		
		tomatoes	tomatoes	sweetcorn		
		zucchini	zucchini	tomatoes		
				zucchini		
Sow direct	beetroot	beetroot	beetroot	beetroot	beetroot	beetroot
	cabbage	cabbage	cabbage	cabbage	cabbage	cabbage
	carrots	carrots	carrots	carrots	carrots	carrots
	celery	celery	celery	celery	celery	celery
	cress	climbing beans	climbing beans	climbing beans	climbing beans	cress
	leeks	cress	cress	cress	cress	dwarf beans
	parsnip	cucumber	cucumber	cucumber	cucumber	leeks
	peas	dwarf beans	dwarf beans	dwarf beans	dwarf beans	lettuce
	radish	eggplant	eggplant	eggplant	leeks	parsnip
	silverbeet	leeks	leeks	leeks	lettuce	radish
	spinach	lettuce	lettuce	lettuce	parsnip	silverbeet
	spring onions	parsnip	parsnip	parsnip	radish	spinach
		peas	radish	radish	silverbeet	spring onions
		radish	silverbeet	silverbeet	spinach	
		silverbeet	spinach	spinach	spring onions	
		spinach	spring onions	spring onions		
		spring onions	sweetcorn	sweetcorn		
		sweetcorn	zucchini	zucchini		
		zucchini				

MARCH	APRIL	MAY	JUNE	JULY	AUGUST
cabbage	cabbage	silverbeet	spring onions	spring onions	cabbage
cauliflower	cauliflower	spinach			lettuce
celery	celery	spring onions			silverbeet
chicory	leeks				spinach
leeks	lettuce				spring onions
lettuce	silverbeet				
silverbeet	spinach				
spinach	spring onions				
spring onions					

MARCH	APRIL	MAY	JUNE	JULY	AUGUST
beetroot	beetroot	beetroot	cress	cress	cress
cabbage	cabbage	carrots	peas	peas	lettuce
carrots	carrots	cress	radish	radish	peas
celery	celery	parsnip	spring onions	spring onions	radish
cress	cress	radish			
leeks	leeks	silverbeet			
lettuce	lettuce	spinach			
parsnip	parsnip	spring onions			
radish	radish				
silverbeet	silverbeet				
spinach	spinach				
spring onions	spring onions				

Flowers and vegetables in a cottage-style garden.

VEGE CALENDER — COLD CLIMATE

	SEPTEMBER	OCTOBER	NOVEMBER	DECEMBER	JANUARY	FEBRUARY
Sow in trays	broccoli	broccoli	broccoli	broccoli	cabbage	cabbage
	cabbage	cabbage	cabbage	cabbage	lettuce	lettuce
	celery	capsicum	cauliflower	cauliflower	silverbeet	silverbeet
	chicory	cauliflower	celery	leeks	spring onions	spring onions
	silverbeet	celery	cucumber	lettuce		
	spinach	chicory	eggplant	silverbeet		
	spring onions	cucumber	leeks	spring onions		
		leeks	lettuce	sweetcorn		
		lettuce	silverbeet	tomatoes		
		silverbeet	spring onions			
		spinach	sweetcorn			
		spring onions	tomatoes			
		zucchini	zucchini			
Sow direct	beetroot	beetroot	beetroot	cabbage	cabbage	cabbage
	cabbage	cabbage	cabbage	climbing beans	cress	cress
	carrots	carrots	carrots	cress	dwarf beans	lettuce
	cress	celery	celery	dwarf beans	lettuce	radish
	peas	cress	climbing beans	eggplant	radish	silverbeet
	radish	cucumber	courgette	leeks	silverbeet	spring onions
	silverbeet	eggplant	cress	lettuce	spring onions	
	spinach	leeks	cucumber	parsnip		
	spring onions	lettuce	dwarf beans	radish		
		parsnip	eggplant	silverbeet		
		peas	leeks	spring onions		
		radish	lettuce	sweetcorn		
		silverbeet	parsnip			
		spinach	peas			
		spring onions	radish			
		sweetcorn	silverbeet			
		zucchini	spring onions			

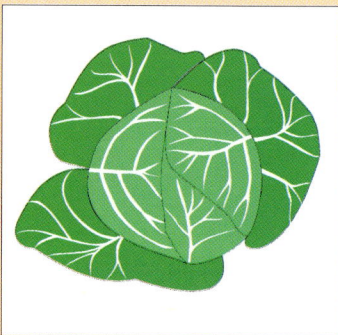
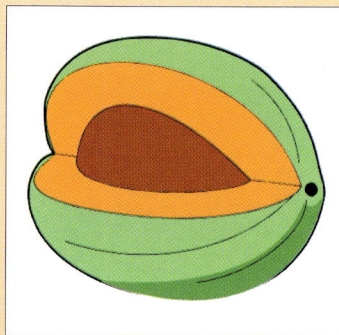

March	April	May	June	July	August
lettuce					cabbage
spring onions					

March	April	May	June	July	August
carrots	broad beans	broad beans		cabbage	beetroot
cress	carrots	carrots			cabbage
lettuce	cress	cress			cress
spring onions					peas
					radish

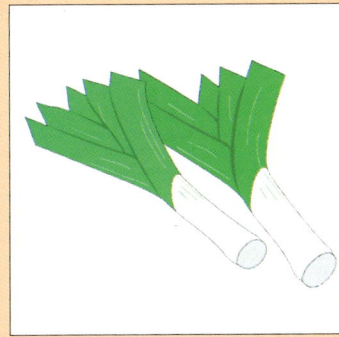

Culinary Herbs

Once you've experienced the pleasure and convenience of cooking with herbs from your own garden, it's hard to do without them. It's just as well they are so easy to grow. Even the tiniest gardens will have space for herbs, and most of them are very successfully grown in pots.

Herbs are as decorative as they are useful. Whether you set aside a separate area for herbs or include them in the flower or vege garden, they will contribute to the overall beauty of the garden with colour, texture, fragrance and form. Take rosemary, for example; it makes a fantastic hedge or background shrub.

To start with, it helps to know which herbs are perennial and which are annual. Perennial herbs need only the occasional cut back, but annuals are resown (or purchased as seedlings) at least once a year. While your mint will keep growing indefinitely, there's nothing you can do to stop your parsley going to seed. The trick with parsley is to sow fresh seed or plant new seedlings regularly.

BASIL

Ocimum basilicum

Basil is a summer-growing annual, a herb to make the most of when it is in season by planting more than you think you'll need. It's a shame that this all-time favourite won't grow through the winter, but it is with summer foods (tomatoes, new potatoes, green salads, cheeses, fresh pasta dishes . . .) that basil is at its most delectable. To enjoy basil in winter harvest what's left of your crop in autumn, before the first frost, and freeze it. Better still, make it into pesto and then freeze.

There are a number of basil varieties, the most popular being sweet basil, which has large bright green leaves and grows to about 50 cm tall. Basil seedlings of various grades become available in the garden centres with the onset of the warm spring weather. Alternatively, you can grow basil from seed.

> Growing from seed:
> Go to page 209.

Basil will not germinate in a cold soil so for direct sowing wait until November. In trays, seed can be sown earlier in spring and kept in a warm place such as a greenhouse until it is warm enough to plant the seedlings in the garden or outside in pots. Early planted seedlings may well do better in a terracotta pot; the potting mix will be warmer than the garden soil.

Like parsley, basil enjoys a well-drained composty soil but does not like dry conditions. Keep the soil moist with ample watering through the summer. Plants in pots will need extra care with watering up to twice a day. The smaller the pot, the more you will have to water. Plant no more than three plants to a 25 cm pot. Plants in the garden should be spaced (or thinned to) about 25 cm apart.

Basil is touted to be good for keeping the bugs away from tomatoes and is offensive to mosquitoes and flies, but snails are not so fussy. They will devour your tender young basil plants as soon as you turn your back. Laying bait after planting is crucial.

Once plants are established, constant picking will help to keep them bushy. Pinch out flower heads as they appear to encourage maximum leaf growth.

BASIL LOVES:
- ✓ A rich, moist soil
- ✓ Compost
- ✓ Good drainage
- ✓ Sun
- ✓ Warm weather

CHIVES

Allium schoenoprasum

Chives are a perennial herb that will grow all year round in a warm climate. Where winters are cold the leaves will die back in winter but return in spring. They grow best in a well-drained moist soil with plenty of compost, in sun or part shade.

The flowers are attractive lavender-coloured pompoms, making chives a very pretty border for the herb garden. Flowers are also edible and make an attractive garnish. But if you want to maintain leaf production you'll need to remove the flower heads as they appear. For the best of both worlds grow enough chives to allow some for flowers and some for continuous picking.

Produce new plants by dividing the clumps in spring. Simply dig up the clumps and divide them into smaller clumps of a few plants each. Replant into freshly dug, composty soil. A handful of general garden fertiliser is also worth adding at this stage. If you are doing everything right but your chives still lack vigour, try a handful (about 30g per square metre) of garden lime. If you don't have access to existing clumps to divide, you can start off by sowing your own seed. Chives can be either direct sown and thinned to 15 cm apart, or raised in a container.

> Growing from seed:
> Go to page 209.

The easiest method is to buy a potted clump of chives, ready to transplant straight into the garden or a terracotta pot. It may be big enough to divide into two or three plants straight away. Alternatively, you can buy a punnet of young seedlings. The best idea is to do both so you have some to use immediately with more plants coming along for later.

Chives will repel aphids, so it's worth planting lots of them around vulnerable garden plants such as roses. Garlic chives (*Allium tuberosum*) has white flowers, which may be more to your liking for this purpose than the lavender flowers of common chives, depending on the colour of your roses. Of course, if you still have to spray your roses, reserve another spot in the garden for the chives you are going to eat.

CHIVES LOVE:
- ✓ A rich, moist soil
- ✓ Compost
- ✓ Good drainage

CORIANDER

Coriandrum sativum

For those of us with a passion for the taste of fresh coriander leaves, it's hard to believe that it is not enjoyed by everyone, such is the distinctive flavour of this herb. Essential in Thai cooking, coriander leaves go well with curries as well as salads and are sensational in a chicken sandwich.

Coriander is an annual growing to around 40 cm tall. Success in growing it has eluded many otherwise green-fingered gardeners. This is probably because the plants do not transplant easily. The trick is to sow seed directly into the ground and keep them moist at all times. Sow the seeds in early spring in a warm sunny position with light, fertile, well-drained soil. Germination takes about 2 weeks and is assisted by covering to create darkness. Invert a box or pot over the seed bed, but watch carefully and remove it once seeds have sprouted. Also, don't allow them to dry out.

> Direct sowing:
> Go to page 209.

Plants should be kept well watered during dry periods to maintain healthy leaf growth. To delay seed production, trim off the top growth. The seeds, of course, are also used in cooking. These are ready for harvest when they change from green to brown in late summer. Cut off the seed heads and allow the seeds to dry for a couple of days before storing.

CORIANDER LOVES:
- ✓ A rich, moist soil
- ✓ Compost
- ✓ Good drainage
- ✓ To be grown direct from seed

TOP CULINARY HERBS

DILL
Anethum graveolens

The beautiful feathery foliage of dill makes it worth growing to use as a garnish alone, but its mild aniseed flavour goes superbly with fish and salads. The seeds are used in pickles.

Dill is a tall-growing annual, easy to grow in a sunny well-drained position, in soil that is kept well watered. A member of the carrot family, dill has a long tap root, so is best grown in the garden or in a deep pot. Transplant pot-grown seedlings with care or, better still, sow seeds directly in the garden, thinning plants to about 25 cm apart when they have four leaves. Sow seed every few weeks for a continuous supply of leaves. Seeds are ready for harvest when they have turned dark brown.

Direct sowing:
Go to page 209.

FRENCH TARRAGON
Artemisia dracunculus

French tarragon is a perennial that dies down and disappears from sight in winter. New growth appears in spring, in the form of soft stems bearing narrow green leaves. By mid-summer the stems become woody and branched. In late autumn it is cut right back, but the flavour can be preserved for year-round use in the form of tarragon vinegar.

Fresh leaves, which must be chopped to release the flavour, can be used with a wide range of foods, including omelettes, chicken, fish, salads, and cooked vegetables such as carrots. In the latter case it should be finely chopped and stirred quickly around the just-cooked vegetables.

Tarragon needs a warm sunny position in a well-drained soil with added compost. If the soil is too wet over winter the dormant roots are likely to rot, so a pot is a better place for growing tarragon if you have heavy soil.

Plants need lifting and dividing every few years to prevent over-crowding of the roots. This is also the means of propagation, as French tarragon cannot be grown from seed.

French tarragon grows best in cool climates. Russian tarragon is easier to grow but lacks the flavour of French tarragon.

LEMON BALM
Melissa officinalis

This is one of the easiest herbs to grow. Once established all that is needed is an annual cut back in autumn and watering during dry periods. Lemon balm is a perennial that continues to provide its crop of bright green, lemon-flavoured leaves all year round. It makes an attractive leafy filler for the herb garden and will grow in full sun or part shade.

Grow lemon balm from cuttings or divisions or from seed. It readily self-sows if plants are left to flower and set seed in autumn.

The flowers of lemon balm attract bees. *Melissa* comes from the Greek word for bee.

MINT
Mentha spicata

When it comes to mint the choice can be daunting — spearmint, pepper-mint, apple mint, rustless mint, etc. Spearmint (*Mentha spicata*) is the most commonly grown and has a good strong flavour. All mints are perennials and have creeping stems. They are easy to grow in just about any soil as long as it doesn't dry out.

As with many easy-to-grow plants mint can be more difficult to stop growing than to get growing. It is therefore best given an area of its own away from other plants. It can be grown around the base of a climber (such as wisteria) whose deep roots won't suffer too much from the competition. Mint will grow in full sun or semi-shade. Alternatively, grow your mint in a pot, the bigger the better to prevent drying out. Pots can be planted in the garden to contain the roots but keep them cool. This way you can have the foliage of the mint blended with other herbs without the risk of overcrowding them, but watch out for runners (bits of stem that may escape over the sides of the pot and take root).

If your mint becomes straggly or is attacked by rust (orange spots on sickly looking leaves), cut it right back, disposing of any diseased material, and it will soon recover with a fresh sprouting of green growth. Rust tends to affect mainly the old leaves so constant trimming to promote new growth is a good way to keep it at bay. A bad infestation is best dealt with by digging up the whole plant

and burning it. Site the new plant in a different place if possible.

Propagate mint by planting rooted divisions or runners taken from mature plants.

PARSLEY
Petroselinum crispum

Parsley is a biennial, perishing once it has flowered and set seed, but taking two growing seasons to do so. Biennial or not, parsley has the annoying habit of going to seed just when you need it most. For a continuous supply of parsley, new seeds or seedlings should be planted regularly, at least twice a year — in spring and again in autumn. Most cooks can't get by without at least three good-sized plants growing at a time.

If buying plants you have the option of bigger plants in single pots or punnets of six to ten young seedlings. The larger-grown potted variety are more instant and suffer less transplanting shock than those in punnets, which must have their roots prised apart. Punnets, however, give you more plants for your money, even if you lose a couple in the early stages.

Parsley likes the sun, but grows best when its roots are relatively cool. In the hottest part of summer, part shade is a good idea. For winter and spring a sunnier position is better. The soil should be constantly moist. If plants become too dry they will bolt to seed. This can pose problems if growing parsley in pots in summer, where the potting mix tends to be warmer and dries out more quickly than garden soil. Get around the problem by having a decent-sized pot, say 25 cm diameter with one parsley plant in the centre. A trio of dwarf marigolds could fill out the perimeter of the pots until the parsley is big enough to look the part on its own. Keep pots away from the hottest midday sun, at least while the parsley gets established.

Parsley enjoys a fertile soil. A good handful of blood and bone mixed into the soil at planting time is a good idea especially if you have been growing parsley in the same spot for a few years. For potted parsley or as a boost to plants growing in the soil, apply a nitrogen-rich liquid fertiliser such as Nitrosol® at least monthly.

Young parsley seedlings sometimes protest when it comes to transferring them from their nursery container into the garden. Take special care not to damage the roots of seedlings. Handle the stems rather than the roots and leave as much potting mix around each plant's roots as you can. Transplant into moist, compost-rich-soil that is friable and well drained.

The same applies for sowing seed directly in the garden. Prepare the soil well with plenty of compost and water before sowing, and keep it moist, especially while the plants get established. Soaking seed overnight prior to planting is an extra precaution to keep seeds moist. Parsley is a slow germinator, taking up to 3 weeks from sowing so don't think you've failed if the seedlings don't pop out of the ground in a hurry.

Growing from seed:
Go to page 209.

Last, but not least, resist the temptation to pick leaves from your young parsley plants until they have had a chance to establish (at least eight leaves).

PARSLEY LOVES:
✓ A rich, moist soil
✓ Compost
✓ Good drainage
✓ A cool root run
✓ Part shade during hot months
✓ Full sun during cool months

ROCKET
Eruca sativa
Rocket leaves add a spicy tang to summer salads, usually combined with lettuce and dressed with an olive oil and vinegar dressing. It's also good in sandwiches.

An annual herb, rocket will grow all year round in a mild climate but has a better flavour when grown quickly, so it is best planted in spring for use over the warmer months.

Start sowing directly in the garden in early spring in full sun or part shade. The soil should be worked to a fine tilth with plenty of compost and kept moist. Thin the young plants to about 15 cm apart and start picking when they are about 20 cm tall. A dry soil will encourage plants to go to seed so

encourage lush growth by keeping them well watered. In warm weather plants will go to seed quite quickly so sow every few weeks for a continuous supply. Once you've discovered the taste, one plant will never be enough.

When the plant has flowered, the leaves are not as tasty and the plant stops growing. Remove the flower heads as they appear to keep the leaves going as long as possible. The flowers are also edible and can be used in salads. Left to its own devices in an undisturbed soil rocket will self-sow easily, but be careful not to pull out the young seedlings along with weeds.

Direct sowing:
Go to page 209.

ROSEMARY
Rosmarinus officinalis
Rosemary is a shrub worth having in the garden even if it wasn't such a marvellous culinary herb. It is hardy and easy to grow, preferring a dry soil that is not too fertile, the main ailment being dieback and eventual death when the roots become too wet.

Plant advanced shrubs for a more instant effect or grow your own from cuttings (a good method for a hedge), which need no special treatment. Just place cuttings directly into position in well-drained garden soil, and water them in. Protect young plants from frost.

Trim rosemary bushes or hedges well to keep them in shape with plenty of fresh young growth. This is a shrub that can grow up to 2 m but is easily contained around 1 m with pruning.

Traditionally used to flavour roast lamb and other rich meat dishes, rosemary is also fantastic with vegetables, especially if you roast them in olive oil with generous scatterings of chopped rosemary leaves. Rosemary together with olive oil, garlic and tomatoes makes a wonderful sauce for fresh pasta. Sauté a sprig long enough to flavour the oil (a few minutes) and discard before adding the rest of the ingredients.

ROSEMARY LOVES:
✓ Well-drained soil
✓ Not too much fertiliser
✓ Full sun
✓ Being trimmed

SAGE
(Salvia officinalis)
Common sage is a distinctive-looking plant with distinctively flavoured leaves for seasoning rich meat dishes. It is wonderful with kebabs and in stuffing, but take care not to overpower them by using too much.

The plants grow about 50 cm tall with a covering of velvety, grey-green leaves. The lavender-blue flower spikes appear in summer and are attractive to bees.

Sage prefers a light sandy soil and will perform poorly in a soil that is wet in winter. If your soil is too heavy you can happily grow your sage in a pot, where it will thrive in the well-drained potting mix. Generally known as a sun lover, common sage tends to grow better in northern New Zealand gardens if it has some shade.

A perennial, sage is best renewed every 3 or 4 years. The easiest way is to purchase potted plants, but you can also sow seeds or grow new plants from stem cuttings. Prune lightly after flowering to retain a nice bushy habit.

Purple sage (*Salvia officinalis* 'Purpurea') makes a stunning garden partner for common sage and other green-foliaged herbs. It has rich purple foliage and deeper-coloured flowers than common sage and is shorter growing. There is also a green-and-gold variegated form.

Direct sowing:
Go to page 209.

SORREL
Rumex acetosa
Sorrel leaves are used to add zing to salads. Sorrel has a lemony character, which makes it nice with oily fish such as salmon.

A hardy perennial, sorrel can be grown from seed sown in spring, from division of existing plants in the autumn or buying a potted plant from a garden centre. Sorrel can be grown in a pot or in the garden but grows best in a rich moist soil with partial shade.

Growing from seed:
Go to page 209.

SWEET BAY
Laurus nobilis

The sweet bay (or bay laurel) is a beautiful tree from the Mediterranean that will reach up to 15 m tall. Fortunately, it is easily contained with pruning to a more appropriate scale for the average garden, where it can be maintained in its natural pyramid shape, trained as topiaries or made into a standard. It is a classic ever-green specimen for a large pot. Sweet bay also makes a good hedge. A bay tree makes the perfect centre-piece for a formal herb garden or can simply be worked into the shrub and flower borders as part of the overall structure of the garden.

So valuable is this plant as an ornamental, the ability to pick your own fresh bay leaves for cooking almost comes as a bonus. Bay leaves are an important year-round herb, especially wonderful in bouquet garni (parsley and thyme wrapped in a bay leaf added to soups and casseroles). At Christmas time the dried or fresh leaves can be used to make traditional Christmas wreaths.

Where summers are hot, try to locate your bay tree in part shade.

SWEET MARJORAM
Origanum majorana

Sweet marjoram is an easy-to-grow perennial for a sunny location. It is wonderfully fragrant and a very useful herb for many dishes including pizzas, pastas, salads, omelettes, tomato dishes, and soups. To retain the flavour it should be added towards the end of cooking.

The sweet marjoram has tiny green leaves and dainty white flowers. Common marjoram (*O. vulgare*) is also attractive with larger leaves, a more spreading habit and pretty pink flowers. It is somewhat easier to grow, but its flavour pales in comparison to sweet marjoram.

Grow sweet marjoram from seed raised in a tray or transplant potted plants obtained from a garden centre. A well-drained but well-watered soil is the order of the day for marjoram. It should not be too rich so go easy on the fertiliser with this herb.

Sweet marjoram will behave like an annual in a cold climate where it will not survive the winter, nor will it fare too well in warm climates if the roots become too wet in winter. In such situations it is best to grow sweet marjoram in pots, which can be moved into a sheltered spot in the autumn. Common marjoram is less fussy.

Replace plants every few years and prolong useful leaf growth by trimming off the flowers, pretty though they are.

> Growing from seed:
> Go to page 209.

THYME

There are numerous different thymes, all highly aromatic and all edible. With their different growth forms, foliage and flower colours, they are as valuable as landscaping plants as they are in the kitchen. They are perennials that enjoy hot dry conditions, making them ideal for growing in pots.

Two of the most useful as culinary herbs are common thyme (*Thymus vulgaris*) and pizza thyme (*Thymus nummularius*). Common thyme makes a small mounding shrub, 20 to 30 cm tall with tiny grey-green leaves and pink flowers in summer. Pizza thyme has glossy green leaves with a marjoram-like flavour, and pink flowers.

Thyme likes full sun and a well-drained soil that is not too rich. Although it must have excellent drainage, watering will be necessary in the driest weather, especially for newly planted plants.

Replace plants every few years if old plants become too woody, but prolong their life with constant trimming at least once a year after flowering. New plants can be produced by division.

THYME LOVES:
- ✓ Well-drained soil
- ✓ Growing in pots
- ✓ Full sun
- ✓ Being trimmed

> Direct sowing:
> Go to page 209.

A range of thymes.

Citrus

ighly ornamental citrus belong in every warm-climate garden, where they are the easiest fruit trees to grow. They have good form and dense, glossy evergreen foliage. As lawn specimens, background plantings or in tubs they look good throughout the year with a minimum of fuss. They have deliciously fragrant flowers and fruit that looks as good as it tastes, adding colour to the garden in winter.

The majority of citrus will not grow outdoors where winters are cold. All need protection from frost, but there are a few that will grow and fruit in cooler climates. The cold-hardiest citrus are kumquat (the most cold hardy), Meyer lemon and mandarins.

In Europe, citrus have been grown for centuries as container plants, moved undercover for the winter. In southern regions of New Zealand growing citrus in pots is the ideal way to beat the cold.

Because good drainage is essential for citrus, pot culture is also the answer for gardens with heavy soils. The smaller-growing trees — Meyer lemon, kumquat, mandarins and navel oranges — are the most suitable for containers. Provide a large container, 40 to 60 cm in diameter, and feed and water more frequently than you would for citrus in the ground.

As well as a warm temperature, citrus need a well-drained soil rich in organic matter. In poorly drained soils use raised beds or pots. Poor fruiting is usually a result of dry periods in summer or erratic watering of plants in pots.

Yellow leaves are usually a sign of nutrient deficiency. Feed your citrus regularly. Three times a year is ideal: in spring, summer and autumn. Plants in the ground should receive citrus fertiliser, spread in a ring about half a metre in from the outermost leaves but well away from the main trunk. At planting time mix a slow-release fertiliser into the soil. For potted plants use a slow-release fertiliser supplemented with liquid fertiliser once a month from spring through autumn. Foliar feeding is also beneficial. However, never use powdered citrus fertiliser on plants growing in containers.

Well-grown citrus are relatively trouble free when it comes to pests and diseases. A regular spray programme using Super Copper is the best way to prevent disease. Combine this with regular removal of damaged branches and fallen fruit. Mites can be a problem in mid to late summer. They are deterred by spraying the undersides of the leaves with water. Bad infestations should be controlled by using a mite spray.

Pruning is rarely necessary with citrus except occasionally to control their size or shape or remove damaged wood. Prune only lightly after harvest (or as you harvest) by trimming back to a healthy shoot. Lemon trees will tolerate heavier pruning than other citrus. It is a good idea to remove most of the fruit from newly planted trees (especially heavy-bearing ones) to redirect the plant's energy into vegetative growth.

More about soil preparation:
Go to page 190.

More about fertilisers:
Go to page 200.

More about pests and diseases:
Go to page 215.

TOP CITRUS

CLEMENTINE MANDARIN
Citrus hybrid 'Clementine'
Small tree
'Clementine' has a neat rounded habit and dense glossy foliage. Fragrant flowers are followed by lots of small, round, bright orange fruit. This is a tree of maximum ornamental value in the garden or containers.

GOLDEN SPECIAL GRAPEFRUIT
Citrus xparadisi 'Golden Special'
Medium to large tree
The best grapefruit for a coolish climate, 'Golden Special' has large, pale yellow fruit with a tangy flavour. Cooler climates will produce tangier fruit with a lower sugar content, and they will take longer to ripen. It is a vigorous-growing heavy cropper that needs plenty of space.

JAMAICAN WHEENY GRAPEFRUIT
Citrus xparadisi 'Jamaican Wheeny'
Medium-sized tree
'Jamaican Wheeny' bears large golden yellow fruit that are very juicy and quite sweet, and are produced in mid-winter. This grapefruit is not so good for cooler climates.

LEMON GENOA
Citrus limon 'Genoa'
Medium-sized tree
More compact than 'Yen Ben', this tree is quick to bear medium-sized, very juicy fruit with a good sharp flavour that ripen over a long winter season. Almost seedless and almost thornless, 'Genoa' makes a nice evergreen tree for the smaller garden.

LEMON YEN BEN
Citrus limon 'Yen Ben'
Medium to large tree
A taller-growing lemon tree but one of the best. It produces lots of seedless fruit with an excellent sharp flavour that are good for cooking. Though not without thorns, 'Yen Ben' is quick-growing and densely foliaged. The main fruiting time is autumn and winter.

MEYER LEMON
Citrus limon 'Meyer'
Small tree
This is the best, if not the only, lemon worth considering for a pot, and also the most hardy to cold. It has attractive, bright yellow fruit all year round and a sweet mild flavour — great for gin and tonics. The bright green foliage is bronze when it first unfolds and there are no thorns.

NAVEL ORANGE
Citrus sinensis 'Washington Navel'
Small tree
This is a compact tree with dense glossy foliage and fragrant spring blossoms. It is very ornamental and a lovely shaped tree for a large pot. The medium-sized, thin-skinned fruit is very juicy, rich flavoured and ripens in early summer.

SATSUMA MANDARIN
Citrus hybrid 'Satsuma Miagawa'
Small to medium tree
'Miagawa' is a relatively new Japanese cultivar, with intensely fragrant flowers and the characteristic flat, easy-peel fruit of the satsuma mandarins. It is very productive and early fruiting, ripening in May and June. The fruit is sweet with good keeping qualities.

TAHITIAN LIME
Citrus latifolia
Small tree
Tahitian lime is the best lime for New Zealand gardens and needs warm subtropical conditions in order to do well. It is a compact, almost thornless tree bearing seedless juicy fruit. It is suitable for a large container.

TANGELO
Citrus hybrid 'Seminole'
Medium tree
Tangelo fruit are extremely sweet and juicy, unbeatable for juicing. The fruit holds well on the tree after ripening in late summer.

VALENCIA ORANGE
Citrus sinensis 'Harwood Late'
Medium tree
A New Zealand-raised form of the world's most loved orange, 'Harwood Late' is a vigorous-growing tree producing heavy crops of larger-sized, thick-skinned fruit in autumn and early winter.

EDIBLE BUT MAINLY FOR SHOW

KUMQUAT
Fortunella japonica
Small tree
The kumquat grows to a mere 1.2 to 1.5 m tall and is the cold-hardiest citrus. It is a very adaptable ornamental plant, exceptionally good for containers. The small round fruit ripens to golden orange, mainly in winter, when you need it most. The fruit is great for indoor decoration. It is both delicious and attractive in special desserts.

ORNAMENTAL ORANGE
Citrus aurantium
Small tree
Ornamental oranges (or 'bitter oranges') are ideal container plants or as a feature in the potager garden. They have small dark green leaves and small, perfectly spherical, bright orange fruit. The fruit makes good marmalade, but is not generally recommended for eating raw. Wonderfully fragrant flowers precede the fruit.

Container
gardening

Tubs, barrels, pots, window boxes and hanging baskets have fantastic potential as places to grow plants. Filling them up with attractive plants is easy. The tricky part is usually keeping them looking good for any length of time. Success depends on catering to the needs of plants whose life-supporting root system is confined to a limited space.

WATERING PLANTS IN CONTAINERS

Plants in containers need extra care with watering. The smaller the pot or the bigger the plant, the more you will need to water.

In spring and summer, daily watering is the general rule. In very hot, dry weather you may need to water twice a day. Windy weather will increase the demand for watering as water loss is increased both through the leaves and the sides of some containers. Hanging baskets are particularly vulnerable to drying out, so make them as big as you can. One really big hanging basket will be a much wiser investment than two small ones, with much more spectacular results.

Conveniently located taps and the right hose attachment make a big difference. A long-handled watering wand is ideal. But if you find that the watering of your pots is demanding too much of your time, first make sure your pots are large enough for their plants, then consider some time-saving devices:

❑ *GROUP POTS TOGETHER*. This way they shelter each other from wind and heat, slowing down the water loss.

❑ *USE FIXED IRRIGATION*. If pots are grouped together, it's easy to run a length of irrigation tubing between them. To totally automate things, a programmable timer can be installed to turn the water on and off at appropriate times and you can even pre-set the dates for watering while you are on holiday.

❑ *USE WATER CRYSTALS*. These are for containers, especially for the hot summer months. The crystals act as mini reservoirs. It is best to add water crystals to the potting mix in the gel state by pre-mixing them in a bucket of water. It is a mistake to add too many, especially in a wet season, but water crystals are like guardian angels for those who forget about watering from time to time.

❑ *USE WETTING AGENTS*. These are an excellent development for containers. Not just for the home gardener, they are used commercially to save on irrigation and maximise the shelf life of plants sitting in the nursery. Dry potting mix is difficult to rewet because the dry organic matter within it repels water. Well-developed root

Dracaena draco and *Metrosideros* 'Tahiti'.

systems will add to the problem. With the limited space in a container, it is important that as much of it as possible is engaged in providing water and nutrients to the plants. When a wetting agent, such as Saturaid, is added to the potting mix, the wettable area increases fourfold and the water spreads across the pot rather than washing straight out the bottom. Saturaid can be mixed in at repotting time or simply sprinkled over the top surface of the potting mix and watered in. Only a very small amount is used. Saturaid works well in conjunction with water crystals.

❏ *PAINT THE INSIDES OF TERRACOTTA POTS WITH A SEALANT*. This slows water loss through the pots' sides. Terraseal is the trade name of a natural terracotta pot sealer.It significantly reduces water loss while still allowing the pot to 'breathe'. It is made from sodium bentonite, which swells when wet to form an impervious gel that sticks tenaciously to the sides of the pot.

FEEDING PLANTS IN CONTAINERS

The best way to keep up with the nutritional demands of your container plants is to use a combination of controlled-release fertilisers and liquid fertilisers. As a general rule, include controlled-release fertiliser in the potting mix, and supplement it with a liquid fertiliser through the main spring and summer growth period. Fast-growing flowering plants, such as annuals, need extra applications of a fast-acting liquid fertiliser, such as Nitrosol® or Phostrogen®. Always make sure your potting mix is moist before feeding with a liquid fertiliser as it will simply wash through dry potting mix, and may place undue stress on the plants. Reputable brands of potting mix already contain a well-balanced mixture of nutrients, and so only liquid feeding during the growing season should be necessary. Eventually these nutrients will become used up, in which case repotting may be required.

Trees and shrubs will do well with a spring booster feed and another in autumn. In spring, a good way to do this is to gently remove the top few centimetres of potting mix and replace it with fresh potting mix containing controlled-release fertiliser. For large tubs you can use a narrow stake to make holes at about four evenly spaced intervals around the plant, to half to two-thirds the depth of the pot, and deposit a sprinkling of fertiliser into each hole.

PLANTING IN CONTAINERS

Planting in a container is instant and convenient. It can be done at any time, in any weather. There is no ground preparation to worry about. It is important to use potting mix, not garden soil. Purpose-designed potting mixes are available for outdoor container gardening. They contain a balanced mix of materials to give optimum drainage and water-holding capacity.

METHOD:

❏ Prepare the pot. Clean it thoroughly to remove any possible pests or disease. If necessary, paint the insides with a sealer such as Terraseal®. If you are concerned about potting mix escaping through the drainage holes, cover them with a piece of open-weave wire mesh or fabric.

More about fertilisers: Go to page 200.

- Prepare the potting mix. If you are using water crystals, pre-soak them to form a gel and then mix them thoroughly into the potting mix. Add a slow-release fertiliser or wetting-agent granules at the same time if desired.

- Water the plant thoroughly by steeping it in a bucket of water until the bubbles stop rising. Remove it from its nursery container.

- Fill the pot with enough potting mix so that when placed on it, the root ball of the plant reaches to a few centimetres below the pot rim. This allows room for water to pool at the top of the pot instead of spilling over the sides at watering time.

- Sit the plant in the centre of the pot and fill around the sides with potting mix, carefully firming it around the root ball by pushing down into the potting mix with your fingers.

- The final surface of the potting mix should not be more than a few centimetres above the original level of soil of the nursery pot.

- If underplanting a tree or shrub with annuals, plant the seedlings around the edges of the pot.

- Annuals can be planted by filling the pot to just below its final soil depth and making holes for the seedlings as you would if planting in the garden. Plant closer than recommended for garden planting to achieve a fast cover of flowers and foliage.

- Immediately after planting, water the mix thoroughly until water begins to emerge from the drainage holes.

REPOTTING

If your container plants are requiring a lot of watering and feeding but still fail to thrive, it could be time to repot. Repotting is essential when a plant's root system becomes pot-bound.

To remove a shrub or tree from a large pot, let it dry out slightly first and then lie it on its side. Gently tap the pot around the rim and pull the plant free. To prevent cracking, cushion the pot on a cloth or other soft surface. Removing a shrub or tree from a container will not be difficult if the pot is tapered towards the bottom. Pots that curve in at the top can cause problems.

You may wish to repot the plant into the next-sized pot if you want it to keep growing larger. Alternatively, you can return the plant to the same pot. This way you are restricting the ultimate size of a tree or shrub to suit your requirements by restricting its roots. In either case, it is important to replenish the soil and nutrients around the roots. Once the plant is out of its pot, remove up to a quarter of the old potting mix from around the roots. For tightly matted roots use a knife to shave about 5 cm from the sides and 10 cm from the bottom of the root ball. Pruning the top of the plant at the same time will be appropriate for most shrubs. Return the plant to the pot and add fresh potting mix containing a slow-release fertiliser. The best time to repot is when plants are dormant, which is usually in winter.

Pansies, perennial portulaca and celosias colour up the background to a large potted cycad.

TOP CONTAINER PLANTS

ANNUALS

BOTANICAL NAME	COMMON NAME	FLOWERING SEASON
Impatiens walleriana	Busy Lizzie	summer
Lobelia erinus	Lobelia	spring, summer, autumn
Lobularia maritima	Alyssum	all year
Lychnis viscaria	Viscaria	summer, autumn
Pericallis xhybrida	Cineraria	spring
Petunia xhybrida	Petunia	summer
Primula malacoides	Fairy primrose	winter, spring
Primula vulgaris	Polyanthus	winter, spring
Salvia splendens	Salvia	summer
Tagetes cultivars	Marigold	summer
Tropaeolum majus	Nasturtium	summer
Viola cornuta	Viola	spring, autumn
Viola xwittrockiana	Pansy	autumn, winter, spring

Annuals:
Go to page 127.

PERENNIALS

BOTANICAL NAME	COMMON NAME	FLOWERING SEASON
Agapanthus 'Streamline'	African lily	spring, summer
Argyranthemum 'Elfin' hybrids	Dwarf marguerite	spring, summer
Brachyscome 'Break O'Day'	Swan river daisy	all year
Cerastium tomentosum	Snow-in-summer	spring, summer
Convolvulus sabatius	Bindweed	summer
Dianthus cultivars	Border pink	spring, summer
Erigeron speciosus cultivars	Fleabane	spring, summer
Felicia amelloides	Blue marguerite	spring, summer, autumn
Gazania hybrids	African daisy	spring, summer, autumn
Helianthemum cultivars	Sun rose	summer
Helipterum 'Paper Cascade'	Paper daisy	summer
Hosta cultivars	Plaintain lily	spring
Pelargonium xdomesticum cultivars	Regal pelargonium	summer
Pelargonium xhortorum cultivars	Geranium	summer
Pelargonium peltatum cultivars	Ivy geranium	summer
Phlox subulata cultivars	Alpine phlox	spring, summer
Thymus spp. & cultivars	Thyme	summer
Succulents and cacti cultivars		

Perennials:
Go to page 102.

Succulents and cacti:
Go to page 138.

SPRING-FLOWERING BULBS

Anemone

Babiana

Crocus

Daffodil

Freesia

Hyacinth

Ipheion
Lachenalia
Muscari
Ranunculus
Tulips

TREES AND SHRUBS

BOTANICAL NAME	COMMON NAME	HEIGHT
Acer palmatum cultivars	Japanese maple	1 m
Adenandra uniflora	China flower	60 cm
Agave attenuata		1 m
Anigozanthos hybrids	Kangaroo paw	60 cm–1 m
Astelia chathamica 'Silver Spear'		1.5 m
Aucuba japonica	Japanese laurel	1.5 m
Azalea evergreen hybrids	Azalea	75 cm–1 m
Buxus sempervirens	English box	1 m
Callistemon 'Little John'	Dwarf bottlebrush	75 cm
Camellia cultivars	Camellia	up to 3 m
Citrus cultivars	Citrus	various
Hibiscus Hawaiian hybrids	Hibiscus	various
Juniperus chinensis 'Kaizuka'	Hollywood juniper	2 m
Laurus nobilis	Bay tree	4 m
Metrosideros 'Tahiti'		1 m
Rhododendron vireya hybrids	Vireya rhododendrons	1 m
Rosa hybrids	Roses	various
Xeronema callistemon	Poor Knights lily	1 m
Yucca filamentosa	Adam's needle	1.5 m

Bulbs:
Go to page 112.

Trees:
Go to page 15.

Shrubs:
Go to page 29.

Roses:
Go to page 85.

Azaleas.

Tropical waterlilies.

Water gardening

As anyone who has spent time with small children will know, there is something very captivating about water. Children will play happily with water for hours. Taps are irresistible, and on a trip to the zoo, a toddler will often be far more interested in a small waterfall than the liveliest of monkeys.

The attraction to water is in all of us. It's not surprising that it has been included in gardens since ancient times. Water is central to most of the grand gardens of Europe, in the form of huge and extravagant man-made fountains, waterfalls and canals. In New Zealand we are surrounded by water. Few live far from a beach, lake or river, and many of us have the great fortune of enjoying a water view without having to create our own.

Such a bounty of natural waterways is perhaps one reason why New Zealanders have been in no hurry to adopt the passion for making water gardens. Until recently, it has been considered the domain of the expert or wealthy gardener, but more and more, water gardening is becoming accessible to everyone.

The range of water-gardening gear is ever expanding, with an emphasis on easy installation and low maintenance. Expert advice is easy to find. From a simple fountain to a grand pond there are water features to suit any garden style or budget.

SIMPLE WATER FEATURES WITHOUT PONDS

Pools are not always a desirable option, especially where small children must be considered, but the tranquil, cooling effects of water can be enjoyed in other ways.

A BIRDBATH is the simplest and easiest water feature to install. It is a garden ornament as well as a water feature and is ideally positioned at the end of vistas or used as a centrepiece. It gives added interest with the birdlife it might attract and takes the water above toddler height. If possible, avoid putting your birdbath close to over-hanging tree branches or other places within handy pouncing distance for cats.

A WALL FOUNTAIN in its most traditional form is a lion's head. Wall fountains are often situated above pools, but they can also spout on to a bed of pebbles with a hidden collecting tank underneath. Another option is to purchase a self-contained unit complete with hidden pump and attached basin, a mini pond at eye level. The water is collected in the pool and recirculated via the pump back out the lion's mouth.

PEBBLE POOLS can also be purchased as self-contained units. The pool has a covered sump to hold the pump and collect the water. Pebbles cover the whole apparatus once installed so that the central fountain appears to spout out from the ground over the pebbles. The units themselves are usually round, but the pebbled area could be irregular or formal in shape depending on the style of your garden.

A waterlily pot is the ideal way to enjoy waterlilies when you don't have a pond. It adds a touch of water-garden atmosphere to the smallest of spaces.

A TALL URN adds elegance to any garden setting especially when planted with a tall water plant, such as *Cyperus haspan* or *Pontederia cordata,* coupled with a waterlily.

Other suitable containers include old coppers or wine barrels. They can be surrounded by plants such as hostas or ferns, which will help blend the container into the garden setting.

More about waterlilies in pots: Go to page 185.

MAKING A POND

If you are installing a pond in your garden, think first about what style and size of pond will best suit your garden before getting yourself tied up in knots over the practicalities. These will come later as you modify the original dream pond to suit your budget and what is practical. Because water is so attention-grabbing by nature, a badly designed pond will stand out as much as a good one. So it's worth much deliberating (or paying a good designer) to ensure that your pond design is as perfect as it can be for your garden.

THE SHAPE most popular for garden ponds is the irregular shape of a natural pond, and if installed properly with appropriate natural-style planting it will look lovely in an informal-style garden. But the irregular shape is not always best for the smaller garden. Even in a cottage garden with informal planting, a straight-sided or circular pond is the better choice. A geometric-shaped pond is the obvious choice for the formal garden, fitting in with symmetrically arranged paving and planting schemes.

THE SIZE of the pool should also be in scale with the size of the garden. A good size if you have room is around 4.5 to 5 m^2 of water surface (i.e., 2 m long by 2.5 m wide or a circle roughly 2.5 m in diameter). This has been shown to be an optimum size for a stable ecological environment with minimum temperature fluctuation and is better for fish. Smaller pools are more susceptible to algal attack.

POSITIONING is of premium significance. One of the most beautiful qualities of a pond or pool is reflection. They will reflect surrounding plants as well as larger trees, buildings, ornaments or the sky. The reflection depends on where you are standing when you look at the pond. So reflection may be one of the influencing factors when it comes to positioning of the pond in relation to the house, pathways and the various viewing points around the garden.

In practical terms, the pond needs to receive at least 5 hours of sunshine if it is to be kept clean and weed free with thriving fish. Although trees look wonderful as a reflection, they are best not overhanging your pond to the extent that they drop too many falling leaves into the water, causing pollution and sometimes even poisoning the fish life.

Other things to consider will be the proximity to electricity for pumps or lighting, and to taps for filling and topping up the water level.

RAISED POOLS have an enhanced reflective quality by being brought closer to eye level. Formal pools need not be at ground level. They can be positioned at any level that suits your site. A change of level allows the opportunity for waterfalls. Sides of raised pools may also double as seats. Safer where children are concerned, a raised pool could even be made out of reach of small children.

Irregular-shaped pools are designed to look natural and risk looking ridiculously unnatural if positioned above ground level. On the other hand, beware of placing your pool in a waterlogged hollow. While it might seem the obvious choice for a natural pond, excavation will be difficult and damage by water pressure from beneath the pond is very likely.

With out-of-ground pools it is important to make sure that the sides are designed to cope with the weight of the water. Ready-made fibreglass ponds can be installed with the top half out of the ground, building up the surrounds with a low retaining wall and backfilling with well-compacted soil. If necessary a rim of concrete may be added around the top edge of the pond for extra support.

THE IDEAL DEPTH for a small pond is 45 cm. This caters for the requirements of the majority of water plants as well as the fish. The larger the pond, the deeper it can be. However, even very large ponds need not be over 90 cm deep.

Very shallow water is prone to algae, which quickly reduce the pond to a slimy mess, but to accommodate bog plants a shelf of 20 cm depth may be included around the perimeter of the pond.

Slope the sides of the pond steeply. Gently sloping saucer shapes leave you with too much shallow water.

THE EDGES of a natural pond will be made of rock, as natural-looking as possible. Those of a formal pool will be made of any material that is in keeping with the garden itself, whether it be stone, brick, concrete or timber. The important thing is that the edges cantilever over the edge of the water. An overhang of at least 50 mm will hide the inside pond walls and disguise the rise and fall of the water level due to rainfall and evaporation.

POND GADGETS

PUMPS

Moving water enhances the beauty of a pond. It also makes for a healthier pond by circulating the water, increasing oxygen levels and creating a healthier environment for plants and fish. Consult a reputable stockist to ensure you get the right pump for the job. This will depend on the size of your pond and the demands of filters, waterfalls or fountains. A pump specially designed for water gardens is best.

FILTERS

If you want your pond to be low maintenance, a filter is an exceptionally good idea. These ensure healthier cleaner ponds and are either mechanically or biologically based. It is important to have the right-sized filter for your pond and to install it correctly. Advice is the key, ideally at the design stage.

POND CONSTRUCTION

The most popular way to construct a pond is by using a flexible liner. This allows complete flexibility of design — you can have any shape or size you want. It is also a cost-effective option with a range of materials available. Seamless, tear-resistant and flexible, today's liners are much improved on those of days gone by, with even the cheapest versions lasting ten years when properly installed. Whatever you do, use a purpose-designed material guaranteed against ultraviolet breakdown. It is false economy to use ordinary black polythene. Black, however, is the best colour to go for. It offers a more natural finish and a contrasting background for plants and fish and gives rise to the best mirror images.

Making a pool using a flexible liner is by no means difficult, but by far the easiest way is to purchase a pre-formed pond. Such concerns as the correct depth are taken care of. Pre-formed ponds are extremely hardy and there is a vast range of shapes and sizes to choose from. They come in both irregular and formal shapes with built-in shelves for marginal plants. Some even come with a built-in waterfall. For most newcomers to water gardening, the little extra it costs will be more than covered by the time saved and convenience.

INSTALLING A PRE-FORMED POND

1 **EXCAVATE** the ground to the required depth and 15 cm wider than the pond perimeter. Cover the base with 5 cm of sand to protect the pool from stones.

2 **POSITION** the pond using a spirit level to check that the top of the pool is level in all directions.

3 **BACKFILL** around the sides ensuring that the soil is worked under the shelves to provide firm support all round. Add water to the pond as you backfill to ensure even placement of the pond.

4 **DECORATE** the pond surrounds with the chosen edging and planting.

Pond edging:
Go to page 182.

Pond planting:
Go to page 184.

ULTRAVIOLET CLARIFIERS

These relatively new electrical devices are used in conjunction with a filter to keep ponds clear by destroying green algae. They are expensive to install but worth investigating for big-budget projects.

PLANTING

Apart from looking great next to water, plants are vital to the overall natural balance of a pond, helping to keep the water clean and clear, and some generating oxygen for the fish. Ideally, a half to one-third of the water surface should be covered by plants — this cuts out sunlight, too much of which encourages undesirable algal growth. The fish also appreciate the shelter afforded by a good covering of plants.

Planting can be done any time from spring to autumn when plants are in active growth and the water is warm. Essentially the planting season begins when the plants begin to grow. When planting a new pond, leave the water to de-chlorinate and stabilise for a few days before introducing plants.

All plants should be in containers, ideally baskets. Don't place a layer of soil over the base of the pond unless you want to turn your pond into a bog garden. Specially designed baskets for water gardening are best as they allow free movement of water through the root system with roots growing through the sides. Plants in baskets can also be easily moved around.

Normal potting mix is too light for water gardens. Buy a planting mix specially formulated for water plants or use a heavy garden loam. After planting, top off the mix with a layer of pebbles or stones to prevent soil spreading into the pond.

Water plants, especially flowering ones, need feeding just like any other plants, but normal fertilisers can aggravate algal problems, so feed your water plants with a special water-plant or waterlily fertiliser. These are available in small sachets, which are easily inserted into the basket at planting time or into the baskets of established water plants.

As for those plants surrounding your pond or water feature, the scope is only limited by your imagination. However, your garden soil does not magically convert to the perfect habitat for bog plants just because you have created a pond. In fact, the soil may well be on the dry side if the pond is correctly sited in a sunny position. It may be more appropriate to select ordinary garden plants, especially a few of those that flower in the autumn and winter when most of the bog and marginal plants are dormant, such as azaleas, camellias and hellebores.

WATER PLANTS

Plants that grow in watery environments can be categorised according to the depth of water they are best adapted to:

BOG PLANTS grow in permanently damp but not saturated soil. Many can be grown as ordinary garden plants.
Astilbe spp.
Primula prolifera (syn. *P. heladoxa*) and other candelabra primulas.

MARGINAL PLANTS grow partly submerged in shallow water 5 to 8 cm deep, or in constantly moist soil at the edge of a pond or stream. Many of them will also grow as ordinary garden plants.

Japanese irises (*Iris ensata* cultivars)
Louisiana irises (*Louisiana* hybrids)
Cyperus haspan.

DEEP-WATER MARGINALS are those plants that grow with all but their tops fully submerged. Most prefer a water depth of around 15 cm, but this varies between species. The right depth is easily achieved by raising the plant's container to the required height on blocks at the base of the pond.

Waterlily (*Nymphaea* spp.)
Pontederia cordata.

OXYGENATING PLANTS release oxygen into the water creating a suitable environment for other plants and fish. They also absorb excess mineral salts and nitrates from the water, thereby starving algae of their food source and keeping the pond clean. They must have strong light to do their job efficiently. There are two types:

Iris and dwarf calla lily (*Zantedeschia*).

❑ Submerged oxygenators grow fully submerged with their roots in soil and their tops below the water surface.
   Oxygen plant (*Elodea canadensis*) is sold in pet shops for aquariums — 10 bunches per square metre is the recommended planting rate.
   Water milfoil (*Myriophyllum propinquum*) — 10 bunches per square metre is the recommended planting rate.

❑ Floating oxygenators literally float and grow on the water surface, roots and all. They tend to be quite rampant but are easily netted out if they begin to take over.

A healthy pond contains a well-balanced planting with plenty of oxygenators. For example, a larger pond of around 5 m² surface area would ideally be stocked with three waterlilies, a couple of other deep-water marginal plants and about 50 oxygenators, plus marginal plants.

A tiny pond of less 1 m² in surface area would have room for one waterlily (a pygmy waterlily for the very tiny pond), with six or seven oxygenators, and at least marginal plants to complete the picture.

WATERLILIES

The first thought of making a water garden often springs from the desire to grow waterlilies. Romantic and exotic in flower, they are beautiful with just their lovely round leaves floating on the surface of the water.

There are 3 main types of waterlily:

HARDY WATERLILIES grow to a diameter of about 1 m and are good for a deeper pond, preferring to have 20 to 40 cm of water above the top of their basket. The flowers sit on top of the water alongside the leaves.

TROPICAL WATERLILIES grow to an average spread of about 2 m and prefer shallow water, with only 10 to 15 cm above the top of their basket. The flowers are held above the foliage on tall stems. These are the waterlilies used as cut flowers. Tropical waterlilies are generally no less hardy than 'hardy' waterlilies in New Zealand conditions.

PYGMY (OR MINIATURE) WATERLILIES, as their name suggests, have smaller flowers and smaller leaves, spreading up to a metre across. They like to have 10 to 30 cm of water above the top of their basket. These are the best waterlilies to grow in large pots, when you don't have a pond.

Waterlilies are not difficult to grow. Above all, they are sun lovers; the more sun they get, the better they will flower. They need still water that warms up quickly in spring or after a cold night, hence they are best in water that is not too deep. Running springs and streams are unsuitable and waterlilies should be positioned away from waterfalls or fountains.

Hardy waterlilies.

WATERLILIES LOVE:
- ✓ Full sun
- ✓ A rich planting mix
- ✓ Still water that warms up quickly in spring

Plant waterlilies in containers, ideally baskets. Use blocks to achieve the correct depth for your variety. Use a soil mix of 1 part garden loam to 1 part compost, or a specially prepared water-gardening mix. Waterlilies are gross feeders. The easiest method of feeding is to add special water-plant sachets to the baskets at planting time and replace with a new sachet each spring.

Waterlilies look best if they cover one-third of the pond surface. A pond completely covered is not a healthy environment for fish or the important oxygenating plants. In large ponds with more than one waterlily plant, space the pots about 2 m apart for tropical waterlilies, 1.5 m apart for hardy waterlilies, and 1 m apart for miniatures.

A WATERLILY IN A POT

YOU WILL NEED:

One pygmy waterlily plant.

A waterproof container of at least 50 cm diameter (e.g., glazed terracotta with hole plugged, wine barrel, old copper).

Waterlily planting mix.

Water-plant fertiliser sachet.

Waterlily basket (medium size).

Stone chips or pebbles.

Bricks or blocks to fit in the bottom of the water container.

1. Fill the basket with planting mix up to 5 cm below the top.

2. Insert the fertiliser sachet into the middle of the planting mix.

3. Plant the waterlily firmly so that its crown (the junction between roots and shoots) is just emerging from the soil mix.

4. Fill to the top of the basket (a layer of 4 to 5 cm) with pebbles.

5. Water thoroughly to ensure the mix is saturated.

6. Add any bricks you need to the bottom of the water container so that the top of the basket sits 20 to 30 cm below the top of the container.

7. Position the basket in the water container and gently fill it so that the crown of the waterlily is just below the surface of the water. If the waterlily has already sprouted young leaves, these should be just floating.

8. After about a week add more water, filling to the top of the container.

FISH FACTS

Fish add interest to a pond but they are not essential. In fact they are not always recommended because they breed furiously and must be culled periodically. They can also add to algal problems by way of nitrate-rich waste.

Fish need unpolluted, well-oxygenated water. Too little oxygen goes hand in hand with too much carbon dioxide, which can be lethal. Plenty of oxygenating plants are thus essential.

Water movement is not essential for fish but they tolerate it. They enjoy playing in splashing water while the mixing of air and water increases the amount of dissolved oxygen.

Fish do not require deep water. The oxygen they need to survive is present in ever-decreasing quantities with increasing depth. They do, however, tolerate cold water as long as it doesn't ice over for prolonged periods. If this happens (in very cold climates), pierce a hole in the ice to allow toxic gases from decaying matter to escape. The fish do not die from the cold but from suffocation due to trapped carbon dioxide.

It is important to wait until plants are well established (at least a month after planting) before you introduce fish to your pond. They are likely to destroy young plants before they have a chance to grow.

Shelter is important to fish, another reason to get the planting established first. Submerged oxygenator plants provide an ideal breeding ground for fish. This may not be such a good thing if you have a population-control problem.

POND PROBLEMS

ALGAE occur when there is a high presence of nitrates, on which they thrive, in the water. Like most pond plants, they also thrive on plenty of sunlight. Algal outbreaks are common in spring, but in a well-balanced pond will last only until the fresh spring growth of oxygenators and other pond plants begins.

The best way to discourage algal growth is to control the level of nitrates in the water. Nitrates come from any form of debris, including leaves, fish excreta and (it has to be said) dead fish! So, first of all, keep these things to a minimum.

The next thing is to make sure you have sufficient oxygenating plants to absorb excess nitrates. Waterlilies and other floating plants help too. A plant cover of a half to two-thirds on the water surface is ideal. This cuts down the amount of light reaching the algae underneath.

A filter attached to a pump is an excellent way of controlling the pollutants algae thrive on. It is worth considering, especially if you are installing a pump anyway.

In theory, a well-balanced pond should not possess algal problems, but commercial algae killers are available as a last resort. A better alternative than chemicals is an ultraviolet clarifier. It is more expensive initially but environmentally friendly and harmless to fish and plants.

COMBATING ALGAE:
- ✓ Less fish
- ✓ Clear debris from surface
- ✓ More oxygenating plants
- ✓ Install a filter
- ✓ Two-thirds covering of waterlilies

MOSQUITOES are a horrible thought — enough to put anybody off water gardening. But they don't have to be a threat. Position ponds away from shady corners. If mosquitoes still occur, try dropping a couple of teaspoonfuls of vegetable oil on the pond surface. This will smother the larvae without any adverse effect on the pond.

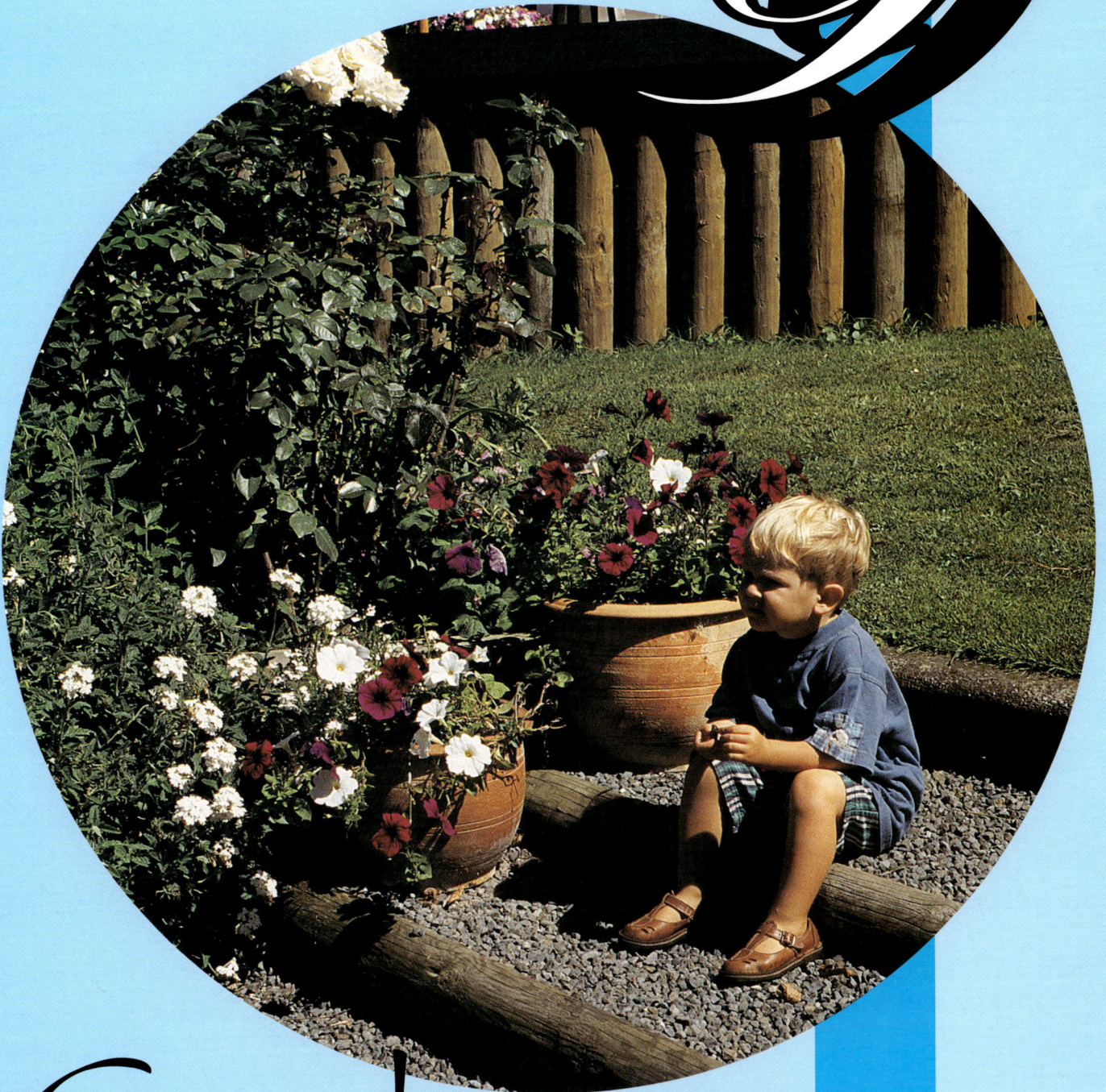

Gardening in action

Soil Preparation

Once you have planned your garden, you'll be keen to start planting, but it pays to put some effort into preparing the ground before you rush out to the garden centre.

Putting in new areas of garden usually requires some kind of soil cultivation. The more compacted the soil has become through its previous use, the more digging will be required to make it a satisfactory environment for plants. Compacted soils are poorly drained, poorly aerated and difficult for plant roots to penetrate. A rotary hoe is useful, especially for large areas, but it will only cultivate to a limited depth so is best reserved for lawns that have shallow roots.

Vegetable and flower gardens need particular attention and are best dug by hand to at least a spade's depth. Digging when the soil is wet is not only hard work but bad for the soil. On heavy clay soils, digging immediately after a period of heavy rain is best avoided. Wait until the soil is moist but not soggy. A fork is better than a spade for soils that are on the wet side.

Avoid mixing the topsoil with the subsoil. Bulk up shallow topsoils with extra compost.

SOIL IMPROVEMENT

Improving the structure of the soil is an ongoing process, which begins at the digging stage when good volumes of compost can be conveniently added. Thereafter, it is a case of adding more organic matter whenever you have the opportunity — at planting times or as a mulch.

Plenty of organic matter is the answer to improving both clay and sandy soils. Add as much as you can to the topsoil when preparing a garden. Compost can be bought by the trailer load or in bags, depending on the scope of your project. Make sure that any material you are adding to the soil is well broken down (i.e., in composted form). Animal manures, in particular, can be damaging if added in their raw state. Bark or lawn clippings can strip the soil of nitrogen if not broken down properly first. There are various other soil-conditioning products available, each with their own particular blend of organic materials.

RAISED BEDS

When drainage is poor, one of the easiest remedies is to raise the planting site above ground level. This also gives rise to a warmer soil in the early spring, ideal for getting summer vegetable crops off to a good start.

For shallow-rooted crops, digging is often not necessary. Raised vegetable gardens can be made by building a bed of compost and/or fresh topsoil directly on top of the soil. In this case, perennial grasses and other invasive weeds should be cleared from the site first.

When the subsoil is compacted, especially if you want to grow deeper-rooting

Soil preparation for lawns: Go to page 146.

More about mulching: Go to page 204.

How to make compost: Go to page 196.

plants, it pays to first remove the topsoil and break up the subsoil. The existing topsoil can then be replaced along with additional topsoil or compost to make the raised bed. If you buy in topsoil, make sure it is of good quality (not mixed with subsoil) and weed free (at least free of weeds such as oxalis).

Raised beds that are mass planted in trees and shrubs may simply be mounds. In smaller gardens, and for vegetables and flowers, which must be tended to on a regular basis, the beds are more likely to have sides. These may be built from timber, concrete, bricks, concrete blocks or rocks, or may be a good place to use up broken concrete from an old pathway. Sides that are wide enough to sit on make for convenient gardening. For vegetable and flower beds, life will be easier if you can reach every part of the raised bed from its sides.

Bearded iris enjoy well-drained soil.

LAYING DRAINS

A heavy soil will not necessarily be improved dramatically by the installation of drains, as the problem lies with the soil's inability to let water drain through its structure. Good drainage can, however, prevent soils getting too wet in the first place by diverting excess water away from the garden. They are also necessary to keep water away from the house and lessen earth movement on sloping or retained areas.

The best time to install drains is during preparation of the soil. Paved areas will affect the positioning of drains, as will the slope of the property. Soak pits are necessary when there is not access to storm-water drains. It is best to employ an expert, as badly layed drainage systems can be worse than none at all.

Plants for the water garden: Go to page 184.

If your site proves to be too difficult or expensive to drain, consider a bog garden and grow plants that like damp conditions. Trees that tolerate wet feet will help remove excess water by taking it up through their roots and releasing it through their leaves.

PLANT BUYERS' GUIDE

Not all plants are equal when it comes to how they will perform in your garden. A strong, healthy young plant will establish much more quickly and have a superior long-term performance in your garden than a lesser example of the same variety. Shape is also important.

If you can avoid it, it pays not to buy the last plant in the row. Unless, that is, you are a kind, nurturing soul who usually goes for the runt of the litter. At least be wary of such a specimen and check it out before you buy.

THINGS TO LOOK FOR:

✓ **A HEALTHY ROOT SYSTEM.** This is the most important criterion of all. Some roots coming out the bottom of the bag is a good sign, but a hard, tightly packed mass of roots, growing in a circular pattern around the container, is not.

✓ **EVIDENCE OF RECENT GROWTH**, especially with trees and shrubs in spring, and especially those that have been grown in the open ground and had their roots trimmed to get them into their containers (e.g., spring roses and some deciduous trees).

✓ **GOOD COLOUR**. Unless you are looking at a variegated or golden-leaved cultivar, yellow is not a good sign. Rich green is generally what you are looking for.

✓ **GOOD FOLIAGE COVER**. A spindly plant that lacks foliage near the bottom may be genetically disposed to legginess, but it may also just be an unhealthy specimen that has been in the garden centre too long. Of course, you wouldn't expect to find leaves on a deciduous plant in winter.

✓ **GENERAL LACK OF DISEASE**. Spots and brown blotches on leaf margins should be queried.

✓ **NOT TOO MANY FLOWERS**. This depends very much on the plant. Flowers in great volume are appropriate for an indoor chrysanthemum, but not necessarily for a young shrub. Too many flowers may be at the expense of strong foliage growth. Fruit on young fruit trees are similarly not always ideal. If it is the flowering season for a particular shrub, choose the one with an average number of flowers.

✓ **GOOD SHAPE**. This depends on what you want from your plant. If you wish to create a standard, a straight central stem will be important. If it is a bushy shrub you want, look for an even shape with lots of branches. A shade tree should have a straight central trunk. You can correct the shape later with pruning and staking, but it is best to start off with a shape as close as possible to the ultimate goal. Pull plants out of the row and line them up so you can deliberate on the best shape for you. Ask for help.

✓ **WEEDS AND FADED LABELS**. These could well mean that the plant has been sitting around for too long.

White-flowering *Cistus* with annuals and perennials against an evergreen backdrop.

Planting is easy, fun, and very satisfying. Assuming you have already prepared the ground to a satisfactory degree, it's as simple as this:

1 WATER THE PLANT. Do this thoroughly, even sit it in a bucket of water until it is thoroughly saturated. This is especially important for plants that have dried out in their containers.

2 DIG A HOLE. The bigger the better so that there is plenty of crumbly, freshly dug and compost-enriched soil around the plant's roots. Dig at least twice as wide and one and a half times the depth of the size of the plant's container. Backfill the bottom of the hole to the depth of the container, firming down gently. In heavy soils plants such as rhododendrons like to sit a little higher then they were in their bag, the soil mounded up a few centimetres above ground level.

3 MIX SOME GOODIES INTO THE SOIL. Compost and fertiliser is an optional extra but will generally give faster, healthier results. Mix compost and a slow-release fertiliser into the soil before it is returned to the planting hole (including the soil at the bottom of the hole). Exact quantities depend on what you are planting, the state of your soil, and how well you prepared it beforehand.

4 REMOVE THE PLANT FROM ITS CONTAINER. Unless you are planting invasive plants like mint or bulbs to lift at a later date, never plant without removing the container bag or pot first. If the plant has been in its container too long, the roots may be tightly packed and spiralling around in the shape of the pot (i.e., pot-bound). In such cases, gently loosen and lightly prune the roots, removing damaged parts with a clean cut. (Note: do not do this with containerised roses.)

5 PLACE THE PLANT IN THE HOLE. It should be at the same level as it was in its pot. Grafted plants, such as roses or citrus trees, need to be placed so the graft (the lumpy nob on the stem just above the roots) is a centimetre or two above the soil. Position stakes at this point if they are needed. This saves the roots from being damaged by driving stakes in later.

6 **REPLACE THE SOIL.** Place the soil, containing its added compost and fertiliser, around the root ball of the plant, firming it gently with your hand or foot as you go. Add a layer of mulch if appropriate, remembering to keep it clear of the main stem.

7 **WATER AGAIN.** This ensures that the soil in and around the planting hole is well watered and helps to push the soil in snugly around the plant's roots.

Soil preparation: Go to page 190.

Compost: Go to page 196.

Fertilisers: Go to page 200.

Mulching: Go to page 204.

STAKING

Staking is important for plants such as trees, standard roses and tall perennials. When newly planted trees are subject to wind movement, the consequent rocking of the roots prevents them from becoming established properly in the ground. Taller perennials often need staking to prevent them from blowing over and damaging their flowers. It depends very much on the plant and the amount of shelter.

In very windy locations, stakes may have a damaging effect, causing abrasion and breakage to stems and branches. In this situation it is often better to anchor the plant by placing a large rock at its base. The rock can double as a 'leaning post'.

Stakes can be dead tree branches and twigs, tanalised timber or bamboo, or expensive metal renditions. Prominent wooden stakes don't always suit the pretty cottage garden where twigs and branches may be better disguised among the flowers. For feature plants such as weeping standard roses, a top-quality, purpose-built metal stake would be worth the investment. Wooden stakes are ideal for tomatoes and trees.

When staking trees, it is best to place two stakes, one each side of the tree. Tie with a flexible tie, such as an old nylon stocking or a specially designed alternative from a garden centre, not string. Pieces of old tyre tube make great ties.

Making Compost

Homemade compost is not only a cost-effective way of improving your soil. It is also a convenient way to recycle garden waste such as lawn clippings and prunings. Aim to have at least one good load of compost to put on the garden each year. Spring is a good time to spread compost as a mulch or mix it into the soil before planting.

THE INGREDIENTS

There are various ways of making compost, but the ingredients common to all successful composts are:

❏ ORGANIC MATTER HIGH IN NITROGEN, such as kitchen wastes, lawn clippings, and other soft greens.

❏ ORGANIC MATTER HIGH IN CARBON, such as prunings, autumn leaves, and other coarse materials. Bulky prunings need to be cut up or ideally put through a shredder.

❏ SOIL MICRO-ORGANISMS, which are the workers in the composting process, 'good-guy' bacteria and fungi that break down the raw organic matter, turning it into usable compost. Have the heap in contact with the ground so that soil micro-organisms can enter. Alternatively, add thin layers of soil to the heap or use a commercial compost activator.

❏ OXYGEN (AIR) so that micro-organisms can 'breathe' while they work. The kind that don't need oxygen are the anaerobic bacteria, which make a putrifying smelly mass, not good compost. Consequently, adequate coarse material is needed to keep air spaces open. For this reason lawn clippings alone don't make good compost.

❏ HEAT for effective decomposition. Without it a compost can take a long time before it is ready. A perfect compost heap generates enough heat to kill diseases and weed seeds, but such temperatures are difficult to sustain in a normal situation. It is a matter of striking a balance between ventilation and insulation to prevent heat loss at cold times of the year. The main reason for turning the heap is to give every part of the compost heap some time in the middle, where it is hottest. A shady, out-of-the-way corner is a likely position for a compost heap, but a sunny site is best, especially in winter. Summer-made compost is ready for use in a shorter time than that started in autumn or winter.

❏ *MOISTURE*, for the micro-organisms to function properly. In dry windy weather you may need to water the compost heap occasionally, but remember, wet compost is cold and more oxygen-deficient. A cover to keep out excessive rain is advisable.

BENEFICIAL EXTRAS INCLUDE:

❏ *ANIMAL MANURES.* These are a valuable source of nitrogen on which the micro-organisms thrive and add to the overall soil fertility. Add up to a quarter of the total bulk of the compost.

❏ *BLOOD AND BONE.* This also promotes bacterial activity and speeds up decomposition. Add up to 5 kg per cubic metre of compost.

❏ *LIME.* Lime encourages the activity of earthworms and soil micro-organisms. It is usually added to the compost heap with a thin layer of soil.

WORTH EXCLUDING ARE:

❏ Invasive weeds like oxalis, perennial grasses and onion weed.

❏ Weeds that have gone to seed.

❏ Diseased plant material.

❏ Plants that have been sprayed with long-life chemicals.

❏ Meat scraps (which attract rats).

❏ Wood ash.

❏ Inorganic waste products (plastic, glass, etc).

❏ Sawdust from treated timber.

THE COMPOST BIN

The design of your compost bin will depend a lot on the size of your garden. Compost can be made in a heap without a bin at all, but most gardens need a tidier alternative.

An ideal compost bin consists of a row of three bays, each approximately 1 m² and 1 to 1.5 m tall. The front of each bay should be removable for easy spade access.

The first bay is for collecting the raw materials, the second is for breaking down, the third for storing the ready-to-use compost. In a smaller garden you will get away with two bays: one for collecting while the bottom layer breaks down, the other for turning the contents of the first bay into so that the most mature compost is nearest the top while the bottom layer continues to break down. In a very small garden, one bay may be all you have room for. In this case it's easiest to build your heap as quickly as possible, wait for it to mature, use it all up and start again.

If your needs are for a small compost bin, you may be better off with a preformed plastic bin. The biggest advantage of these is that they are ready made and easy on the eye when you have nowhere to hide them. They are also vermin-proof.

The walls of the homemade compost bin are commonly timber boards, allowing air spaces between each board. Wire netting supported by metal or timber posts is another option. Corrugated iron can also be used as long as air holes are drilled. Whatever material is used, ventilation is important.

MAKING THE COMPOST

The best compost comes from a heap put together all in one go, in carefully worked out, even layers. This is fine if you have the time and the place to stockpile the ingredients. Most people haven't. So, you should do your best to approximate the ideal.

Start the heap with a layer of coarse materials such as hedge clippings to keep the bottom well aerated. Each time you add a layer of lawn clippings add some coarser material, such as chopped-up prunings or dead leaves. Every 50 cm or so, add a thin layer of soil, or sprinkle some blood and bone or compost activator. Keep the worst of the rain off with some kind of cover (polythene will do), especially in winter. Turn the heap at least once during its life if you can.

Compost takes from a few months to a year to mature. In summer it will be a lot faster than in winter. When ready, a good compost is a sweet-smelling, moist, black and friable homogeneous substance resembling a perfect topsoil. It should not be slushy with hunks of raw material still recognisable, except perhaps for the odd partially decomposed stick that can simply be raked out and put back into the next heap.

Compost as a soil conditioner: Go to page 190.

Fertilisers

Without adequate nutrients, plants beome yellow and sickly, growth is painfully slow or stunted, flowering and fruiting may be retarded, and the plants are likely to be more susceptible to pests and diseases. This is hardly surprising, but we often forget about feeding our plants and wonder why they don't thrive.

Fertilisers can be applied during soil preparation and prior to planting. However, to maintain soil fertility and plant vigour in the long term it is crucial to replenish the soil nutrients taken up by plants or lost through microbial activity and soil leaching. To achieve this it is best to fertilise at intervals while plants are actively growing, especially at the onset of spring.

Nutrients can be supplied via a wide range of organic and inorganic fertilisers, however for a healthy garden it is advisable to mainly use balanced fertilisers.

WHAT IS A BALANCED FERTILISER?

A balanced fertiliser contains the three major nutrients needed by plants in large doses: nitrogen (N), phosphorous (P), and potassium (K). It also contains 'trace elements', those nutrients needed in smaller quantities (e.g., iron, magnesium, zinc) but just as essential for a plant's wellbeing.

Different plant groups have slightly different nutritional requirements, and while a general garden fertiliser will generally do for all of them, there are also special purpose fertilisers available that better meet these requirements. With names like 'Rose Fertiliser', 'Citrus Fertiliser' and 'Acid Plant Food' the job has been done for you when it comes to sorting out what you need.

Overuse of single-nutrient fertilisers, organic or inorganic, can lead to chemical imbalances in the soil. This can affect the plant's ability to absorb the right nutrients or a particular nutrient may reach toxic levels in the soil. A common problem with excessive use of nitrogenous fertilisers is too much lush vegetative growth at the expense of flowers or fruit, and increased vulnerability to pests and diseases.

ORGANIC OR INORGANIC?

Organic materials are best for the environment overall. They help maintain good soil structure and are best for the wellbeing of soil micro-organisms, those invisible 'garden elves' who turn soil nutrients into palatable forms for the plant.

Compost, the ultimate organic soil conditioner, does not by itself supply the nutrients required to support a garden. Nevertheless, well-made compost will return to the soil a range of nutrients that will gradually become available to the plants. Unlike inorganic fertilisers, it also replenishes soil humus levels, an important factor in maintaining long-term soil fertility. Organic fertilisers take the form of fishmeal, animal manures, blood and bone and other natural waste products. Because most organic fertilisers require microbial activity to release their valuable nutrients, they are generally slow-acting and the risk of burning is minimal, as long as they are properly decomposed before use.

However, no single organic fertiliser contains a complete range of essential nutrients. A purely organic garden should therefore receive a range of different organic fertilisers to ensure a balanced diet.

Inorganic ('man-made') fertilisers are easy — easy to use, easy to understand and easy to obtain. All have their nutritional make-up clearly described on the bag. Some are instantly soluble and hence give rapid results. Some provide a useful 'quick fix' for when a plant or the soil is deficient in a certain nutrient. Others are true slow-release fertilisers. The main downfall of inorganic fertilisers in the garden is that they do nothing for the soil structure or for the long-term livelihood of the soil. However, for potting and seed-raising mixes they are second to none.

The best advice for an easy, healthy garden is to use both. Use plenty of compost, organic fertilisers when you can get them, and chemical fertilisers for extra support.

FAST ACTING OR CONTROLLED RELEASE?

The fast-acting fertilisers are liquid fertilisers (such as Phostrogen® and Nitrosol®) and powdered forms that come in bags, such as general garden fertiliser, rose fertiliser, etc. These work like a tonic, quickly sending a tired plant into renewed growth and virility. They work brilliantly with plants that produce heavy crops of flowers or fruit over a short period, such as annuals and perennials. Long lasting they are not, however. It is therefore pointless to add too much at a time. Most of what is not taken up by the plants is quickly washed through the soil and wasted. Worse, overdosing with fast-acting fertilisers, especially the powdered forms, risks burning the roots. For this reason, the powdered fertilisers should not be used for container-grown plants.

Globe artichoke.

Controlled or slow-release fertilisers release nutrients to the soil gradually, at a rate that approximates the needs of the growing plants. They are ideal for potting mixes and are the best plant foods to use at tree and shrub planting time. They can also be used as a side dressing for growing plants in the garden. They are generally very clean and easy to use in convenient small packages that are easy to carry home and store in the garden shed. Only small amounts are used.

Examples of slow-release fertilisers are Nutricote®, Osmocote® and Triabon®. Slow-release fertilisers last anything from three months to two years in the soil. There is now a complete range available, individually formulated for different plant groups: citrus, roses, lawns, bulbs, tomatoes, pots, houseplants . . . and one for general use in case you don't have the storage space for a complete collection! These fertilisers contain a combination of products that result in immediate as well as long-term results. They work by responding to changes in soil temperature and moisture. Controlled-release fertilisers are environmentally friendly because leaching of excess nutrients is minimal.

Watering

Water is not just a matter of life and death. There is a vast difference between plants merely surviving and those really thriving. From the taste of your lettuces to the growth rate of your shelter trees, water may be the deciding factor.

Of course, different plants have different water requirements and soils have widely varying water-holding capabilities. Some climates provide high volumes of natural water through rainfall and others practically none when it is most needed.

Watering (or irrigation) balances the equation between what the plant needs and what its environment is giving it. When plants are actively growing they need more water. When the weather is warm or windy, water lost to the air needs replacing. A plant with water excess to its requirements suffers just as much as a thirsty one, and in this case needs shifting to a drier garden position or a pot.

Watering is not altogether a bother, in fact it can be quite a relaxing task, but the truth is, you may not always be ready to spend the time when your garden needs you most. The first thing is to minimise the water demands of your garden as much as possible, then to make watering as easy as you can afford. The difference between an automatic watering system and a watering can speaks for itself, in terms of time saved as well as cost. There are lots of options in between.

The thought that goes into making it easy for yourself will also go towards better water conservation.

WAYS TO MINIMISE THE WATER NEEDS OF YOUR GARDEN:

❑ Concentrate on trees and shrubs. After the first few years of establishment, trees and shrubs need negligible watering. Roses, perennials and annuals will always need regular watering, as will vegetable gardens and lawns.

❑ Choose plants with low water requirements or those that tolerate periods of drought.

❑ Use mulches. A layer of bark, straw, compost, stones or broken shells all cut down on water loss from the soil.

❑ Cover the ground. Bare soil loses water to the air via evaporation more rapidly. Use lots of groundcover plants and you'll also cut down on weeding.

❑ Have more paved or decked surfaces and less lawn.

❑ Provide shelter for your garden. Wind makes a huge difference to the amount of water lost to the air.

❑ Improve the water-holding ability of light soils by conditioning with compost, added generously prior to planting and thereafter as a mulch.

❑ Use a wetting agent and/or Crystal Rain in pots and hanging baskets.

❑ Paint the insides of terracotta pots with a sealant such as Terraseal.

❑ Choose large pots in preference to small ones. The smaller the pot the more often it will need watering.

Soils:
Go to page 3.

Plants for problem soils:
Go to page 72.

More about mulches:
Go to page 204.

Groundcovers:
Go to page 56.

Shelter planting:
Go to page 24.

Soil preparation:
Go to page 190.

Pots and watering:
Go to page 172.

WAYS TO MAKE WATERING EASY:

❏ Invest in easy-to-use hose attachments such as watering wands.

❏ Position taps where they are needed most.

❏ Group pots together.

❏ Group plants with high water needs together, for example, roses, perennials, annuals and vegetables.

❏ Shape lawns for easy watering (and easy mowing too).

❏ Install a fixed irrigation system. Use it for your pots as well as the main garden.

Lawns:
Go to page 143.

FIXED IRRIGATION SYSTEMS

Planning is the key. Don't just rush out and buy a prepacked kit. Each garden has its own individual needs. That's why there are so many different components sold separately. Planning your system is a lot easier than it looks at first glance. Suppliers of home garden irrigation systems offer comprehensive manuals and planning guides, even videos to explain the various components of their systems and how to install them. Ask at your local garden centre.

The basic parts are polythene tubing to carry the water, tap attachments and joiners, sprinklers or drippers to deliver the water where it is needed, filters to prevent blockage, and optional extras such as automatic timers.

The best kind of water disperser depends on the planting. Pop-up sprinklers are for lawns. Micro-jet spray nozzles are useful for shallow-rooted plants or those that like wet leaves. For deep-rooted trees, shrubs, roses, and pots and hanging baskets, a drip system is best. There is minimum water loss through evaporation and, with moisture kept off the foliage, reduced disease risk. The number of dispersers depends on the type of planting and your water pressure.

Irrigation tubing can be laid on top of the ground or hidden under soil or mulch. It is best to use it above ground until you have it running properly. Polythene tubing deteriorates in sunlight so is best buried in the long run.

Drip irrigation can save time with pot watering.

Mulching

Plenty of gardens exist without it, but it's a fair assumption that most would perform better with a measure of mulch. Take a look at any garden of excellence and mulching will quietly abound, in flower gardens, along vegetable rows and around trees and shrubs.

A mulch is a layer of material spread on the soil surface. It protects plant roots from temperature extremes, conserves moisture by slowing down evaporation, may inhibit or suppress weed growth and usually adds to the structure of the soil over time. In reducing the need for weeding, a mulch protects plant roots and stems from the ravages of hoes, trowels, and lawn mowers.

A mulch may be compost, animal manure, sawdust, leaf litter, grass clippings, peat moss, straw, or even stones. Plastic weed mat is also a form of mulch. Mixtures or combinations are also used.

An effective organic mulch is between 5 and 10 cm thick. Avoid thick layers in contact with the stem or trunk of plants.

Mulched gardens need to be watered carefully so that the water soaks into the ground below and is not all absorbed by the mulch. Trickle or soak-hose irrigation is ideal with mulches, as long as it is not over-utilised causing the opposite problem.

The pros and cons of various organic materials used for mulching are outlined below.

More about Irrigation:
Go to page 202.

Compost making:
Go to page 196.

COMPOST

Compost is an ideal mulch, improving the soil with each application. The only disadvantage is that weed seeds will germinate on the surface. At least these are easy to pull out.

PEAT MOSS

Peat is an excellent soil conditioner but as a mulch it tends to be difficult to wet once it becomes dry and will blow away.

BARK

Bark comes in many grades from chunky to finely granulated. It is important that it has had nitrogen added to it (i.e., nitrogen stabilised) or it can rob the soil of nitrogen as it breaks down. It is a decorative mulch, good for keeping weeds at bay, especially if used in combination with weed matting. Bark is slow to break down and improve the soil structure (fine grades are best at this), but is therefore longer lasting and needs replacing less often. Fine bark is the most popular for cottage-style gardens because it looks like soil and doesn't detract from the planting. It is an attractive dark colour, which helps to trap the warmth of the sun.

HAY OR STRAW

Good as mulches or for adding to the compost heap. The disadvantage is the possibility of weed seeds in hay.

Autumn leaves

Leaf mould is partly decomposed leaves from deciduous trees, closely approximating the natural mulch of forest floors. It is best to at least partially compost the leaves before using as a mulch, otherwise simply add them to the compost heap. Beware of some tree species, which have toxins in their leaves that inhibit other plants from growing, for example, walnut trees.

Stones

Stones and pebbles suppress weeds, conserve soil moisture and are very good soil insulators, but they won't do much to add to the soil structure in your lifetime. They are a good mulch for permanently planted areas of trees and shrubs or for creating special effects, making an interesting alternative to lawn or paving.

Lawn Clippings

Ready at hand, lawn clippings are better as one of the components of a mulch (mixed with a coarser material) than used by themselves. They are best composted at least partially before use. Fresh lawn clippings will rob the soil of nutrients and may form a crust over the surface, preventing the entry of rainwater. They may also heat up to the extent that they burn plant roots. Never use lawn clippings too thickly or allow them to build up around the trunks of trees and shrubs.

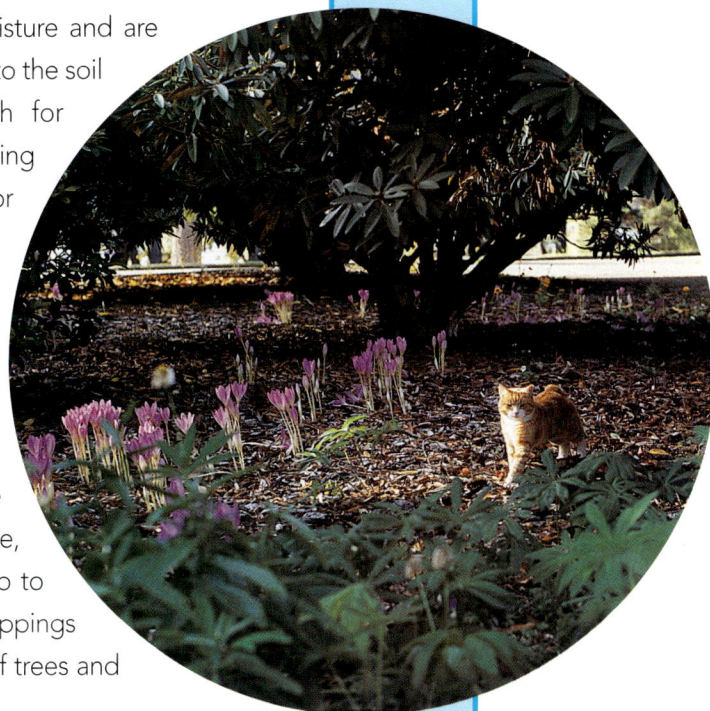

Pine needles

Pine needles make a good mulch for acid-loving plants like camellias. They are slow to break down so, if adding them to the compost heap, use thin layers only.

Animal manures

Best mixed into the topsoil as organic soil conditioners and fertilisers than used as mulches, pure animal manures are ideally added to the compost heap. If pure animal manures are to be used directly on the garden, they should first be stacked in heaps to partly decompose. Cover heaps to keep the rain off. Lightly mix them into the topsoil. Those mixed with straw, such as stable manure, make a good mulch.

Sawdust and wood shavings

As long as they do not come from treated timber, these make good mulches or can be added to the compost heap.

Newspapers

A cheap way to suppress weeds, newspapers need to be used in conjunction with a layer of bark or similar-weighted mulch. Wet them before use.

Pruning

Pruning is as fundamental as weeding, feeding and watering to keep a garden looking good. With regular pruning, plants remain bushy and healthy looking, with better overall shape, more flowers, more fruit and fewer disease problems. If pruning is often the most neglected task it is because of the fear of doing it wrong. The first thing to know is that it is very unlikely that you will harm a plant by pruning it. The more you prune, the more you will come to understand how each plant responds and the more confident you will become.

Pruning is not difficult. The basic science of it is very simple: if you chop off the end of a branch, it will sprout new growth below the cut, very often from the bud directly below your cut and to the exclusion of any growth from buds below it. Armed with this knowledge you can control the shape of your trees, shrubs and roses to your heart's content.

Pruning tools for the average garden include a good quality pair of secateurs (you get what you pay for), a pair of loppers, a saw for bigger branches, and hedge trimmers (electric or otherwise). It is advisable to keep tools sharp and clean as a precaution against the spread of disease.

One of the first jobs to do when you prune is to remove all dead or diseased wood. Then see to the overall size and shape and shorten branches to encourage renewed vigour. Cuts should be made on an angle sloping away from a bud 5 mm to 1 cm above it. Too close and you risk damaging the bud. Too far away and the wood above the bud will die, risking further dieback down the stem. Look at the position of the bud on the stem. Where is the new shoot going to grow: toward the middle of the bush or towards the outside? With few exceptions, the latter scenario is the right one. The idea is to let light and air in, encouraging growth and discouraging disease. So make your cut above an outward-facing bud.

All this talk about cutting to a bud becomes academic when dealing with densely branched shrubs, including those used for hedges. All that is needed here is an overall trim with the pruning shears. Topiaries are trimmed this way too.

How hard should you prune? Generally, the harder you prune, the more vigour you will inject back into the plant, but don't prune so hard that you cut into old wood that is past sprouting new growth. Fast-growing evergreen shrubs like lavenders and hebes need regular pruning to retain a compact bushy shape, but always leave some green leafy growth below your cut. Many perennials are best cut almost to ground level for renewed vigour.

When should you prune? Obviously, you don't want to prune when plants are at their flowering best. If in doubt, prune straight after flowering (when they look as if they need a bit of a tidy up). It helps if you can tell whether a plant produces its flowers

'Sexy Rexy' blooms best with pruning.

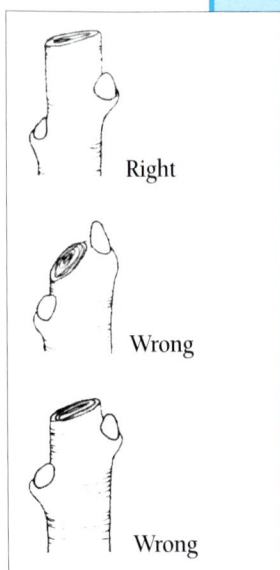

Right

Wrong

Wrong

on wood produced the previous season or on current season's growth. Those that flower on wood produced the previous season, such as early spring-flowering shrubs like rhododendrons, should not be pruned in winter unless you are prepared to do without flowers the coming spring. Otherwise, winter is the best time to prune cold-hardy plants. Frost-tender shrubs should not be pruned until after the last frost in spring.

SPECIAL PRUNING

TOPIARY

Topiary in its traditional form involves the creation of living sculptures via the clipping and pruning of evergreen shrubs. English box, because of its small, closely set foliage and slow growth is by far the most widely used plant. Apart from the common species, *Buxus sempervirens*, there are many other kinds of *Buxus*.

To create your first topiary it's usually best to start off with a simple shape. Simple globes, cubes and pyramids never fail to look good. If things start to get a bit lopsided it might be time to start getting creative. There is no reason why all topiaries have to be symmetrical — artistic licence reigns. The lollipop shape is also quite easy to achieve. The method is the same as that used to create any standard shrub.

Since the English box has a naturally even shape, a globe topiary is not too difficult to achieve with a good eye, though more top trimming than side trimming will be necessary. A pyramid shape is easiest to achieve if a frame is used as a template. A pyramid is made from four wooden stakes joined at the top and covered with wire mesh. This sits over the shrub as it grows and any protruding sprigs are trimmed off at the point they pass the mesh.

Once the topiary fills the frame completely it is removed but may be used again as a guide in maintenance trimming. A trim at least twice a year (more often in warmer regions) is necessary to keep this type of topiary in shape.

To compensate for the loss of energy from constant trimming, topiaries (especially those in containers) need plenty of feeding.

'INSTANT' TOPIARY

Topiaries made in the traditional clipped manner take time to mature. The short-cut method of making a topiary involves quick-growing plants that are trained over a specially shaped wire frame. The most common plants used are the small-leaved ivies (*Hedera* cultivars) and the creeping figs (*Ficus pumila* and its cultivars).

Frames for instant topiary can be homemade out of wire or wire mesh or they can be purchased ready-made. Many shapes and sizes are available, from simple cones to the more elaborate spirals, teddy bears and birds. You can even buy them planted if you are one to whom instant has to mean just that.

The easiest way to make this kind of topiary is to plant one or more plants in the pot at the base of the frame and train them to cover the frame, trimming as required.

Buxus cultivars
Go to page 31.

How to make a standard:
Go to page 208.

A slender stem topped with a mop of foliage and flowers in the style of a small tree makes an elegant subject when something a bit special is called for in pots or in the garden.

Finished specimens can be purchased for instant effect but it is surprisingly easy to make your own, and a lot of fun. Some plants, most notably roses, are trained into standards by grafting a shoot on to a tall root stock in the nursery, but most shrubs will respond to the following method:

❏ For a first attempt, try something fast growing such as a fuchsia or a Marguerite daisy. Other plants that make excellent standards are lavender, English box, camellias, trailing rosemary, conifers, pelargoniums, lantana, bay and gardenias.

❏ Start in early spring with a young plant with a strong straight main stem. Position a strong stake as close as possible to the main stem without damaging the roots.

❏ Secure the plant to the stake with flexible ties (pieces of nylon stocking will do) at intervals up the main stem.

❏ Remove all side branches.

❏ As the plant grows, keep removing the side shoots, leaving the main shoot intact and tying the stem to the stake as it grows. This encourages the plant to grow upwards. Check that the ties do not become too tight as the main stem thickens. In the early stages any single leaves growing directly out from the main stem should be left on as they still provide the plant with energy. The side shoots to remove appear between these leaves and the main stem.

❏ Once the stem reaches the desired height, it's time to pinch out the growing tip. This encourages the plant to branch out at the top.

❏ Each of the resulting branches should in turn have their growing tips removed to encourage further branching and to develop a dense, bushy top.

❏ Continue to remove any side shoots that appear from the main trunk and keep trimming the top growth to keep it bushy.

Growing Plants From Seed

Growing your own plants from seed is very satisfying. It saves money, especially if you want large quantities of flowers to fill every corner of the garden and allows you to grow varieties that may not be otherwise purchasable.

Seeds are either sown directly into position in the garden or in trays for later transplanting. Seeds that are sown direct are generally larger-sized seeds or plants such as root vegetables that do not respond well to transplanting. Many flowering plants grow very easily from seed sown directly into the garden. These tend to be plants that also self-seed quite readily, such as forget-me-not, alyssum, calendula and honesty. Sowing in trays means that you can control the environment for germination and often have plants ready earlier in the season.

Growing plants from seed is easy. Here's how:

The annual *Echium* 'Blue Bedder' is grown easily from seed.

SOIL AND POSITION

To germinate, seeds need moisture and warmth. Once they have their first leaves (called seed leaves or 'cotyledons') they need light and a little later on, when all their stored food has been used up, they need food. A good soil or seed-raising mix must have a fine crumbly texture that holds moisture without becoming too wet. Overly damp conditions lead to a fungal disease called 'damping off', which causes young seedlings to collapse. For direct sowing prepare the soil well, working it into a fine tilth. It is important to wait until the soil is warm and friable before sowing.

When sowing in containers, use a specially prepared seed-raising mix such as Yates Black Magic. Other mixes may be too coarse or contain the wrong balance of fertilisers. Since warmth is required for germination, a sunny position is ideal, but you will need to protect young seedlings from direct sun in summer.

SOWING DIRECT

1. Prepare the soil well before planting, adding plenty of compost. Peat can also be added to improve soil texture.

2. Level and smooth the soil surface to a fine tilth with a rake.

3. Moisten the soil well a few days prior to planting, unless rain does this for you.

4. If planting in rows, make furrows to the depth recommended on the seed packet.

5. Sow seeds at the specified spacing along the row and cover with fine soil (a sieve can be useful here) or seed-raising mix. Firm gently with a rake head. Sow fine seed by holding the foil packet horizontally between your thumb and third finger and tapping gently with your forefinger.

6. Water well after sowing and ensure the soil does not dry out prior to germination.

SOWING IN TRAYS

You will need a specially prepared seed-raising mix, such as Yates Black Magic, and a seed tray or recycled punnets which have been thoroughly washed. Ensure any container used has adequate drainage holes.

1. Fill the container with seed-raising mix to 1 cm below the top. Level the surface and firm it down gently. Water thoroughly but gently without disturbing the level surface.

2. Sow the seed by holding the foil pack between your thumb and middle finger and tapping with your forefinger. Larger seed can be placed at the recommended spacing if you wish to leave out the pricking-out stage.

3. Lightly cover with seed-raising mix to the required depth. Follow instructions on the back of the packet. The finer the seed the less cover you need; the finest seeds need no covering. If not done prior to sowing, water the mix with a fine rose watering can or by sitting the trays in a tub with a few centimetres of water.

4. Cover the tray with glass and paper to maintain even moisture and to protect against direct sunlight, and place it in a warm position until the seeds germinate.

5. Remove the cover to allow light in and to allow good air circulation as soon as the seeds have germinated.

6. When the seedlings have their first true leaves (those that appear after the cotyledons) they can be 'pricked out'. Alternatively, if you only need a few plants they can be thinned.

   ❏ Fill a container or small individual pots with potting mix.

   ❏ Loosen the soil around the seedlings (a kitchen fork is ideal for this) and carefully lift each, holding them by their leaves rather than the delicate roots. Aim to disturb the roots as little as possible.

   ❏ Make a hole in the potting mix and place the seedling in the hole. Then gently firm the soil around it.

   ❏ If using a single container for pricking out, ensure the seedlings have adequate spacing to allow growth before they are large enough to plant out or pot individually.

   ❏ Water the seedlings gently and place the containers away from direct sunlight and draughts for several days to allow the seedlings to 'harden off'. In three to four weeks the young plants will be ready for transplanting into the garden.

GOLDEN RULE
Read the Packet

HANDY HINT
If not using all the seed in first sowing, open packet from the bottom to avoid destroying available information.

White alyssum (foreground) is also grown easily from seed.

CHECKLIST FOR SUCCESS

EIGHT REASONS FOR POOR GERMINATION:

1. Planting too deeply — check the instructions on the packet.

2. Too wet — mix should be damp but not saturated. Check drainage and don't have the seed bed too firm.

3. Too dry — cover to prevent drying out and don't have the seed beds too loose.

4. Wrong temperature — many plants have different requirements (e.g., parsley likes it cool, beans like it warm). Always check the packet and don't be tempted to plant summer plants too early if sowing outdoors.

5. Slugs and snails — use Slug Slam or Baysol.

6. Soil diseases — encouraged by poor drainage, over - watering, or poor ventilation. Use a sterilised mix and clean containers. Rotate crops to prevent disease build up in the garden when sowing directly.

7. Fertiliser burn — don't apply fertiliser until after transplanting.

8. Old seed — a seed is a living thing; the older the seed the less viable it becomes. Store seed in a cool dry place, and use fresh seed for very best results. Once the foil sachet is open, the seed should be used within six months. Check the use-by date on the seed packet.

WHEN TO SOW

Always read the back of the seed packet. Sowing time will always vary depending on climate with warmer climates having a longer season.

SOW IN SPRING (For mid-summer flowering or harvesting)

FLOWERS	VEGETABLES	HERBS
Alyssum	Beans	Basil
Cosmos	Beetroot	Borage
Dahlia	Broccoli	Chamomile
Gypsophila	Cabbage	Chives
Hollyhock	Capsicum	Coriander
Larkspur	Carrots	Dill
Livingstone daisy	Cress	Marjoram
Lobelia	Cucumber	Parsley
Love-in-a-mist	Eggplant	Sage
Marigold	Leeks	Thyme
Nasturtium	Lettuce	
Petunia	Parsnip	
Phlox	Peas	
Salvia	Radish	
Scabiosa	Rocket	
Statice	Silverbeet	
Stock	Spinach	
Sunflower	Spring onions	
Verbena	Tomatoes	
Viscaria	Zucchini	

SOW IN SUMMER (For autumn flowering)

FLOWERS	VEGETABLES	HERBS
Alyssum	Beans	Basil
Calendula	Beetroot	Borage
Cineraria	Broccoli	Coriander
Cornflower	Cabbage	Dill
Cosmos	Capsicum	
Dianthus	Carrots	
Forget-me-not	Celery	
Gypsophilia	Cress	
Larkspur	Cucumber	
Livingstone daisy	Leeks	
Marigold	Lettuce	
Pansy	Onion	
Petunia	Parnsip	
Phlox	Pumpkin	
Scabiosa	Radish	
Snapdragon	Silverbeet	
Sweet pea	Spinach	
Viola		
Viscaria		

SOW IN AUTUMN (Winter and spring flowering)

FLOWERS	VEGETABLES	HERBS
Alyssum	Broad beans	Chamomile
Calendula	Cabbage (warm climates)	Chives
Cornflower	Carrots (cold climates)	Coriander
Cineraria	Cress	Marjoram
Cosmos	Onions	Parsley
Delphinium	Radish (warm climates)	Thyme
Dianthus	Spinach (warm climates)	
Forget-me-not	Silverbeet (warm climates)	
Gypsophila		
Larkspur		
Lobelia		
Pansy		
Polyanthus		
Poppy		
Primula		
Scabiosa		
Snapdragon		
Stock		
Sweet pea		
Sweet William		
Viola		

'Flower Carpet', a disease-resistant rose.

Pests, Diseases, and Sprays

Pests and diseases are a fact of life. They will always be present in a garden to some degree and tolerated up to a point. How you cope with them when they pass that point is up to you. Some gardeners are prepared to spray, others are not. There are a number of ways to minimise any need for spraying. Mostly, it's a matter of general health and hygiene:

❑ Keep plants well fed and watered.

❑ Avoid creating humid conditions with overhead watering or poor ventilation.

❑ Although close planting can look great it provides an ideal environment for pests and diseases.

❑ Prune plants to keep them open and well ventilated and remove all dead or diseased material. Do not put it on the compost heap.

❑ Remove leaf litter or dead fruit and flowers from around disease-prone plants such as roses and fruit trees.

❑ Keep weeds to a minimum.

❑ Plant disease-resistant varieties.

❑ Choose plants that grow well in your climate.

'Rose Pearl' drift.

Control is easier and more effective if something is done before the problem gets too overwhelming. You first need to identify the culprit and eliminate the possibility of other causes, such as lack of water, lack of food, or frost or wind damage. Then determine whether the damage is being done by a pest or a disease, and ideally what particular pest or disease you are dealing with. A trip to a garden centre with a leaf from the affected plant is the easiest way.

DISEASES make spots, blotches, and rusty or powdery deposits on the fruit or leaves. Most garden diseases are fungal infections and are controlled by spraying with fungicides. Most of these kill a range of diseases. A spray called Fungus and Mildew Spray is an example of a good broad-spectrum disease spray. Combined insect and disease sprays, such as Gild or Shield, will also control most common disease problems. Some diseases are caused by bacteria and are notoriously difficult to control by spraying. Pruning out infected branches is often the only solution.

INSECTS make leaves yellow by sucking the sap from them or there are tell-tale holes and nibbled edges. Aphids are very common insect pests. They have soft bodies you can squash with your fingers. They conveniently cluster together on young shoots or flower buds, doing considerable damage. If you have a small garden you might be able to keep them under control manually. Spraying with soap suds is another way to kill soft-bodied insects like aphids. For bad infestations of aphids or other insect pests, there is a range of general and more specific insecticides as well combination insecticide/fungicide sprays, such as Gild or Shield. These are good preventative sprays for plants and roses.

SNAILS AND SLUGS, perhaps the most common garden pests, also take chomps out of the leaves, easily devouring entire young plants. They particularly relish the new shoots of emerging spring bulbs and perennials such as hostas. There are various alternatives when it comes to slug and snail bait: weather resistant or short term, and small granulated forms that are difficult to see once sprinkled and too small to attract toddlers' fingers. Most snail baits have a pet repellent in them but determined animals are still at risk. The best idea if you have concerns is to loosely cover the bait with a piece of drainpipe or a cut-off plastic drink bottle.

MITES are minute insect-like creatures that make leaves yellow and unhealthy looking by sucking the sap from them. They prefer hot dry weather and congregate on the undersides of leaves. They are not controlled with a regular insecticide and need a special mite killer or oil spray. Mites are common on citrus trees and roses in summer. An effective deterrent with citrus is to spray the undersides of the leaves with water, as mites hate being wet. This is not so good for roses, which are more susceptible to disease if humidity builds up around the foliage.

Modern sprays for the home garden are generally of low toxicity and very safe to use, but you should always take precautions. Don't spray when there are children or animals around. Always wear protective clothing. Avoid spraying on a windy day and *always read the label on the pack*. Only spray when you need to. Remember that pests and diseases have a habit of building up resistance to repeatedly used chemicals.

10

Indoor gardening

Living greenery adds interest and vitality to indoor spaces. Some houseplants also act as clean-air machines, improving the air we breath in enclosed spaces.

While healthy plants add ambience and make you feel good, not-so-healthy ones do the opposite and, sadly, through ignorance or neglect, indoor plants are capable of becoming sick a lot quicker than those outside. The indoor environment is artificial, with plants entirely dependent on you to provide the necessities of life.

It's really very easy if you restrict yourself to a few well-chosen, hardy houseplants and pay attention to a few basic requirements. Factors to consider are light, food, water, humidity, room temperature, draughts, pests and diseases and, something that is a special problem for indoor plants — dust.

HUMIDITY AND ROOM TEMPERATURE

Indoor environments are designed with human comfort in mind being warm and dry. Plants generally prefer more moisture in the air. Artificial heating creates dry conditions unfavourable to many houseplants. For most, the higher the temperature of a room, the higher the humidity should be. The humidity level around a plant can be increased by mist spraying or by standing the plant in a tray of pebbles (or gravel) and water. The pebbles hold the base of the pot above the water so that the plant is not sitting in it. Make sure the pebbles are not completely under water.

Houseplants do not cope well with extreme changes in temperature. Avoid draughts and do not place plants next to heaters. If you have underfloor heating, place plants above floor level.

LIGHT

Light is crucial to all plants. Those lacking light will become thin, straggly and pale. Generally houseplants have to contend with relatively low-light situations. Many indoor plants are jungle plants in their natural habitat, with large glossy leaves designed to catch any light that is offering, but each plant has its own lighting needs. Some tolerate a dark hallway, others need to be near a sunny window. The great majority grow best with a generous helping of indirect light. This means a bright room but not in the path of direct sunlight. A plant that has been growing in relative darkness will protest if brought straight out into bright light. It needs first to be acclimatised in a slightly brighter position. Flowering houseplants and those with coloured leaves generally need the brightest positions. Plants that can survive in poor light include *Dracaena*, *Spathiphyllum* (peace lily), *Aspidistra*, *Ficus* (figs) and palms.

WATER

No plant can survive without water. There are always cacti and succulents for those who find the job of watering houseplants too time-consuming. But even these need some water and they do like lots of light. More plants actually die from overwatering

Poinsetta.

than underwatering. Remember that plants need a lot less water in winter than in summer when they are actively growing. Cut right back on watering in winter or the cold wet roots will soon turn up their toes. Similarly it is important to have a well-drained pot with a well-drained potting mix (not garden soil). Plants in rooms with gas heating will need more water. Some plants need more water than others.

So, how do you tell if it's time to water? The instructions on a houseplant's label will give you some indication. If the soil surface is dry to touch and the pot feels light or gives a hollow ring when tapped, it is generally time to water. If the leaves are drooping it's definitely time to water — unless the plant has been so overwatered that the roots are now dysfunctional! Overwatering can be difficult to cure. A new plant might be the best solution, but you can try putting the plant in a shady place, letting the soil become almost dry and then watering very gradually in very small doses while new roots form. It might also be appropriate to prune the foliage.

Use water at room temperature rather than very cold water. Rainwater is ideal. A plant can be given a tonic by placing it outside in a shower of rain to rinse out all the excess minerals that have built up in the potting mix. (Mind you, don't leave it out in bright light for too long.) Except for plants like African violets and furry-leaved begonias that do not like water on their leaves, mist spraying with water is beneficial to many houseplants (especially those from the tropics) by increasing the humidity around the leaves.

FOOD

The potting mix your plant comes with or that you repot it into will have a good three to four months' supply of slow-release fertiliser. After that you will need to feed it, especially in the warmer months when the plant is growing. Liquid fertilisers are the easiest to use. Make sure they are balanced plant foods. It is a good idea to lightly water the plant prior to feeding as a thirsty plant might absorb the plant food all in one go and suffer from a nutrient overdose. Fast growers and flowering plants need more frequent feeding than others. Always read the advice on the pack.

More about fertilisers:
Go to page 200.

PESTS AND DISEASES

Yellow leaves can mean a number of things. Your houseplant could be suffering from too much or too little water, a nutrient deficiency, lack of light, or a cold draught. It might also be under attack from an insect, virus or fungal disease. Usually with pests and diseases there are other tell-tale signs.

Diseases usually occur as a result of overwatering, and sometimes overcrowding or poor ventilation. They may show up as wilting, or as mouldy or powdery areas on the leaf surfaces. The best thing to do is get rid of the plant before the disease spreads to others. Fungicides may help save valuable plants but the sick plant should be moved well away from others.

Insects like warm, sheltered indoor conditions. Common examples of houseplant harassers are: mealy bug, easily identified by its cottonwool-like coating; aphids, whose soft fat bodies can be seen in crowded clusters on young soft growth; and scale insects, which look like tiny limpets clinging to stems and leaves, especially of ferns. They all suck the sap from the plant and should be sprayed with a recommended insecticide. Mites are difficult to see with the naked eye. They also suck the sap but are not strictly insects, but spider relatives. The upshot is that they are unharmed by most insecticides. For mites you need a miticide. Better still, do what you can to prevent an attack. Mites thrive in warm dry conditions, so discourage them by keeping up the humidity. Mist spray with water, especially the undersides of the leaves.

Dust

Dust is a common hazard for the poor houseplant. Plants need to breathe to survive. If the pores on the leaf surfaces are clogged with dust, this becomes pretty difficult. It doesn't look very nice either. So do your plants justice by occasionally wiping the leaves. Sponge them gently with plain water (at room temperature) or use a special leaf polish. This removes dust and other pollutants, makes the leaves look nice and shiny, and may also contain a special insecticide or fungicide to guard against pests and diseases. Serious dust problems can be avoided if you mist spray the leaves daily with water. Polishes may also be applied by spraying.

Repotting houseplants

As plants grow, so do their roots, eventually outgrowing their pots. One way of preventing a plant from growing larger than you want it is to confine the root system in a pot. Many indoor plants thrive on being rootbound. However, it is amazing what fresh potting mix will do for a tired-looking houseplant. Even if your houseplants have reached the desirable size, they will still benefit from repotting. Old potting mix lacks useful nutrients and is likely to have a build-up of other, less-than-useful chemicals. So, even if you put them back into the same pot, it is essential to the health of your plants that you do repot them periodically. Many plants, such as ferns, can be divided at repotting time to produce new plants. Others, such as weeping figs, can have their roots lightly trimmed. At the very least, scrape off the outside layer of mix and replace it with fresh mix. Repotting is best done once a year in early spring, just before the onset of new growth, or in autumn, but for most plants the timing is not critical. Always use fresh potting mix, never garden soil. The new pot should ideally be no more than 3 cm larger in diameter than the old one. An oversized pot can lead to problems with the excess potting mix sitting like a cold damp cloak around the roots.

Water the plant thoroughly an hour before repotting. Invert the pot and remove the plant. Carefully tease out any matted roots and use a sharp knife or secateurs to remove any that look rotten or unhealthy. An unhealthy plant may have its top growth trimmed too. Place a layer of potting mix at the bottom of the new pot and position the plant so that the top of the root ball is a centimetre or two below the rim. Fill in the sides and tap the pot on the table to settle the mix, then water it carefully.

If lush healthy specimens still elude you, there are always the low-maintenance artificial varieties. The other option is to decorate your indoor environment with cut flowers or flowering houseplants such as chrysanthemums, which last a lot longer than cut flowers and are usually less expensive — so you need not feel guilty when you discard them at the end of their useful life.

More about pests and diseases: Go to page 215.

FOLIAGE HOUSEPLANTS

DRAGON TREE
Dracaena

Dracaenas are among the most stunning plants for dramatic architectural effects. They do not come cheap and are an investment that need looking after, but are well worth the effort. Position dracaenas with care. Droughts, heaters and direct sunlight are all no-nos, and they are averse to being moved about. Overwatering is to be guarded against and while they like plenty of humidity, they don't like too much water sitting on their leaves. Water dracaenas when the top 2 or 3 cm of the mix becomes dry, reasonably regularly in summer but slowing right down in winter.

Feed fortnightly in spring and summer with liquid fertiliser. The true dragon tree, *Dracaena draco* has a cluster of green sword-like leaves topping a thick bare trunk. *D. marginata* has smooth slender stems and narrow spiky leaves, dark green with a red margin. It is relatively easy to grow. *D. deremensis* 'Warneckii' has strappy green leaves with white stripes. *D. fragrans* (corn plant) has ribbon-like leaves curving downwards. There are various variegated cultivars.

DUMB CANE
Dieffenbachia

The variegated leaves of *Dieffenbachia* make an attractive contrast when used with plain green plants. They are easy to grow but must not be overwatered. Mist spray the leaves occasionally and feed every few weeks over spring and summer with a liquid fertiliser. A warm brightly lit position away from direct sun is best. Repot in spring. The sap of *Dieffenbachia* is highly poisonous, so they are not a good choice where there are small children.

GRAPE IVY
Cissus

There are various species of *Cissus*. Highly recommended is *C.* 'Ellen Danica', with serrated glossy leaves. It is a climbing plant, good supported on a ponga stake or perfect cascading from a basket. *Cissus* is quick growing, long lived and very tolerant of imperfect conditions. It enjoys frequent summer watering (a little often), slowing down in winter. Feed every few weeks during the warm months with liquid fertiliser and repot every second spring.

PEACE LILY
Spathiphyllum

If you were to have just one houseplant, a peace lily would be an excellent choice. There are a number of species and cultivars. All are outstanding performers and very easy to grow. They produce stunning flowers but have been included here as a foliage plant because of their permanent year-round good looks. The most important thing to get right with a peace lily is the watering. They need lots of water in summer when they are actively growing and much less in winter. Peace lilies tolerate lower light than most plants and won't look their best in full sun. They enjoy humid conditions and liquid feeding. Sponging the leaves every so often and repotting each spring will keep them growing heartily for years.

SYNGONIUM

The Syngoniums are attractive climbing or cascading basket plants with attractive coloured and patterned leaves. They like filtered light, good humidity, regular summer watering and weekly feeding with a dilute solution of liquid plant food during the spring/summer growing period. Mist spray regularly with tepid water to keep the leaves healthy.

UMBRELLA TREE
Schefflera, Tupidanthus

Where a value-for-money large-scale plant is needed, the tropical umbrella trees are ideal. *Schefflera actinophylla* and *Tupidanthus calyptratus* (syn. *S. pueckleri*) are so similar that they could easily be mistaken for the same plant. They also like the same growing conditions and are grown in subtropical gardens. As indoor plants they are easy to care for as long as

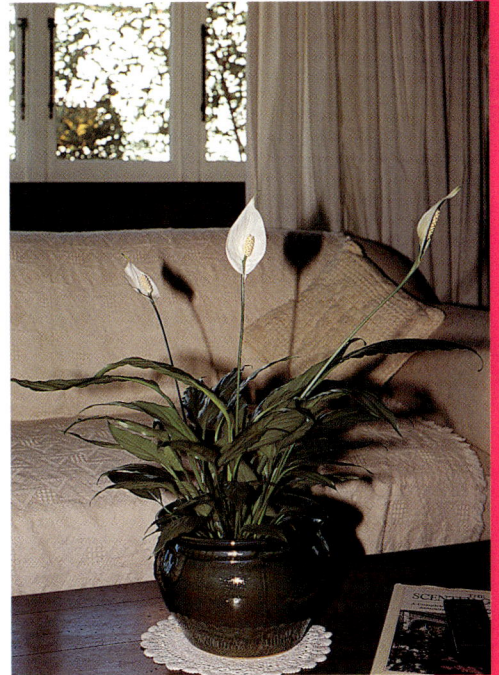

Peace lily.

you follow the basic rules. Give them good light away from direct sun, but don't overwater. Mist spray to simulate the humid conditions they love. *S. arboricola* is a more compact plant with smaller leaves, generally more shrub-like than tree-like. Care for it in the same way as *S. actinophylla*.

WEEPING FIG
Ficus benjamina

These small trees from tropical climates are among the most popular of indoor specimens. At any size they add grace and charm to a room. The weeping fig of 10 or 20 years ago was a much less robust plant than those you can buy today. Modern strains are very hard to kill. With basic care, they will look good all year round. To prevent leaves turning yellow and dropping, the rules are: water without waterlogging, keep away from direct sun and from draughts and heaters, and feed once a month in spring and summer with a liquid fertiliser. Mist spray with water to increase humidity and keep the leaves dust free. Repotting in spring every couple of years is also a good idea.

FERNS

Bird's Nest Fern
Asplenium nidus

This beautiful fern will add a touch of drama to your collection. The foliage is unusual for a fern in that it is undivided. The fronds have attractive wavy margins and unfold from the centre of the plant. Periods of neglect can lead to the broad glossy leaves becoming tatty and discoloured. The best idea is to treat it just as you would a maidenhair fern. Bird's nest fern loves warm humid conditions. Position it, if you can, below eye level to make the most of the architectural effect of the fronds.

Boston Fern
Nephrolepis

Boston ferns are extremely well mannered. They will tolerate neglect more than any other fern. They will, however, reward you for your efforts if you give them a well-drained potting mix, even watering, an occasional liquid feed with an organic liquid fertiliser and a position away from direct sun or draughts. Like all ferns, Boston ferns do not appreciate dry air, a point worth noting if you have them in a gas-heated living room. Mist spraying and saucers of pebbles with water may be in order. Of the numerous different *Nephrolepis* species, *N. massii* is one of the most popular and well known for growing indoors.

Button Fern
Pellaea rotundifolia

An engaging little New Zealand native fern with unusual fronds like double rows of dark green buttons. Button fern prefers to be on the dry side so avoid overwatering. Good drainage is essential and low indirect light is preferred.

Hen and Chickens Fern
Asplenium bulbiferum

This versatile New Zealand native does well indoors or out. Looking appealing in pots, hanging baskets or in a moist sheltered position in the garden, its graceful soft appearance belies its hardiness. The lovely arching fronds are light green and finely cut to give a lacy texture. The name bears witness to the interesting way this fern reproduces itself. Baby plants appear on the mature leaves. These can be removed and grown on. Give good drainage, even watering (little in winter, lots in summer), mist spray for humidity, and organic liquid fertiliser. They like lots of light but not direct sun.

Maidenhair Fern
Adiantum

The most well known of the many different maidenhair ferns is the very beautiful *A. raddianum*. There are many different cultivars available. 'Ocean Spray', a compact bush form, is one of the best. Your experience may well suggest that maidenhairs are not easy to grow, but they are given no special treatment and are grown in exactly the same conditions as any other fern. The most common mistakes are overwatering or erratic watering, lack of humidity and cold draughts. They also have an aversion to direct sun. What maidenhair ferns do like are a humid atmosphere and indirect light. Keep them in a bathroom, kitchen or by an indoor spa, or mist spray the foliage regularly. Place them on a bed of pebbles and water as described above. Once you find a good position for your maidenhair, leave it there. They do not like to be shifted around. Keep your maidenhair evenly moist, but avoid overwatering in winter. Feed once a month during spring and summer with diluted liquid fertiliser. Strong solutions can burn the roots. Natural products like fish fertiliser are ideal. If the foliage goes brown, cut it all off and repot the plant into new potting mix. Keep it evenly moist and it should soon spring back into life.

Maidenhairs love:
- ✓ A warm humid atmosphere
- ✓ Good drainage
- ✓ Indirect light
- ✓ Even moisture
- ✓ Organic liquid fertiliser

FLOWERING HOUSEPLANTS

African Violet
Saintpaulia

These natives of tropical Africa are very easy to grow. They are long-term houseplants, flowering year after year. Watering is the most important thing. In summer they need to be kept moist but not continuously saturated. In winter they need only infrequent watering. Leaves can become marked or diseased if in contact with water for too long so it is generally recommended that African violets should be watered from the bottom by filling the saucer they sit in. Full sun can burn the leaves, but a warm position with bright light is best for flowering. Avoid draughts. Liquid feeding with a balanced plant food will keep the flowers coming and, to keep plants really thriving, you might want to repot every year into fresh potting mix. At the same time plants can be divided to make new plants. Do this when the plant is not in flower (usually winter). There are thousands of cultivars of African violets, in various shades of pink, purple, blue and white. The flowers can be small or large, single or double, frilly or plain. They look their absolute best flowering *en masse*. Try repotting a number of plants into one large container or window box.

Begonia
REIGER AND BLUSH TYPES

These special begonias have lush green foliage and a continuous entourage of richly beautiful tropical flowers. Colours include intense reds and oranges, dreamy apricots, sunny yellows and crisp pure white. Like most indoor flowering plants, begonias like good light but not direct sun, and to be kept moist but not wet, with greater watering requirements in the warmer months. To maximise the flowering performance, feed occasionally with liquid fertiliser and remove spent blooms.

Blush begonia.

CHRYSANTHEMUM

Potted chrysanthemums are widely available all year round in a huge range of colours and flower forms. They are an ideal gift and just the right thing to brighten up a room in an instant. Compared to a bunch of flowers, they are very reasonably priced and long lasting. Once past their best they can be planted in the garden, for those of thrifty persuasion, otherwise they can make their final contribution to the compost heap, having lived a useful life. Plants grown for indoors have been grown in an artificial environment with special lighting and growth regulators to keep them compact. Planted out in the garden, potted chrysanthemums will grow as perennials reverting to their natural, tall form. Purchase plants with lots of tight buds, just enough flowers open so you can see the colour. Place them in a brightly lit position, away from direct sun and preferably not too warm, keep the soil moist and they will last a month or more. Mist spraying the foliage and an occasional liquid feed will also keep them going longer.

CYCLAMEN

Classic winter-flowering houseplants, cyclamen used to appear in stores in time for Mothers' Day. They are now available in flower from late summer onwards. What they need most is a cool position. They will enjoy the occasional mist spray but detest overwatering. It is best to let them become almost dry and then give a good soaking in the sink. If you wish to keep your cyclamen for next year, turn the pots on their side in a dry place over summer. When the new leaves appear in late summer or autumn, repot and start watering.

KALANCHOE

Easy-care kalanchoes are very colourful and very long flowering. They make wonderful table plants. Most flower naturally in winter and early spring but they can be grown to flower all year round. In mild climates they will grow very successfully outdoors. Inside, they need a bright, sunny position. Kalanchoes need lots of water in spring and summer, tailing off to very little in winter. Prune back by at least half the plant's height after flowering and repot once a year.

POINSETTIA

Euphorbia pulcherrima
Poinsettias flower for Christmas whichever side of the world you live on. Naturally they are winter flowerers, but can be made to flower at any time via carefully engineered, artificial-light conditions in the nursery. The flowers themselves are small and insignificant. It is the bracts surrounding them that give the spectacular colour. Red is the traditional Christmas colour and by far the most widely grown, but there are also white, cream, pink and attractively mottled forms. To look after your poinsettias and keep them flowering for as long as possible, put them in a brightly lit room, away from direct sun. Water in moderation, avoiding overwatering. In summer, a cooler indoor position is preferable to a very warm one. The top of the television is not the best place at any time of the year.

Like chrysanthemums and cyclamen, poinsettias are generally regarded as disposable houseplants. Once the show is over it is disposed of and replaced with something new. If you are one of those people to whom this is sacrilege, continue to water and care for it as a green houseplant. When the leaves have fallen (late winter), cut the stems back to a few centimetres long and put the plant, pot and all, in a cool dark place without water. In spring, repot, place it in a warm, light position, and start watering. In a mild climate, poinsettias can be grown in a warm outdoor position, in a pot or well-drained garden soil. In cold climates they need to be grown on undercover. Bright, indirect daylight and at least 14 hours of darkness each night is needed for flowering. The coloured bracts will appear again in winter, on a plant that is less compact than the original you started out with.

ZYGOCACTUS

Zygocactus are great for hanging baskets or high ledges so that the colourful cascading flowers can be appreciated from below. They must have good drainage, not be over-watered and require 12 hours of darkness to flower, so don't keep them in a room that is used at night. The flowers, in shades of orange, red, pink, purple or white, appear mainly in winter. Water regularly except in autumn. Liquid feed once a fortnight.

Index